Digital Supply Chains

This book provides a practical guide to digital supply chain modelling, demonstrating an agile approach to how such models can be applied to any manufacturing company to build competitive advantage, facilitate new business models and drive towards Industry 4.0. The agile approach of the book provides an attractive alternative to the conventional country-by-country deployment of S/4 HANA and other relevant technologies.

This book contains the expertise Götz G. Wehberg has amassed over 20 years as a senior partner in a leading consulting company, working across industries and with globally recognized clients, advising on digitization. In it, he explains the scientific roots of digital supply chain management such as holism, cybernetics, self-organization and evolutionary theory to inform a deep understanding that can drive a supremely innovative strategy for Industry 4.0.

Beyond strategy, Wehberg introduces the practical tools and technologies used in supply chain modelling, for example, sensors, big data, artificial intelligence and the Internet of Things, as well as a reference framework that categorizes the technologies, together with the latest concepts and tools, such as DDMRP, predictive S&OP, pattern recognition, autonomous logistics and Lean. This framework supports decision making for developing supply chains in an end-to-end and cross-functional fashion, providing clear guidance for executives and managers on how to design supply chains for the future.

Götz G. Wehberg is an Executive Vice President and global sector leader at Capgemini. Wehberg is an expert in supply chain management. He has worked on supply chain topics in many industries, including automotive, process industries, life science and manufacturing. Wehberg works for major clients such as BMW, BASF, Bayer, Siemens and Volkswagen, among others. Besides supply chain management, he is an expert in M&A and digitalization. Today, he works predominantly in Europe. He has worked for a number of years in the Americas as well as the Middle East.

Digital Supply Chains

Key Facilitator to Industry 4.0 and
New Business Models, Leveraging
S/4 HANA and Beyond

3rd edition

Götz G. Wehberg

Routledge
Taylor & Francis Group

LONDON AND NEW YORK

Third edition published 2021
by Routledge
2 Park Square, Milton Park, Abingdon, Oxon, OX14 4RN

and by Routledge
52 Vanderbilt Avenue, New York, NY 10017

Routledge is an imprint of the Taylor & Francis Group, an informa business

First edition published by Gabler 2015
Second edition published by Wehberg 2018

British Library Cataloguing-in-Publication Data
A catalogue record for this book is available from the British Library

Library of Congress Cataloging-in-Publication Data
Names: Wehberg, Götz G., 1967– author.
Title: Digital supply chains : key facilitator to industry 4.0 and
    new business models, leveraging S/4 HANA and beyond /
    Götz G. Wehberg.
Description: Third edition. | Abingdon, Oxon ; New York,
    NY : Routledge, 2021. | Includes bibliographical references and index.
Identifiers: LCCN 2020009840 (print) | LCCN 2020009841 (ebook) |
    ISBN 9780367457815 (hardback) | ISBN 9781003036678 (ebook)
Subjects: LCSH: Business logistics—Information technology. |
    Inventory control—Data processing. | Materials management—
    Data processing.
Classification: LCC HD38.5 .W445 2021 (print) | LCC HD38.5 (ebook) |
    DDC 658.7—dc23
LC record available at https://lccn.loc.gov/2020009840
LC ebook record available at https://lccn.loc.gov/2020009841

ISBN: 978-0-367-45781-5 (hbk)
ISBN: 978-1-003-03667-8 (ebk)

Typeset in Bembo
by Apex CoVantage, LLC

For Alexandra, Finn and Ole in love.

Contents

Preface

Over the past 20 years, a variety of new technologies have been developed. Under the heading "Industry 4.0", Germany and other countries want to leverage these opportunities, with the goal of securing competitiveness and prosperity. The first industrial revolution introduced mechanization. Then, mass production (second revolution) and automation (third revolution) followed. The focus was on large-scale production and efficiency of human resources. Now, the fourth revolution aims at the flexibility of the value chain. This means mobilization of machines and objects. And it offers great opportunities for the management of the flow of goods and associated information. It is time for digital supply chains!

Four figures are valuable in establishing the context. It is estimated that there are currently some 20 billion connected devices worldwide, of which 25 percent of these are industrial appliances (IHS Technology 2015). By 2025, this number of connected things is expected to be some 100 billion, and the industrial share will be around 50 percent. The role of supply chain management for such a world of connected things is rather underestimated.

Taking into account these new possibilities, I would like to combine technology and business perspectives with this publication. Supply chain management is complex in nature, and it is becoming more and more difficult to deal with such complexity. If you look into the details, you will find that today supply chains are challenged by mass customization, and thus an increasingly complex product portfolio and a higher number of rush orders or change requests. Disruptions along the chain, for example, because of breakdowns of logistics infrastructure, electricity blackouts, biological catastrophes and terrorist attacks, are becoming more difficult to handle. In addition, factors from the inner value chain are becoming more volatile in terms of unplanned production shutdowns, bottlenecks at suppliers or sickness of staff. Moreover, supply chain management is a key facilitator for new digital business models.

Current practices, however, do not respond to these challenges properly. Established supply chain planning tools, for example, typically refer to traditional concepts of material resource planning. They do not leverage the latest technology, such as low-cost sensors and predictive analytics. Oftentimes such tools are not able to effectively address these challenges. In addition, a mature supply chain theory is lacking, but would be useful from an academic stand-point. This is why I have complemented this discussion with relevant concepts and theories, where available. As I suggest, there is value in understanding the roots of digital supply chains in terms of their scientific rationale.

The gap between the explosive increase of supply chain complexity on the one hand, and the lack of solutions on the other hand, is the starting point for this volume. The first part of this volume seeks to clearly present the interrelations between complexity and supply chain management. Because both physical and information flow must be considered together, the latest information processing technology must be taken into account. Various aspects of modern IT, such as the Internet of Things, the digital twin and cloud computing, are placed into context, as well as relevant IT standards, such as big data reference architecture.

Because digital supply chain management has to build on existing approaches, in the second part of this volume the existing understandings of supply chain management are briefly systematized. Building on this, a reference framework for digital supply chains is introduced.

The subsequent remarks in the third and fourth parts of the volume aim to fill this frame of reference with content. The analysis focuses on the information and planning systems of supply chain management. The reference frame reflects essential patterns with regards to supply chain profiles, the knowledge of which forms the basis for handling complexity. Selected use cases illustrate the frame and point the way towards digitalization. While the first edition of this book was published in German in 2015, the second edition has been translated to English and enriched by further practical experience and use cases. It has been the basis for further development, including a peer review via my think-tank website and the associated supply chain community. Based on this review and quality improvements associated with it, I am now publishing the third edition.

Part 4 highlights the development of supply chains over time in terms of concrete life cycles and phases. Based on this, guiding principles for the development of digital supply chains are explained. Perspectives for a future supply chain management will follow in the course of the fifth part, which concludes the presentation.

This publication is the result of teamwork. My thanks to my customers as well as the supply chain community, my family, friends and colleagues. Particularly noteworthy in this context are Prof. Ingrid Göpfert, Prof. Stefan Spinler and Prof. Ulrich Thonemann. Without them all, this publication would not have come about.

To get started – three videos on digital supply chains

Video 1: **Principles of nature**
(www.youtube.com/watch?v=FeGvYP4yZyY)

Video 2: **Supply chain design in the future**
(www.youtube.com/watch?v=drP6u6RZ9Zw)

Video 3: **Digital twin of supply chains**
(www.youtube.com/watch?v=WZvGPXLhhSA)

In a nutshell – ten theses on digital supply chains

The following are summaries for the ten theses presented in this text. They are offered here to encourage additional reading and to provide food for thought:

1 **Digital supply chains mean innovation**. Without digital supply chains, new business models do not work. For example, the Internet of Services offers additional potential for differentiation in competition.
2 **Digital supply chains cope with complexity**. The digital twin provides answers to increasing complexity, asking for more resilience. It answers to an increasing number of disruptions along the supply chain and the individualization of products in particular.
3 **Digital supply chains are more than cyberphysical systems**. Digital supply chains are not limited to new technologies, but rather are holistic business solutions. Customers are more and more often looking for total transparency and immediate delivery.
4 **Digital supply chains set efficiency standards**. They reduce transaction costs and support resilience, as well as flexibility, for example, with respect to single batches and scalable structures. Future supply chain organizations will require significantly fewer resources.
5 **Digital supply chains need a concept**. A frame of reference provides design support for managing complexity and closing the integration gap. Supply chain management in many organizations is pre-mature, so that a proper concept supports both to fix the basics and to make use of digitalization.
6 **Digital supply chains leverage on self-organization**. The leadership sets guidelines for steering, design and development and works through shared values and management by exception. Supply chain operations are highly automated.
7 **Digital supply chains are based on pattern recognition**. To cope with complexity, artificial intelligence and big data are used to identify effective algorithms. While artificial intelligence helped to forecast in the past, it will adopt a forecast methodology in the future.
8 **Digital supply chain management is not limited to delivery**. End-to-end supply chain models help to connect the dots across functions

and borders. Digital supply chains involve sales, production, procurement and R&D in particular.

9 **Digital supply chains must be specific**. The operating model and execution roadmap are to be developed on a company-specific basis, for example, matching the existing IT landscape and meeting individual customer requirements.

10 **Digital supply chains are at the beginning**. Learning new skills will be key to success of the transformation and building a comprehensive digital twin of supply chains. Therefore, we should think big, start small and scale fast.

Part 1

Why supply chain complexity matters

1 The complexity issue

The complexity problem is now on everyone's lips. The increasing scope of coordination, and thus efforts to coordinate supply chains, ultimately results from the growing complexity of both the internal and external environment of enterprises (Ulrich/Probst 1991). *Complexity* presents itself as the product of corresponding dynamics and diversity. The increasing number and variety of relevant variables, as well as the heterogeneity of their relationships, characterize diversity. Dynamics reflect the degree of renewal of supply chain–relevant elements, as well as their relationships and effects over time. A well-known and often used abbreviation is *VUCA*, which stands for volatility, uncertainty, complexity and ambiguity. Slightly different definitions of VUCA have been offered, and there is little value in having a discussion about nomenclature. Dynamics and diversity, therefore, represent substantial drivers of complexity.

If we consider the development of the complexity of supply chain–related parameters in recent years, we can see an overall rising trend. Higher complexity requires more time for analysis and decision making. However, the response time available to supply chain managers decreases with higher dynamics. A kind of *time shear* opens a gap (Figure 1.1).

For supply chain practitioners, the aforementioned time gap appears in the form of a whole series of relevant *megatrends* such as digitalization, individualization, data security needs, scarcity of resources, service competition, terrorism, tax optimization and sustainability. Moreover, unforeseen *disruptions* in the daily business impact the supply chain more often. For example, the production planning and detailed steering (PPDS) cycle traditionally have a freeze. Many companies are facing rush orders, reprioritization and change requests during this cycle. The companies are not able to redo the PPDS as fast as the new requests are coming in. Issues accumulate. Stocks increase, creating bottlenecks within the process, extending response times and making the situation even worse. The so-called bullwhip effect materializes. Examples for potential disruptions include infrastructure breakdowns, biological catastrophes and terrorist attacks. Supply chain management in practice has become increasingly complex in recent years, and will continue to become more so in the future.

In highly complex, non-trivial systems, statements about the effectiveness and efficiency of supply chain management can no longer be described as linear

Lead time

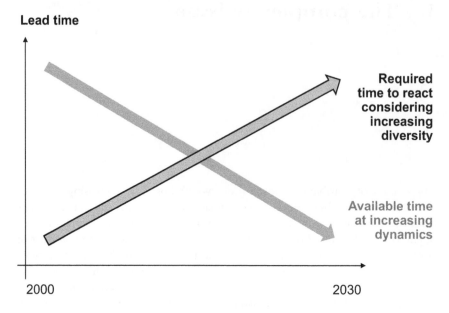

Required
time to react
considering
increasing
diversity

Available time
at increasing
dynamics

2000

2030

Figure 1.1 The time gap of supply chain management (following Bleicher 1995, modified by Wehberg 1997)

if-then relationships. In addition, long-term impacts often do not correspond to short-term effects. As a consequence, a complete analysis of the supply chain system is impossible. Supply chain management acts "blindly" to a certain extent. In other words, *synoptic planning* is no longer possible (Probst 1981).

Ten Hompel (2014) speaks in this context about a *hydrostatic paradox*. The classical planning of material flow systems is essentially based on so-called marginal cost calculation. In this context, the maximum performance has to be provided as the volume delivered per unit of time. The dilemma of this analytical approach in a complex environment lies in the lack of controllability of the marginal power, which means in its barely existing flexibility and resilience.

Supply chain resilience thus means the ability of the supply chain to be able to handle unforeseen events such as logistics infrastructure breakdowns, biological catastrophes or terrorist attacks (see also Weick/Sutcliffe 2001). Over and beyond external disruptions, resilience also includes the capability to cope with increasing internal complexity, such as the climbing number of make-to-order products and rush orders. In a way, of course, such internal disruptors are also a response to external developments. Bottom line, a sufficient resilience allows the companies to maintain a reasonable level of effectiveness and efficiency of their supply chain. Resilience includes both an active dimension being addressed by the concept of agility, as well as a reactive one called robustness. While resilience is a characteristic of supply chain potentials and activities, flexibility means service quality as performance criteria.

Even if the individual system details can no longer be fully grasped or mastered, supply chain management generally tends to increase or decrease the extent of its complexity. *Complexity mastery* is replaced by complexity management or handling. "The need for coping with complexity arises from the realization that every [open] system is embedded in an environment that usually has many behaviours. If a system wants to survive in its environment, it must be able to 'oppose' these behavioural possibilities" (Probst 1981, translated). The extent to which supply chain management deals with complexity determines its efficiency and effectiveness, and thus its contribution to the overall success of the company (Bleicher 1995; Kirsch 1984; Ulrich/Probst 1991).

The traditionally propagated way of supply chain management was the avoidance or reduction of complexity, for example, by external regulation and specialization. However, such an approach is inappropriate to provide the necessary resilience and variety in the supply chain system necessary for the survival of the enterprise. Complexity management should therefore not always mean the reduction of complexity, but it may also imply its conscious increase. The ability to increase complexity is even a central prerequisite for the development and survival of open systems, such as supply chains par excellence (Röpke 1977). On the other side, an unconditional flexibility of supply chains, as is often discussed, is not always appropriate. For supply chains, complexity management in this sense means to handle the interplay between complexity increase and reduction in the form of an *agile development*, such as a trial-and-error process. It must take steps to reduce or increase complexity and at the right time, to the right extent. Although supply chain management does not have complete knowledge of the system's interrelationships, it can recognize certain rules or patterns of order resulting from the interplay of the structures and behaviour of the system or the members of the system, and align its actions accordingly. Such an approach outlines the subject area of digital supply chain management as a whole.

2 Need for a framework

The high importance attributed to the *complexity management of supply chains* raises the question of an adequate design. This problem has not yet been fully addressed by scientific efforts. As will be proved in the course of the second part of this volume, the business sciences offer little theoretical-conceptual support regarding the handling of supply chain complexity. Even if the development of supply chain management is addressed, as for example with *Copacino* in 1992, *Dubbert* 1991, *Ihde* 1991, *Weber/Kummer* 1994 and *Pfohl* 1991, a comprehensive theoretical appreciation of complexity management for supply chains hardly takes place. In addition, the contributions are often limited to selected management subsystems, such as the organization and human resources, or to a subarea of supply chains, such as production logistics. The most comprehensive approaches are provided by the conceptual work of Warnecke, Wildemann, and Fey, as well as Smith and Ptak. In recent years, the platform Industry 4.0, acatech and Fraunhofer emphasize the importance of cyberphysical systems for such complexity management.

Warnecke uses his concept of the "fractal factory" to design a system for production logistics. The fractal structure offers a hierarchizing of the manufacturing organization and enables sufficient complexity in this area via decentralized control loops (Warnecke 1992). *Wildemann* offers the "modular factory" in response to the growing complexity of manufacturing. With his concept of manufacturing segmentation, he offers an organizational principle based on flexibility and process orientation for production (logistics). His concept implies complexity-increasing approaches, in particular in connection with the creation of structured networking and self-regulating, partially autonomous subsystems (Wildemann 1994). The implementation of Warnecke's and Wildemann's ideas are made possible by the use of cyberphysical systems in their pure variety, so that Warnecke's and Wildemann's reflections through the fourth industrial revolution experienced a sort of renaissance for production. From the point of view of supply chain practice, both approaches have been considered very important and relevant. The appreciation and interest of the supply chain practitioner in concepts such as the fractal factory and the modular factory prove that the desire for solutions for dealing with increasing complexity is very strong and increasing. In this respect, Warnecke and Wildemann set the central milestones for the development of complexity management in production. Both approaches offer principles that can also be rolled out to the entire supply chain.

Fey (1989) embeds his concept of integrated supply chain management in the company's management system and derives development steps for supply chains (Kummer 1992). In doing so, he takes aspects of resilience into account as he sheds light on the development of supply chains from a traditional to a cross-sectional understanding. Fey concentrates his statements on the evolution of supply chain management. Like Warnecke and Wildemann, Fey also concentrates mainly on the area of production logistics.

In my publications of 1994 and 1997 (Wehberg 1994, 1997), I am pick up the aforementioned approaches of Warnecke, Wildemann and Fey, amongst others, to design a management concept for the complexity management of the entire supply chain and its resilience, respectively. In the first edition of this publication (Wehberg 2015), I considered the possibilities of Industry 4.0 and digitalization, respectively. By doing so, I sought to combine the principles of a demand-driven and resilient supply chain. This third edition considers further practical experience from another four years acting as a consultant in transforming supply chains (e.g. Wehberg 2018, 2018b; Wehberg/Berger 2018). This includes cooperation with technology providers such as SAP Leonardo and Siemens Mindsphere, in particular.

In 1996, *Beckmann* developed a prototyping approach for supply chain planning based on agile principles. Later on, the resilience of organizations was addressed by Bell (2002), amongst others, in light of the terrible attacks of 11 September 2001. In particular, resilient supply chains became a focus of interest, for example, by Christopher/Pack (2004). These publications focused on the vulnerability of supply chains in cases of unexpected events such as terrorist attacks. While the theoretical fundamentals of these approaches were not broadly elaborated, they primarily focused on risk mitigation. New opportunities generated by digital business models were not incorporated comprehensively.

Smith and Ptak (2011) then deployed the ideas of de-coupling, postponement, etc. to MRP-based standard software for supply chain planning, in terms of demand-driven material resource planning. Their concept helped to develop standard solutions in planning tools and the practical application of relevant concepts. A full leveraging of digitalization potentials, though, still has to be provided from both sides Smith's and Ptak's Demand Driven Institute, as well as respective vendors, which they are working on (e.g. *SAP* has introduced a demand-driven approach within its IBP tool set and others are working on it).

Among others, the Federal Government (through its *Platform Industry 4.0* initiative, with the participation of BITKOM, VDMA and ZVEI), the German Academy of Engineering (*acatech*) and the *Fraunhofer Gesellschaft* (exemplified by acatech 2015; Bullinger/Hompel 2007; ten Hompel 2014) have helped to structure the conception of Industry 4.0 in recent years, emphasizing the significance for supply chain management in particular. For example, ten Hompel early recognized the importance of RFID technology as a kind of precursor of cyberphysical systems (ten Hompel/Bluechter/Franzke 2008). In this context, the federal initiative, acatech and Fraunhofer – each for themselves – are central points of contact for the idea of Industry 4.0 with its technological basis.

Note that there is still a lack of understanding of complexity management for supply chains in many respects. There is a strong need for a frame of reference of digital supply chain management that supports decisions and resilience in particular. From an IT angle, such a framework has been drafted in terms of *RAMI 4.0* (Reference Architecture Model Industry 4.0). It is currently maturing through the development of a big data architecture framework. The latter one typically includes a large number of vendors, while the global players in that market are currently trying to insource, subsequently, and build a track record of use cases. Prospectively, in some years such IT frameworks will be off-the-shelves and commoditized. The business and technological dimensions, however, do not replace one another; rather, they complement each other. Thus, the key question that remains to be answered is how digital technology can support competitiveness and enable new business models.

In particular, a comprehensive empirical foundation of guiding principles on complexity management in supply chains is lacking, with only few initial investigations. For the future, the goal must therefore be to further develop the concept for supply chain management 4.0 or *digital supply chains*, respectively.

A purely theoretical discussion of scientific fundamentals is of little value without being challenged from a practical perspective. *Practical relevance* arises by questioning and putting information into context with application examples. On the other hand, reporting selected case studies in and of itself is not very creative. This is why we will try to consider both perspectives in a balanced manner.

In the following, the terms "supply chain" or "logistics" as well as the expressions "resilient", "evolutionary" or "change oriented" are used in a somewhat interchangeable way. This is not entirely precise from a scientific point of view. However, this blurring should be overlooked insofar as the discussion does not directly refer to its scientific basis.

Literature

acatech/Arbeitskreis Smart Service Welt, Ed., *Smart Service Welt – Umsetzungs-empfehlungen für das Zukunftsprojekt Internetbasierte Dienste für die Wirtschaft*, Abschlussbericht, Berlin 2015.

acatech – Deutsche Akademie der Technikwissenschaften, Ed., *Cyber Physical Systems*, Innovationsmotor für Mobilität, Gesundheit, Energie und Produktion, München, Berlin 2011.

Beckmann, H., Theorie einer evolutionären Logistik-Planung, Basiskonzepte der Unternehmensentwicklung in Zeiten zunehmender Turbulenz unter Berücksichtigung des Prototypingansatzes, in: Kuhn, A., *Reihe Unternehmenslogistik*, Dortmund 1996.

Bell, M. A., *The Five Principles of Organizational Resilience*, Gartner Inc. Stamford 2002.

Bleicher, K., *Das Konzept Integriertes Management*, 3rd ed., Frankfurt a.M., New York 1995.

Bullinger, H.-J., ten Hompel, M., *Internet der Dinge*, Wiesbaden 2007.

Christopher, M., H. Peck, Building the Resilient Supply Chain, in: *International Journal of Logistics Management*, 15 (2004), 2, pp. 1–13.

Copacino, W. C., Time for Change Based Strategy?, in: *Traffic Management*, 31 (1992), pp. 71–72.

Dubbert, M. C., *Strategische Managemententwicklungsplanung, Konzeption und empirische Ergebnisse für den Bereich der Logistik*, Frankfurt a.M. 1991.

Fey, P., *Logistikmanagement und integrierte Unternehmensplanung*, München 1989.

Ihde, G., *Transport, Verkehr, Logistik*, München 1991.

Kirsch, W., *Wissenschaftliche Unternehmensführung oder Freiheit vor der Wissenschaft?*, 2 Bände, München 1984.

Kummer, S., *Logistik im Mittelstand, Stand und Kontextfaktoren der Logistik in mittelständischen Unternehmen*, Stuttgart 1992.

Packowski, J., *Lean Supply Chain Management: The New Supply Chain Management Paradigm for Process Industries to Master Today's VUCA World*, London 2014.

Pfohl, H.-Chr., Unternehmensführungstrends und Logistik, in: Pfohl, H.-Chr. (Ed.), *Logistiktrends '91*, Berlin 1991.

Probst, G. J. B., *Kybernetische Gesetzeshypothesen als Basis für Gestaltungs- und Lenkungsregeln im Management*, Bern, Stuttgart 1981.

Röpke, J., *Die Strategie der Innovation*, Tübingen 1977.

Smith, C., Ptak, C., Lean Finds a Friend in Demand Driven MRP (DDMRP), A White Paper by the Demand Driven Institute, April 2011.

ten Hompel, M., Büchter, H., Franzke, U., *Identifikationssysteme und Automatisierung*, Wiesbaden 2008.

ten Hompel, M., Logistik 4.0, in: Bauernhansl, T., ten Hompel, M., Vogel-Heuser, B. (Ed.), *Industrie 4.0 in Produktion, Automatisierung und Logistik*, Wiesbaden 2014, pp. 615–624.

Ulrich, H., Probst, G., *Anleitung zum ganzheitlichen Denken und Handeln*, 3rd ed., Stuttgart 1991.

Warnecke, H.-J., *Die Fraktale Fabrik, Revolution der Unternehmenskultur*, Berlin u. a. 1992.

Weber, J., Kummer, S., *Logistikmanagement*, Stuttgart 1994.

Wehberg, G., Logistik 4.0, in: *Komplexität managen in Theorie und Praxis*, Wiesbaden 2015.

Wehberg, G., Logistik 4.0 – sechs Säulen der Logistik jenseits nachfragegetriebener Ansätze, in: Göpfert, I. (Ed.), *Zukunft der Logistik – Logistik der Zukunft*, new ed., Wiesbaden 2018, 12th chapter.

Wehberg, G., Logistik-Controlling – Kern des evolutionären Logistikmanagement, in: Jöstingmeier, B. et al. (Ed.), *Aktuelle Probleme der Genossenschaften aus rechtswissenschaftlicher und wirtschaftswissenschaftlicher Sicht*, Göttingen 1994, pp. 73–134.

Wehberg, G., *Ökologieorientiertes Logistikmanagement, Ein evolutionstheoretischer Ansatz*, Wiesbaden 1997.

Wehberg, G., Supply Chain Innovations: From Demand Driven to Digital Twin, Presentation on the Regional Conference of German Association of Logistics (BVL) in Mönchengladbach of 13 September 2018 b.

Wehberg, G., Berger, T., Digital Supply Chains: Leveraging IoT for Managing Supply Chains in Complex Times, BVL Lab in the Deloitte Digital Factory in Düsseldorf, 19 June 2018 (published on www.DigitalSupplyInstitute.com).

Weick, K. E., Sutcliffe, K. M., *Managing the Unexpected: Assuring High Performance in an Age of Complexity*, Jossey-Bass, San Francisco, 2001.

Wildemann, H., *Die Modulare Fabrik*, 4th ed., München 1994.

Part 2

Where we come from

In the first part, key sources of logistics literature were addressed to make clear that the field of digital supply chains has been lightly addressed thus far.

The question of what is special about digital supply chains should not be confused with an investigation into the identity of supply chain management itself. *Supply chain theory* is facing a tough test. Scientists refer to neighboured business studies, such as production, about the original subject of supply chain management (see Chapter 2 of this part). Occasionally, the question arises of whether supply chain management is not just "old wine in new hoses". This shows that a broad consensus on what supply chain management is has not yet been achieved. The attempts to answer the question of what supply chain management is are rare and seldom adequately sound (however, Göpfert 1996).

The following chapters explain why the existing understandings of supply chain management are not suitable for coping with complexity. The various definitions are classified in the sense of an overall view. The understanding of supply chain management has always been influenced by certain megatrends, also referred to as "paradigms" or "myths". Since the end of the last century, five main trends have been identified (Fey 1989; Kummer 1992b).

To a certain extent, as the source of these current paradigms, *scientific management* shaped the functional specialization of companies (Taylor 1911) at the beginning of the 20th century. The core idea of this development was to use task-sharing as efficiently as possible through specialization. The institutional separation of management and execution functions goes back to this Tayloristic approach. For example, one concept that is still applied today and is based on functional specialization is the experience curve effects of companies. Functional specialization was followed by a *product and customer specialization*, which is mainly expressed in today's marketing ideas (Gutenberg 1955; Meffert 1977). This was the basis of *process specialization*, which could significantly contribute to the profiling of supply chain management as an independent business function. In the last 30 years, gaining in importance, but often treated without the necessary theoretical foundations, the change of businesses has been expressed, for example, by slogans like *management of change* or *chaos management*, and dealing above all with the problems of complexity handling and change (Bleicher 1979, 1995; Kirsch 1992).

One main stream of business activity is the specialization of relationships, focusing on the development of a holistic reference framework for the design of highly complex systems (Diller 1994; Sydow 1993). For example, the current development of the *transaction cost theory* is associated with this and tries to explain the functionality of networks or eco-systems. Since the establishment and maintenance of such *eco-systems* can ultimately be understood as a response to a more complex corporate environment, relationship specialization can be interpreted as a specific form of expression of change (Wehberg 1994). If we start from the megatrends of business administration, these can be assigned to the different understandings of supply chain management. The criticism of one approach shows the advantages of others (Weber/Kummer 1994, supplemented by Göpfert/Wehberg 1996).

1   Existing approaches

The *transfer-oriented understanding* of supply chain management characterizes all "transport, storage and transhipment processes in the real goods sector in and between social systems" (Arnold 1988, after Weber 1993b, translated). It is currently the most widespread in the field of supply chain management. It thus understands physical transfer functions in the form of purposeful space and time bridging as the task of supply chain management. It thus focuses on a company's execution system. In many instances, the expression "logistics" is used in this context, rather than "supply chain management". But of course, it is the understanding that counts and not the nomenclature. Today, many supply chain managers decorate their role as supply chain management while following aforementioned understanding.

The transfer-oriented understanding paves the way for a closer study with a group of services that has often been neglected in the past. The mere renaming of already existing functions, such as transport and storage, offers possibly positive loading effects (Weber/Kummer, 1994). However, there is neither great practical benefit nor theoretical cognitive value. Such a functionally specialized task view, at best, offers efficiency advantages, for example due to experience curve effects. The functional specialization also finds expression in technical optimization efforts for individual process steps, such as the construction of dump trucks, industrial conveyors, pre-distribution systems of commissioning, etc. It reflects incompletely the range of tasks of supply chain management.

In contrast to the transfer-oriented approach, *process-oriented supply chain management* includes not only the spatial and temporal transformation functions, but also the operative steering functions relating to the flow of goods. The latter include, for example, production planning and scheduling, as well as dispatch control. The aim of supply chain management in this sense is the coordination of the entire process chain in an end-to-end fashion. The scope goes from upstream suppliers to production and customers right through to the disposal. By avoiding isolated applications, it aims to realize efficiency gains beyond functional specialization. The just-in-time delivery principle (Weber/Kummer 1994) can be cited as a representative example of process-oriented understanding. Just-in-time seeks complete control of a significant part of the material flow and ultimately identifies production-synchronous procurement.

And managing the relationship between sales and manufacturing is certainly at the heart of supply chain management from a process-oriented angle.

As a typical example of such a supply chain management definition that reflects this flow-oriented approach, Pfohl (1990, translated) mentions that of the *Council of Supply Chain Management*: "Supply chain management . . . is . . . the term describing the process from planning, implementing, and controlling the efficient, . . . and cost-effective supply of raw materials, in-process inventory, finished goods, and related information from point of origin to the point of consumption".

Against this background, we can see the *system thinking* of supply chain management; the supply chain is then described as "a number of interrelated parts that operate for a common purpose" (Forrester 1972). From a system perspective, in addition to the elements and relationships of the system itself, it also has to take into account relations with its surrounding system (Pfohl 1990). Process-oriented understanding in this sense tries to holistically grasp the interdependencies and the complexity of supply chain tasks. Due to its limitation to operational tasks, however, it offers only weak design assistance for the development of supply chains. Thus, the complexity management of supply chains has to be regarded as a primarily normative-strategic problem.

Demand-driven supply chain management also considers strategic aspects. It takes into account that relevant parameters do not determine the potential for the whole. Typically, success depends to a large extent on external factors, such as customers, competitors and suppliers (Weber/Kummer 1990). Therefore, this approach is based on the concept of *strategic management* by Ansoff, Declerck and Hayes in 1976. This concept of strategic corporate governance has now reached a high level of diffusion.

In business reality, the discussion about the strategic importance of supply chain management goes back to the 1980s and 1990s. While in the 1960s supplier markets were primarily driven by strong demand, it changed towards *customer markets* at the beginning of the 1980s and 1990s. In addition to the product features, service and supply chain characteristics have increasingly played a role for differentiation in competition. Supply chain service has become the subject of strategic considerations. Concepts such as *marketing logistics* and strategic supply chain management were developed and implemented.

However, there are increasing voices that critically raise doubts about the prevalent mechanistic feasibility or *mastery of control* of aforementioned understanding (Antoni 1985, 1986; Bleicher 1989; Mann 1988, 1995; Servatius 1991; Stachle 1989). The latter seems to be typical for at least a large part of the supply chain theory that corresponds to such demand-driven understanding. Last but not least, it explains the strong need to reduce system complexity instead of increasing it where necessary. It goes hand in hand with the desire to reduce uncertainty and increase control.

In this context, the thesis of the *integration deficit* of logistics applies (Klaus 1994). Countless definitions of supply chain management, as well as declarations of managers, produce the following holistic claim: Flows of material and goods

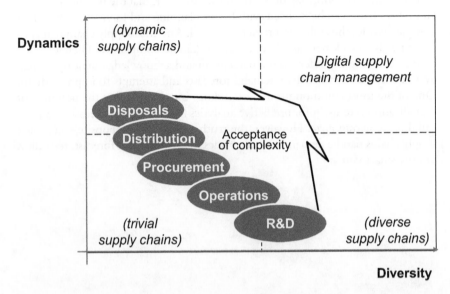

Figure 1.1 Supply chain integration through acceptance and management of complexity

are to be combined across functions and institutions to create a system-wide optimum. However, to date, supply chain management is organized in many companies as "functions" logistics, for example, for SCOR functions. It is common practice to focus on the three planning areas of procurement, production and distribution logistics in a comparatively isolated way. More or less, they are based on their own objectives, optimization rules and databases. Integration is much more often an idea than reality (see Figure 1.1). The potential of supply chain management is far from exhausted. In reality, a significant *knowing–doing gap* (implementation gap) is associated with it.

The knowing–doing gap then results in a chaotic approach to supply chain management. It leads to bullwhip effect and inappropriate service levels for customers. A common reaction in this situation is to increase inventories because management wishes to buffer some of the day-to-day problems; however, that makes it even worse, because lead times prolong and flexibility decreases.

A resilient understanding of supply chain management promises to close the integration gap. "The perceived dynamic plays the role of the trigger for system strategies that cope with complexity" (Bleicher 1994, translated). Good results-oriented strategy exercises always begin with a thorough discussion of trends, disruptions and challenges. Appropriate supply chain strategies find suitable answers to these kind of complexity drivers. In addition to a knowing–doing gap, there is a *seeing–knowing gap* (meaning gap), which describes the delta between data availability and insight, accordingly.

The seeing–knowing gap does not mean, however, that the potential of digital supply chains can be realized with better planning and forecasting only. In a complex world, the ability to predict is limited. And thus supply chain management needs to seek new and better ways to handle complexity. Therefore, the seeing–knowing gap refers to the perception and acknowledgement of the relevant complexity, rather than demand forecasts and attempts to improve them. One of the most common misunderstandings is to believe that the potential of digitalization is to use it for predictive analytics for improving forecasts. You can call this the *forecast myth*. However, the truth is exactly the opposite – complex supply chains handle demand characteristics that you cannot forecast, regardless of how smart you are.

2 Resilient understanding

2.1 Roots

To avoid misunderstandings, the basic concepts of a demand-driven understanding of supply chain management should first be contrasted with the roots
of the resilient approach. The resilient understanding (Göpfert/Wehberg 1996;
Göpfert 2000; Wehberg 1994, 1997) refers to a "holistic-evolutionary management theory" (Servatius 1991).

Mandeville laid a first important cornerstone of this theory through his early
18th-century publication "*The Fable of the Bees*", in which he developed the
twin idea of evolution and the spontaneous formation of order (von Hayek
1969b; Kieser 1988). In 1767, Ferguson brought up Mandeville's idea of the
short-term formula that although order may be the result of human action, it
must not be human intention (Ferguson 1966; von Hayek 1969b). Darwin,
who is today regarded as the co-founder of evolutionary biology and the
theory of evolution in general, was also inspired by these first evolutionary steps
(Darwin 1859, 1967; Riedl 1987). This theory of development builds on the
fundamental idea that a mechanism of multiplication of transferred variants and
competitive selection, over time, produce a wide variety of structures that show
themselves to be suitable in complex environments (von Hayek 1972). This
basic idea is also referred to as the *evolutionary principle*. Consequently, system
complexity becomes the variable of the evolutionary process (Röpke 1977). It
characterizes a system of being able to accept a large number of different states
in a given period of time (Ulrich/Probst 1991). Schumpeter (1950) is probably one of the most important representatives of the theory of evolution in
the context of economic scientific research efforts with his process of *creative
destruction*, which is regarded as the core element of technological change, and
thus as the source of economic development.

The theory of evolution was often misunderstood. Numerous erroneous
interpretations of this theory are responsible for the *misconception* that it consists
of the assertion of the sequence of particular types of organisms that gradually
morph into one another. This is not, however, the theory of evolution, but
the application of the theory to the individual events that have taken place on
Earth for approximately the last two billion years (von Hayek 1972). It is often

misconstrued that evolutionary mechanisms in social systems should act less on the level of individuals and more on institutions and their behaviour (Malik 1984; Sprüngli 1981).

At the same time, nature offers a lot of analogies we can learn from. Consider ants as an example. Harvest ants can promote forestry by accelerating the degradation and conversion of wood. They effectively eliminate other, harmful insects. And the presence of many seed-collecting ants may normally favour production because it counteracts the increase in harmful parasitic beetles.

Ants form highly organized colonies that may occupy large territories and consist of millions of individuals. The colonies are described as superorganisms because the ants appear to operate as a unified entity, collectively working together to support the colony. Their success in so many environments has been attributed to their social organization in terms of swarm intelligence as well as their ability to modify habitats, tap resources and solve complex problems.

What a great supply chain that ants have – it flexibly responds to new challenges, is resource efficient and secures the supply of the colony on the highest level. It is a great example of nature that we can benefit from because we also have to secure supply, be efficient and work flexibly. Our supply chains typically follow the same or very similar principles.

The second historical root of the resilient understanding of supply chain management is *holism*. The essence of this attitude is expressed in the demand for a holistic network of thinking and acting instead of the mechanistic worldview (Capra 1985). The introduction of holistic thinking into business administration has already taken place through the system-oriented approach developed by Ulrich (1968). However, the influence of holistic principles also changed the system theory (Staehle 1989b). If equilibrium-preserving processes are still the subject of first-order cybernetics, cybernetics of the second order is now primarily concerned with imbalances. And imbalances are a necessary condition for changes in a system (Beer 1972; Kirsch/Esser/Gabele, 1979; Vester 1980b; Malik 1984; to Knyphausen 1988; Schulz 1993). The latter can logically be understood as a science of the design and direction of complex, dynamic systems. It establishes a system theory in the broader sense, which is also called *new systems theory* (Probst 1981).

At this point, the transition between holistic and evolutionary approaches becomes fluid (Servatius 1991).

2.2   Integration as core

The adaptation of supply chain structures to changing environmental conditions is usually seen as the task of each subarea, for example, packaging and warehousing. In the context of a holistic approach, however, this is at the heart of *supply chain integration*. The focus of resilient supply chains thus is based on a kind of meta-management. Supply chain integration in this sense must anticipate adjustments that affect the entire supply chain and drive innovation, accordingly (Bleicher 1979; Wehberg 1994). Designing a future supply chain target operating model means both integration of physical flows as well as of supply chain management itself. The one is a prerequisite for the other, and vice versa.

Küpper talks about controlling instead of integration (Küpper 1987, 1995). According to his ideas, *supply chain controlling* plays a central role in the development of a supply chain (management) system. Similarly, Kirsch (1992) uses the term "controlling overlayer". The task of supply chain controlling is characterized by coordinating the management system. It is referred to as secondary coordination, in addition to the primary coordination of the supply chain itself. Moreover, *system forming* and *system coupling* are being distinguished.

Bleicher's (1979) concept, integrated management – which is also known as the *St. Gallen management concept* – forms a frame of reference for management integration and can be transferred to supply chain integration in particular. For doing so, Bleicher offers a technique for analyzing the entrepreneurial situation as a polarized series of tension. This profiling technique supports promising adaptations. It enables statements about the actual and target relationships between intrinsic and external complexity of the supply chain system, which are shown in a simplified way in Figure 2.1. Specifically, the *stabilized supply chain* characterizes a relatively low complexity. The *digital supply chain* represents a higher complexity of relevant structures. In this context, the term "change" continues to characterize the already mentioned interplay between stability and resilience. In a way, it can be seen as a measure of complexity.

The aforementioned profiling framework has to be enriched with *design principles* or concepts to provide guidance for decision making and to facilitate implementation. The theory of evolution does not characterize a closed statement system. Rather, it encompasses a heterogeneous bundle of approaches. Each individual approach regularly includes a cluster of scientists (Wehberg

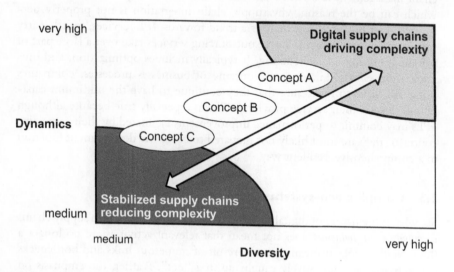

Figure 2.1 Profiling of change (as measure for complexity)

1996, based on Semmel 1984) such as the *population ecology* approach, especially after Aldrich, Hannan, Freeman, Kaufman and McKelvey; the *market process* approach with Fehl, Kerber, Kirzner and Lachmann; the *organizational process* approach, especially with Bigelow, Dyllick, Röpke and Zammuto; the *self-organization* approach with the St. Galler School under Ulrich on the one hand and the Munich School under Kirsch on the other hand; the *psychological approach* according to Weick and others; and the *cybernetics* approach, especially with Ashby. There is no need to address these approaches of organizational theory more precisely at this point. The references made here are sufficient to form a basic understanding of supply chain management based on the literature presented thus far.

Now, a functional perspective (on what resilient supply chain management does) must be differentiated against an organizational one (who is doing it). How supply chain integration is organized and by whom finds very different forms in corporate practice. In *large corporations*, business units or divisions typically orchestrate supply chain operations. The development of supply chain management itself is performed at the group level. From a corporate perspective, supply chain integration aims at identifying trends across business units and enabling functions in terms of size, scale and learning effects. For example, a company-wide consolidation of warehousing or supply chain analytics typically offers such scale. For good governance, it often makes sense to anchor supply chain management as a direct report of the chief finance officer. Here, supply chain integration thus depends on the power and capabilities of the corporate function. In *medium-sized companies*, supply chain tasks are often not explicitly anchored organizationally. Such tasks are performed as part of traditional sales and production functions and responsibilities. Here, the development of supply chain management is often in the hands of the sales or production manager, which can be the reason why supply chain integration is not properly performed. Last but not least, there is a trend towards *4PL* services, fourth-party supply chain management. These outsourcing services take over a large part of planning, control and scheduling. It typically includes optimization, and thus integration efforts. Like any outsourcing of businesses processes, companies using 4PL have to make sure that they continue to have the minimum capabilities to steer their service providers. This is especially true because although 4PLs may commit to performance improvements facilitated by their respective contracts, they are most likely not prepared to cover the development function in a comprehensive, resilient way.

2.3   Complex eco-systems

So, what is the nature of digital supply chains? The transition from supply chains to *supply chain networks* does not mean that relevant activities are no longer a flow. Neither does it mean that as a result of numerous links and bottlenecks that activities are figuratively caught up in a "net". Rather, the emphasis on the network idea points to a new pattern of structural design. Complex supply chain network structures are characterized by the fact that they can serve a variety of relations in different ways. For doing so, they are typically partnering on a need-by-need basis in a broader eco-system. ten Hompel (2014, translated) sums it up as follows: "The supply chain network and its nodes must continually adapt to the conditions. Therefore, nodes should be able to move in the future. This prohibits many forms of classic technical infrastructure".

In a nutshell, digital supply chains can be described as complex eco-systems that are enabled by new technology. From a more academic point of view, a more precise definition of digital supply chain management can look like the following: Digital supply chain management is a special management approach for highly complex eco-systems of object flows, which are based on pattern recognition, generalization as well as self-organization, and leverage on innovative services as well as new technology. Let's discuss the characteristics in more detail.

The special management approach refers to the *resilient* understanding of supply chain management, its roots and integration focus. Object flows include both goods and information. This is, basically, nothing new for supply chain management. However, considering the so-called *digital twins* of a combined virtual and real world such flows are being discussed in a new light and on a new level.

Pattern recognition is the way in which the behaviour of complex systems is being perceived, based on environmental conditions or market requirements. *Generalization* is characterized by comparatively highly differentiated and highly flexible supply chain structures. Such developed supply chain systems offer numerous options to effectively behave in highly complex environments. Generalization does not mean to be a quasi-jack of all trades (or master of none). It can also be expressed to some extent by a multi-specialization. *Self-organization*, then, uses its possibilities by effectively and efficiently linking the subsystems of a supply chain (management). Self-organization is characterized by its recursive, autonomous, redundant and self-referential attachment (Wehberg 1997).

From a business angle, *innovative services* in this context include both new service levels and new offerings themselves, for example, analytics as a service for optimizing product performance. Therefore, digital supply chains are a key enabler for new digital business models. For example, an e-commerce platform will not succeed, sustainably, if the order processing is not being performed in a touchless fashion. And for companies that suffer from a lack of qualified staff, automation can be a key growth factor given they cannot recruit the necessary resources in line with their ambitions. In a digital century, supply chain management definitely upgrades towards a competitive factor from a corporate strategy perspective if it hasn't before from a demand-driven point of view.

Next to new services and macro-economic benefits, digital supply chains can offer the following advantages for companies (Kagermann 2013):

- Individualization of customer wishes.
- Flexibility of supply.
- Improved resource efficiency.

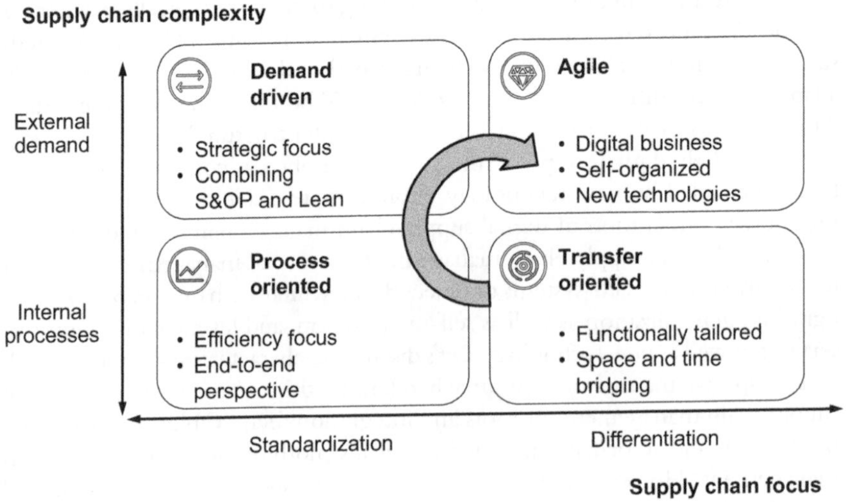

Supply chain complexity

Figure 2.2 Evolution path of supply chain management

A summary of the successive understandings of supply chain management and stages of development is given in Figure 2.2. In particular, the presentation shows the shift in emphasis from fulfilment execution to strategic impact in the course of its development.

Now, what are the key enablers for digital supply chains from a technological and change angle?

2.4   Key enablers: technology and change

As much as a digital twin needs an enabler from a technology point of view, digital supply chains need an IT architecture. Digital twins are enabled by *cyberphysical systems*, which are characterized by the incorporation of computer-aided and mechanical components that communicate via a data infrastructure. In other words, cyberphysical systems represent the fusion of the virtual and the real world (Broy 2010; Bullinger/Hompel 2007; acatech 2011; Vogel–Heuser 2014).

A suitable *IT architecture* is best represented in three dimensions (according to RAMI 4.0, the Reference Architecture Model Industry 4.0 of Platform 4.0 2015):

- Layers or perspectives.
- Life cycle phases and value chains.
- Responsibilities and hierarchy levels (Figure 2.3).

Regarding different perspectives, established planning and operations software such as SAP IBP, EWM and TMS have to be distinguished from new big

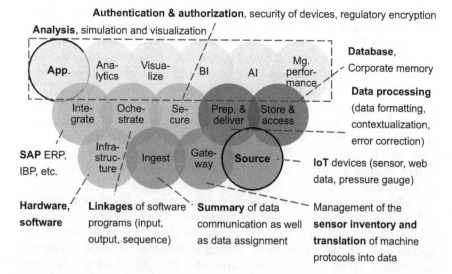

Figure 2.3 Reference architecture for digital supply chains

data applications. Both are tightly linked with the ERP backbone and its data warehouse (e.g. SAP HANA). Figure 2.3 provides an overview of the different layers of such *big data architecture* for digital supply chains. Interestingly, such architecture can be leveraged for other functions over and beyond supply chain management, up to 70 to 80 percent, for example, for procurement, operations and finance, amongst others. In order to connect different things (products, packages, pallets, etc.) it builds on Internet of Things (IoT) platforms such as Leonardo from SAP, ThingWorx from PTC or Mindsphere from Siemens.

While the variety of relevant vendors is currently high, established players insource more and more applications and provide more comprehensive solutions. But even different vendors for the same application, for example, artificial intelligence (AI), typically provide different benefits today, based on the specific use case and the databases being discussed. This is why it is questionable to choose one strategic partner per application field, rather the leveraging the full potential of vendors on a pay-per-use basis. Conclusively, IT architectures for supply chains are on the move. For example, tracking and tracing focused on locations and could refer to SAP TMS in the past. Digital supply chains track and trace many indicators, such as temperature and humidity, amongst others. They use the aforementioned IoT platforms or even blockchain technology for more extended appliances.

Many companies underestimate the necessity of having one coherent big data architecture. For learning the technology, they have started to implement some single use cases as a proof of concept. What they don't have, though, is an overall idea how the end-state architecture should look. They develop proprietary IT solutions for each use case, without having a target picture in mind. Even if they just implement single appliances right now, all these use cases and future ones will not fit with each other in the mid–term. Instead of building one big *data lake*, these companies are dispersing data ponds, which are offering less value, conclusively. For exactly this reason, the motivation to digitalize supply chains can even slow instead of accelerate. Digitalization in this case takes too long, often does not support competitiveness and fails. Thus, a clear idea of the to-be architecture is a real factor for success, which does not mean that the IT has to be built in one step at once. In line with agile IT development, it can be built up stepwise as use cases are implemented. Successful companies are doing it exactly in this way and creating momentum for further use cases. They set up a process for use case creation and implementation, executing dozens or even hundreds of cases a year. This is how a state-of-the-art big data strategy works.

While technology is a key enabler for digital supply chains, other enablers such as *change management* are no less important. The usage of big data technology, for example, can create reluctances of those individuals who use it. Transparency of data facilitates measuring performance of those employees who are generating, using and/or sharing the data. And sharing data means that those humans who are sharing may lose their "monopoly of know-how". Using big data technology may be beneficial for the company; however, it can feel like a threat to respective individuals, which is counterproductive. Ten Hompel (2014) describes the role that humans play within such digital operating models: "Man is connected to the virtual world via an avatar. This software representative communicates with the social community of the CPS and with the cloud". The benefits of digital supply chains for the individual employee in the company is thus an important success factor. Besides use cases, a supply chain manager needs to have a case for change, too.

Over and beyond the usage of big data and the associated supply chain analytics, change plays a major role for the entire supply chain organization as well as for the IT team supporting it. If you consider the extensive automation potential of supply chains, it is easy to foresee that the need for resources will decrease, significantly, while the demand for new capabilities in terms of digital fluency of the supply chain organization is high. In simple words, a supply chain team will manage those systems in the future that push pallets, rather than pushing pallets themselves. Supply chain management develops towards a kind of functional CIO organization just because the impact of new technologies as value drivers is that high. This evolution challenges the way supply chain managers are doing their business and can feel like a threat to individuals. The same applies to the IT organization, who were used to dealing with ERP systems and the infrastructure associated with it in the past. While cloud solutions make a lot of corporate IT infrastructure obsolete, required skills develop from IT towards OT (Operations Technology).

It becomes clear that a state-of-the-art digital supply chain necessarily builds on both a comprehensive understanding of new technologies and its use cases, as well as an effective management of change. Having said that, it is important to understand the concept of digital supply chains holistically and not to limit it to selected technologies or change management. Digital supply chains are not possible without cyberphysical solutions. But first of all, it is a business topic. The life of a supply chain manager was always challenging because of the cross-functional role and interdisciplinary competencies required for it. However, in a digital world it becomes even more challenging.

3 Frame of reference

Digital twin of supply chains

For a sound handling of the numerous tasks and behaviours that are intrinsic to the complexity of supply chains, these are to be brought into a structured order which gives targeted access to specific problems and solutions associated. Although such a *frame of reference* limits the possible observations of the supply chain manager, it is indispensable for the manager's orientation (Probst 1981, in general). The value added of such a frame of reference results from the sum of its logically permissible statements or recommendations. Having said that, a frame of reference for digital supply chains can be structured with means of the following four dimensions (in the following Wehberg 1994, 2018):

- Levels of supply chain management (e.g. on a normative and strategic level).
- Systems of supply chain management (e.g. information and controlling).
- Design of the supply chain, with two poles, complexity and stability.
- Digital twin of the supply chain, including interfaces (e.g. to product design).

Let us start talking about *management levels*: The task assignments attributable to the complexity of supply chains can essentially be attributed to ensuring their fitness. The *fitness* of supply chains can be described on three levels (Bleicher 1995; Schwanninger 1994). The normative level characterizes its developability, which is derived above all from certain values of its employees and the associated basic attitudes. In doing so, it is responsible in particular for making sense and being meaningful in supply chain management, but also influences the viability of the entire company. Being the key facilitator for digitalization and enabling sustainability of a company are examples for such. At the same time, the normative level sets the framework for opportunities at the strategic level, for example, by maturing the understanding of supply chain management from a demand driven to a digital one.

Strategic decisions generally aim to create favourable conditions ("to do the right things") for the operative tasks through the effective design of supply chain structures (Drucker 1963). In this context, we want to describe the effectiveness as the quotient between the actual and target cost level and the level of performance of supply chains. It expresses the contribution that supply chain management can make to the competitive potential of the company. In a way, supply chain strategies aim at shifting, segmenting and forming the *cost-service curve* towards a competitive position (Figure 3.1). While supply chain management has to consider all three levels, its strategy is certainly a focus from a digitalization point of view. Many supply chain managers miss the opportunity to contribute to the company's value from a strategic angle. For example, you just need to ask them whether they sit at the strategy board round table of their company. Most likely not. And many digitalization managers focus too much on technology. They are well integrated within the IT team, but often less connected to the business. Digital supply chains, however, are the result of doing both – addressing the strategic potential as well as approaching it from a business perspective. It redefines the role of the supply chain manager of the future in several regards.

At the heart of the operational level of supply chains is the efficient steering of respective processes ("to do the things right"). The efficiency characterizes the quotient of input and output (Göpfert/Wehberg 1995). It is therefore defined by the ratio of service to costs. With respect to the cost–service curve, supply chain operations want to find the proper position on the existing curve(s) rather than forming a new curve or transforming it. Given a pre-defined design structure and a high degree of automation of digital supply chains, algorithms

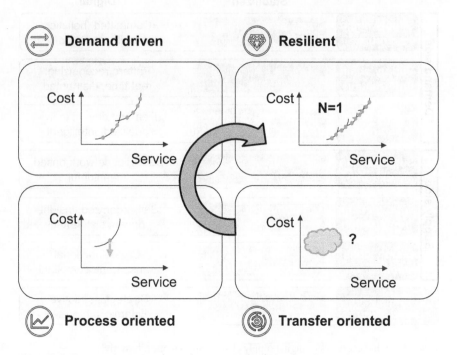

Figure 3.1 Cost-service curve dependent on supply chain maturity

will cover a huge part of this kind of operations tasks in the future. While the cross-functional coordination of capacities and resources within the S&OP process was characterized by personal interactions in the past, for example, such alignment will be subject to algorithms in the future. In other words, it is not so much about volumes, sites and lot sizes anymore, but about algorithms that determine the right volumes, sites and lot sizes.

Subdividing the *management (sub-)systems*, which is also referred to as hierarchization, leads to a profile system that can be refined to the level of individual design parameters of supply chains (Figure 3.2). Basically, demand side–related systems of supply chain management can be distinguished from supply side–related ones. The demand-side view includes key design parameters like supply chain governance, demand analytics and the planning approach, while the supply side refers to its capabilities, infrastructure and facilitators. Because such a system would be too extensive to be fully explained here, the following will focus on selected system-forming elements of the supply chain values, information and planning in particular.

You may ask yourself whether the differentiation of the value system of an enterprise through the formation of a subsystem is expedient. This can be answered against the background of intelligence. *Intelligence* can be understood as the ability to quickly cope in unfamiliar situations, to grasp the essence of

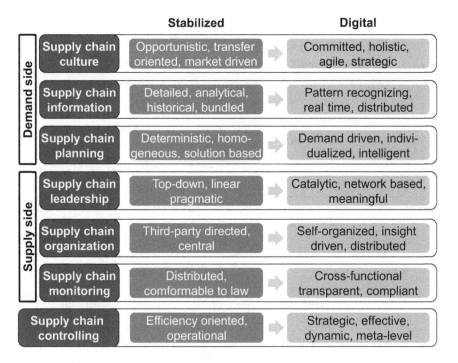

Figure 3.2 Characteristics of digital supply chain management (illustrative)

a fact or process quickly and correctly, mental agility, adaptability, curiosity, and rapid thinking and judgement. With regard to the normative fitness level, it should be noted that the presence of subcultures has a supportive effect on the intelligence of the company (similar to Simon 1989). The expansion and maintenance of separate values of supply chain management can be helpful. The significance of the normative also stems from the fact that "with the advent of the fourth industrial revolution . . . the normative area of supply chain management and the operational real-time area of the machines and the physical material flow are decoupled" (ten Hompel 2014, translated). A steering is then primarily indirectly, virtually possible via guardrails, which are just above values and standards set.

Now, what about *supply chain design* in terms of complexity versus stability? The synthesis of the aforementioned St. Gallen management concept and the coordination-oriented controlling approach leads to the reference structure shown in Figure 3.2. The profile of supply chain controlling represents (graphically) the change (as a measure of complexity) brought about by system coupling. The system forming is represented by all other systems of supply chain management and its change profiles, respectively.

The amount of change in supply chain management over the course of time ultimately depends on its development. However, it should also influence the latter in favour of the company's objectives. As already mentioned, an in-depth investigation of the development of a supply chain takes place within the fourth part of this volume. In particular, we will see what kinds of lessons we can learn from relevant academic approaches, if relevant. Given that holistic-evolutionary theory is at the heart of understanding supply chain management, let's see the relevant design principles it provide that can help. A holistic-evolutionary theory tries to answer the question how much complexity is necessary and how much stability is possible. In other words, it helps to determine the *right degree of change* (as a measure of complexity) based on the extrinsic and intrinsic challenges a company is facing.

Digital supply chains are not sustainable without an overall consistent design advantage. For this reason, all subsystems have to be designed coherently. Figure 3.2, therefore, shows in a nutshell the characteristics of such holistically understood digital supply chain and its associated level of change. The illustration includes one or the other keyword, so they are to be explained in the third part of this volume. By doing so, the frame of reference determines a clear definition of what a complex versus stable design means for key design parameters or systems of supply chain management. This provides a basic orientation and decision support for supply chain managers when developing their operations. At the same time, the target structure will always have to be developed on an enterprise-specific basis. In this sense, the example design of the parameters shown in Figure 3.2 can only be illustrative and directional. There is no "off-the-shelf" digital supply chain; there is no one blueprint that fits all situations. Rather, it is about company- and industry-specific solutions. This is especially true in light of new digital business models. Given that digital supply chains are a key facilitator for such, their design has to be as individual as the digital business model itself. Of course, a discussion about the corporate strategy and new business models associated to a certain extent also refers to common patterns of digitalization.

When it comes to designing *digital supply chains*, today we do it differently than in the past. We don't do one-off exercises to determine the network, but we permanently optimize the structure as a result of our predictions in order to balance capacities and material, globally. Our planning is not a closed system anymore; we must seek new disruptions and try to counterbalance their impacts. We don't even plan ourselves, but rather try to determine intelligent planning algorithms. On the shop floor, we are questioning the traditional MRP logic and introducing demand-oriented steering mechanisms. And our supply chain team is not doing physical transport or warehousing anymore, but managing automatic transport and warehousing systems. This all is based on a strong and independent supply chain governance that supports self-organization and powerful IT.

To do this on a real-time basis and efficiently, we use standard ERP tools and combine it with new technology. A big data architecture complements the classical ERP as well as supply chain IT landscape and makes use of IoT and AI technologies. Process mining helps to identify the relevant use cases that determine the future architecture. We don't do big bang waterfalls but develop in an agile way through consistent architecture cuts. IT develops towards OT.

And then we come up with something that we call a *digital twin of the supply chain*. The digital twin is a complex matter and represents a virtual model of the real chain. Typically, the virtual part includes the process, cost-service, geographical and technological parameters. Like in nature, the digital twin allows us to permanently optimize the structure and evolve it over time. Nature is doing many, many things right and optimizes over millions of years and hundreds of generations. The digital twin, however, allows us to optimize supply chains even within hours. Like in the evolution of nature, the digital twin of a supply chain is a digital twin of performance because it supports the feedback loop for a continuous improvement of the network.

The digital twin of a supply chain adds up to the digital twin of product design, production and the IoT (Figure 3.3). In an end-to-end perspective, new products or design adjustments need to have a proper supply chain network. The digital twin thus includes new designs that make, for example, delivery and maintenance easier. It allows us to plan, source, make, deliver and serve in a way that we have never done before. The evolutionary approach of supply chain management creates examples that enhance service levels or flexibility by 60 percent and decrease working capital as well as cost by 40 percent. These examples are very close to nature, which provides fantastic role models for great supply chains.

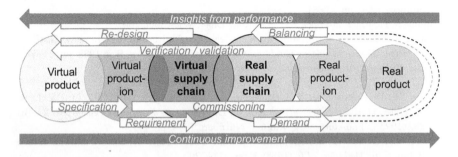

Figure 3.3 Digital twin (Wehberg 2018, based on Mrosik 2018)

Literature

acatech/Arbeitskreis Smart Service Welt, Ed., *Smart Service Welt – Umsetzungsempfehlungen für das Zukunftsprojekt Internetbasierte Dienste fur die Wirtschaft*, Abschluss-bericht, Berlin 2015.

acatech – Deutsche Akademie der Technikwissenschaften, Ed., *Cyber Physical Systems*, Innovationsmotor für Mobilität, Gesundheit, Energie und Produktion, München, Berlin 2011.

Ammelburg, G., *Die Unternehmenszukunft*, Freiburg 1985.

Ansoff, H. I., *Strategic Management*, New York 1979.

Ansoff, H. I., Declerck, R. P., Hayes, R. L., *From Strategic Planning to Strategic Management*, London 1976.

Antoni, M., Innovation durch Evolutionäres Management, Die Antwort auf die Herausforderung der Ingenieure, in: *Congena-Texte*, (1985) 2/3, pp. 49–55.

Antoni, M., Menschliche Arbeit – Grundbedürfnis oder fremdgesetzte Norm? Konsequenzen für die Personalentwicklung, in: Riekhof, H. C. (Ed.), *Strategien der Personalentwicklung*, Wiesbaden 1986, pp. 23–75.

Arnold, U., Stichwort Logistik, in: *Gablers' Wirtschaftslexikon*, 12th ed., 2. Band, Wiesbaden 1988, pp. 170–174.

Beckmann, H., Theorie einer evolutionären Logistik-Planung, Basiskonzepte der Unternehmensentwicklung in Zeiten zunehmender Turbulenz unter Berücksichtigung des Prototypingansatzes, in: Kuhn, A., *Reihe Unternehmenslogistik*, Dortmund 1996.

Beer, S., *Brain of the Firm*, Chichester 1972.

Bleicher, K., *Chancen für Europas Zukunft – Führung als internationaler Wettbewerbsfaktor*, Frankfurt 1989.

Bleicher, K., *Das Konzept Integriertes Management*, 3rd ed., Frankfurt a.M., New York 1995.

Bleicher, K., *Normatives Management*, Frankfurt a.M., New York 1994.

Bleicher, K., *Unternehmensentwicklung und organisatorische Gestaltung*, Stuttgart, New York 1979.

Browning, J., The Power of Process Redesign: A Round Table Discussion with John Hagel, Richard Heygate, Rod Baird and Greg Prang, in: *McKinsey Quarterly*, (1993) 1, pp. 47–58.

Broy, M., Ed., *Cyber-Physical Systems: Innovation Durch Softwareintensive Eingebettete Systeme*, Heidelberg u. a. 2010.

Bruhn, M., Bunge, B., Beziehungsmarketing – Neuorientierung für Marketingwissenschaft und -praxis?, in: Bruhn, M., Meffert, H., Wehrle, F. (Ed.), *Marktorientierte*

Unternehmensführung im Umbruch, Effizienz und Flexibilität als Herausforderung des Marketing, Stuttgart 1994, pp. 41–84.

Bullinger, H.-J., ten Hompel, M., *Internet der Dinge*, Wiesbaden 2007.

Capra, F., Die Auto-Organization im nicht-lebenden Universum, in: Guntern, G. (Ed.), *Der blinde Tanz zur lautlosen Musik, die Organization von Systemen*, Brig 1988, pp. 21–37.

Capra, F., *Wendezeit – Bausteine für ein neues Weltbild*, Bern 1985.

Darwin, C., *The Origin of Species*, Cambridge, MA 1859 and 1967.

Diller, H., Ergebnisse einer Metaplandiskussion "Beziehungsmanagement", in: Backhaus, K., Diller, H. (Ed.), *Beziehungsmanagement, Dokumentation des ersten Workshops vom 27, Bis 28.9.1993 in Frankfurt a.M.*, Münster, Nürnberg 1994, pp. 1–7.

Diller, H., Kusterer, M., Beziehungsmanagement, Theoretische Grundlagen und explorative Befunde, in: *Marketing ZFP*, (1988) 3, pp. 211–220.

Drucker, P. F., Managing for Business Effectiveness, in: *HBR*, (1963), pp. 53–60.

Eigen, M., Schuster, P., *The Hypercycle*, Heidelberg 1979.

Eigen, M., Winkler, R., *Das Spiel, Naturgesetze steuern den Zufall*, München 1975.

Ferguson, A., *An Essay on the History of Civil Society*, Edinburgh 1966.

Fey, P., *Logistikmanagement und integrierte Unternehmensplanung*, München 1989.

Forrester, J. W., *Grundsätze einer Systemtheorie (Principles of Systems)*, Wiesbaden 1972.

Freichel, S. L. K., *Organization von Logistikservice-Netzwerken, Theoretische Konzeption und empirische Fallstudien*, Berlin 1992.

Göpfert, I., *Logistik – Führungskonzeption und Management von Supply Chains*, München 2000.

Göpfert, I., Wehberg, G., *Evolutionskonzept der Logistik: Prozessorientierung durch Veränderungsspezialisierung, Arbeitspapier Nr. 7des Lehrstuhls für Allgemeine Betriebswirtschaftslehre und Logistik der Philipps-Universität Marburg*, Marburg 1996.

Göpfert, I., Wehberg, G., *Ökologieorientiertes Logistik-Marketing, Konzeptionelle und empirische Fundierung ökologieorientierter Angebotsstrategien von Logistik-Dienstleistungsunternehmen*, Stuttgart, Berlin, Köln 1995.

Gutenberg, E., *Grundlagen der Betriebswirtschaftslehre, Zweiter Band: Der Absatz*, Berlin u. a. 1955.

Haken, H., *Erfolgsgeheimnisse der Natur – Synergetik: Die Lehre vom Zusammenwirken*, 3rd ed., Stuttgart 1981.

Haken, H., *Information and Self-Organization: A Macroscopic Approach to Complex Systems*, Berlin 1988.

Haken, H., *Synergetik, Eine Einführung*, Berlin 1981.

Hoffmann, F., Stichwort Organization, in: Grochla, E. (Ed.), *Handwörterbuch der Organization*, 2nd ed., Stuttgart 1980, pp. 1425–1431.

Holling, C. S., Resilience and Stability of Ecological Systems, in: *Anual Review Ecology and Systems*, (1973) 4, pp. 1–23.

Horváth, P., *Controlling*, München 1979.

Kagermann, H., N.N. in: Promotorengruppe Kommunikation der Forschungsunion Wirtschaft – Wissenschaft (Ed.), *Deutschlands Zukunft als Produktionsstandort sichern. Umsetzungsempfehlungen für das Zukunftsprojekt Industrie 4.0. Abschlussbericht des Arbeitskreises Industrie 4.0.*, Frankfurt a.M. 2013.

Kennedy, J. G., *Herbert Spencer*, Boston 1978.

Kieser, A., Darwin und die Folgen für die Organizationstheorie, Darstellung und Kritik des Population Ecology-Ansatzes, in: *DBW*, (1988) 5, pp. 603–620.

Kirsch, W., Evolutionäres Management und okzidentaler Rationalismus, in: Probst, G. J. B., Siegwart, H. (Ed.), *Integriertes Management, Bausteine des systemorientierten Management*, Bern, Stuttgart 1985, pp. 331–350.

Kirsch, W., *Kommunikatives Handeln, Autopoiese, Rationalität, Sondierungen zu einer evolutionären Führungslehre*, München 1992.

Kirsch, W., Esser, W.-M., Gabele, E., *Das Management der geplanten Evolution von Organizationen*, Stuttgart 1979.

Kirsch, W., Meffert, H., *Organizationstheorien und Betriebswirtschaftslehre*, Wiesbaden 1970.

Klaus, P., *Die dritte Bedeutung der Logistik*, Nürnberger Arbeitspapier Nr. 3, Nürnberg 1993.

Klaus, P., Jenseits der Funktionenlogistik: Der Prozessansatz, in: Isermann, H. (Ed.), *Beschaffung, Produktion, Distribution*, Landsberg/Lech 1994, pp. 331–348.

Kummer, S., *Logistik für den Mittelstand*, München 1992a.

Kummer, S., *Logistik im Mittelstand, Stand und Kontextfaktoren der Logistik in mittelständischen Unternehmen*, Stuttgart 1992b.

Küpper, H.-U., *Controlling: Konzeption, Aufgaben und Instrumente*, Stuttgart 1995.

Küpper, H.-U., Konzeption des Controlling aus betriebswirtschaftlicher Sicht, in: Scheer, A.-W. (Ed.), *8. Saarbrücker Arbeitstagung 1987: Rechnungswesen und EDV*, Heidelberg 1987, pp. 82–116.

Lenk, H., *Pragmatische Philosophie*, Hamburg 1975.

Maik, F., *Strategie des Managements komplexer Systeme*, Bern, Stuttgart 1984.

Mandelbrot, B. B., *The Fractal Geometry of Nature*, 3rd ed., New York 1983.

Mann, R., *Das ganzheitliche Unternehmen*, 6th ed., Stuttgart 1995.

Mann, R., *Das ganzheitliche Unternehmen*, Bern 1988.

Maturana, H. R., Varela, F. J., *Autopoiesis and Cognition: The Realization of the Living*, Boston 1980.

Maturana, H. R., Varela, F. J., *Der Baum der Erkenntnis – Wie wir die Welt durch unsere Wahrnehmung erschaffen – die biologischen Wurzeln des menschlichen Erkennens*, Bern 1987.

Meffert, H., *Marketing*, 1st ed., Wiesbaden 1977.

Meyer-Abich, K. M., *Wissenschaft für die Zukunft – Holistisches Denken in ökologischer und gesellschaftlicher Verantwortung*, München 1988.

Möller, K. E. K., Interorganizational Marketing Exchange: Metatheoretical Analysis of Dominant Research Approaches, Working Paper No. 7, Helsinki School of Economics and Business Administration, Helsingfors 1992.

Mrosik, J., Ingenuity Inspired by Biology, presentation of Dr. Jan Mrosik, Futuras in Res conference, Berlin, 28 June 2018.

Pfohl, H.-Chr., *Logistiksysteme, Betriebswirtschaftliche Grundlagen*, 4th ed., Berlin u. a. 1990.

Pfohl, H.-Chr., *Marketing-Logistik, Steuerung und Kontrolle des Warenflusses im modernen Markt*, Mainz 1972.

Pfohl, H.-Chr., Unternehmensführungstrends und Logistik, in: Pfohl, H.-Chr. (Ed.), *Logistiktrends '91*, Berlin 1991.

Plattform 4.0, *Umsetzungsstrategie Industrie 4.0*, Ergebnisbericht 2015.

Prigogine, I., *Introduction to Thermodynamics of Irreversible Processes*, 3rd ed., New York 1967.

Probst, G. J. B., *Kybernetische Gesetzeshypothesen als Basis für Gestaltungs- und Lenkungsregeln im Management*, Bern, Stuttgart 1981.

Riedl, R., *Evolution und Erkenntnis – Antwort auf Fragen unserer Zeit*, 3rd ed., München 1987.

Röpke, J., *Die Strategie der Innovation*, Tübingen 1977.

Schiemenz, B., *Betriebskybernetik, Aspekte des betrieblichen Managements*, Stuttgart 1982.

Schneider, D., Controlling im Zwiespalt zwischen Koordination und interner Misserfolgs-Verschleierung, in: Horváth, P. (Ed.), *Effektives und schlankes Controlling*, Stuttgart 1992, pp. 11–35.

Schulz, D. E., *Ordnung und Chaos in der Wirtschaft: Zur strategischen Lenkbarkeit von Organizationen aus systemtheoretischer Sicht*, München 1993.

Schumpeter, J. A., *Kapitalismus, Sozialismus und Demokratie*, 2nd ed., München 1950.

Schwanninger, M., *Managementsysteme*, Frankfurt a.M, New York 1994.

Semmel, M., *Die Unternehmung aus evolutionstheoretischer Sicht, Eine kritische Bestandsaufnahme der Organizations- und Managementtheorie*, Bern, Stuttgart 1984.

Servatius, H.-G., *Vom strategischen Management zur evolutionären Führung*, Stuttgart 1991.

Simon, V., Soziale Unternehmensentwicklung, in: Seidel, E., Wagner, D. (Ed.), *Organization. Evolutionäre Interdependenzen von Kultur und Struktur der Unternehmung*, Wiesbaden 1989, pp. 339–352.

Spencer, H., *The Principles of Biology*, London 1864/1867.

Sprüngli, R. K., *Evolution und Management, Ansätze einer evolutionistischen Betrachtung sozialer Systeme*, Bern, Stuttgart 1981.

Staehle, W. H., *Management – eine verhaltenswissenschaftliche Perspektive*, 4th ed., München 1989.

Staehle, W. H., Strategie für Visionäre, in: *Management Wissen*, (1989) 12, pp. 48–50.

Sydow, J., *Strategische Netzwerke*, Wiesbaden 1993.

Taylor, F. W., *The Principles of Scientific Management*, New York 1911.

ten Hompel, M., Logistik 4.0, in: Bauernhansl, T., ten Hompel, M., Vogel-Heuser, B. (Ed.), *Industrie 4.0 in Produktion, Automatisierung und Logistik*, Wiesbaden 2014, pp. 615–624.

Ulrich, H., *Die Unternehmung als produktives soziales System*, Bern 1968.

Ulrich, H., Probst, G., *Anleitung zum ganzheitlichen Denken und Handeln*, 3rd ed., Stuttgart 1991.

Vester, F., *Neuland des Denkens*, Stuttgart 1980.

Vogel-Heuser, B., Herausforderungen und Anforderungen aus Sicht der IT und der Automatisierungstechnik, in: Bauernhansl, T., ten Hompel, M., Vogel-Heuser, B. (Ed.), *Industrie 4.0 in Produktion, Automatisierung und Logistik*, Wiesbaden 2014, pp. 37–48.

Von Foerster, H., On Self-Organizing Systems and Their Environment, in: Yovits, M. C., Cameron, S. (Ed.), *Self-Organizing Systems*, London 1960, pp. 31–50.

Von Hayek, F. A., *Die Theorie komplexer Phänomene (Deutsche Übersetzung)*, Tübingen 1972.

Von Hayek, F. A., Ed., *Freiburger Studien, Gesammelte Aufsätze*, Tübingen 1969.

Von Hayek, F. A., *Law, Legislation and Liberty*, Vol. 1: *Rules and Order*, London 1973.

Weber, J., *Einführung in das Controlling*, 4th ed., Stuttgart 1993.

Weber, J., *Logistik-Controlling*, 3rd ed., Stuttgart 1993.

Weber, J., Kummer, S., Aspekte des betriebswirtschaftlichen Managements der Logistik, in: *DBW*, 50 (1990) 6, pp. 775–787.

Weber, J., Kummer, S., *Logistikmanagement*, Stuttgart 1994.

Wehberg, G., Erfassung und Handhabung komplexer Ökologiephänomene in der Logistik, in: Keller, H. B., Grützner, G., Hohmann, R. (Ed.), *Werkzeuge für Simulation und Modellbildung in Umweltanwendungen, Wissenschaftlicher Bericht des Forschungszentrums Karlsruhe*, Karlsruhe 1996.

Wehberg, G., *Ökologieorientiertes Logistikmanagement, Ein evolutionstheoretischer Ansatz*, Wiesbaden 1997.

Wehberg, G., *Supply chain of the Future, Deloitte video presentation*, Youtube, 2018.

Wehberg, G., Logistik-Controlling – Kern des evolutionären Logistikmanagement, in: Jöstingmeier, B. et al. (Ed.), *Aktuelle Probleme der Genossenschaften aus rechtswissenschaftlicher und wirtschaftswissenschaftlicher Sicht*, Göttingen 1994, pp. 73–134.

Wildemann, H., *Die Modulare Fabrik*, 4th ed., München 1994.

Zmarzlik, H. G., Der Sozialdarwinismus in Deutschland als geschichtliches Phänomen, in: *Vierteljahreshefte für Zeitgeschichte*, (1963), pp. 246–273.

zu Knyphausen, D., *Unternehmungen als evolutionsfähige Systeme – Überlegungen zu einem evolutionären Konzept für die Organizationstheorie*, München 1988.

Part 3

What a digital supply chain is

1   Cultural aspects

1.1   Supply chain philosophy

w not used to discussing such factors, preferring instead hard facts and figures. At the same time, we all agree that soft factors can play a major role for the success of a company, and supply chain management in particular. Therefore, let's discuss these soft factors with the aid of some guiding questions, as follows.

What is a supply chain philosophy? The normative tasks anchored in the supply chain value system deal with the values and the resulting norms, the politics and behavioural culture of related employees (similar to Schmidt 1986). Supply chain values characterize a "conception of the desirable" (Meffert 1992), which is "characteristic of an individual or a group [in the supply chain organization] and which influences the choice of accessible ways, means and goals of action" (Kluckhohn 1962, translated). From the actual stock of the values, which represents the current result of a previous development, the *supply chain philosophy* must be distinguished. It marks a grounding in the intended change in normative supply ply chain management. Based on basic paradigmatic assumptions, so-called basic assumptions (Schein 1984), it shapes the future development of value. The roots of such assumptions and model ideas go back to the human and world views of a supply chain manager. Since they are usually neither clearly recognizable nor covered, the supply chain philosophy also includes value enhancement, which deals with the disclosure of the nature and content of existing values (Bleicher 1995).

But why does the philosophy play such an important role for a digital supply chain? The importance of the supply chain philosophy for the flow of goods-related management is derived from the fact that the traditional supply chain goals, such as the maximization of the delivery service at certain supply chain costs, due to the increasing system complexity, are becoming insufficient to provide management with guidance. Such a conventional approach alone does not take into account the personal goals of supply chain employees or social claims, although from a systems theory point of view this would be indispensable for a holistic problem solving. For the ability to develop the supply chain as well as the entire enterprise, therefore, the establishment of shared values that provide a sense of supply chain actions is key. Pointing out *meaningfulness*, normative system-building tasks at the same time do have a constitutive effect for all other management subsystems of supply chain management, which means also for its strategic and operational level (Weber/Kummer 1994 and supplementary Bleicher 1992; Weber 1993; Göpfert 2013).

And how to create meaning or make sense? Meaning can arise if the relationship of the supply chain management to its environment is interpreted correctly, for example, by highlighting the need for an increased sustainability, customer friendliness, quality of care or production flexibility. The supply chain philosophy is thus to be understood as a key integration driver. It goes without saying that it requires harmonization with the other elements of the corporate value system. And it can mean that managers first of all acknowledge that they do not master their highly complex supply chain in a deterministic manner. The concession that "something is not completely under control" can be perceived as very unpleasant and correspondingly difficult, however, has a paradigmatic meaning and is therefore part of the supply chain philosophy. By the way, it shows clear parallels with a shift from an extreme to a *moderate voluntarism* in the sense of Kirsch, Esser and Gabele (1979).

Can business ethics help supply chain management? When defining a specific supply chain philosophy, ethical standards can provide assistance. *Ethics* seeks to find systematic justifications for values that grow out of responsibility towards third parties (Jöstingmeier 1994). The essence of considerations of corporate ethics is expressed by the following principle, which is based on the categorical imperative of Kant: Treat your counterpart as you would like to be treated yourself (similar to Dylick 1992). A deeper reflection of this principle leads to the core concern that both the well-being of man and the protection of the natural environment are the objects. In this context, Servatius (1992) speaks of a balanced relationship of taking and giving between the company versus nature, thus providing the basis for a supply chain philosophy that is sufficiently committed to ethical principles. For example, a "we first" philosophy does not encourage cooperation because eco-system partners might be afraid whether they can rely on their partner and get their fair share or not. On the other side, "sharing" can be a facilitator to liaise, integrate and optimize in a joint fashion (Figure 1.1).

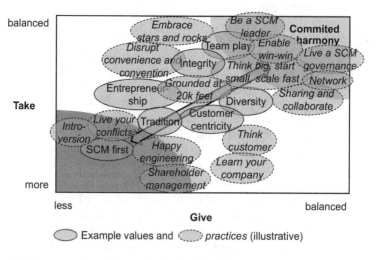

Figure 1.1 Change profile of the supply chain philosophy

The possible significance of the supply chain philosophy as an integration driver is shown in the following example.

Project example: control philosophy

Initial situation: A mechanical engineering company has successfully grown and internationalized over the decades. On the basis of successful technical developments, the business was set up and expanded in various destination countries in terms of service and sales. Over time, the countries have taken on the P&L responsibility in order to ensure the highest possible degree of decentralized entrepreneurship and customer proximity, despite the considerable size of the company. Functions like sales, service, order processing and supply chain management were owned and performed by countries. Only production, R&D and selected G&A functions (accounting, HR, etc.) were organized transnationally in cost or service centres. The P&L of individual countries served as a control tool.

Objective: The company management had to recognize that efforts to increase efficiency were not progressing because of the decentralized control philosophy. The realization of synergies and any kind of cross-country multiplication of proven solutions was not addressed comprehensively. While the structures in the countries were often more or less mature, the holistic, transnational perspective did show room for improvement. For example, the company had significantly higher inventories than its competitors because warehousing was conducted at the country level. If one part was missing in Northern Germany, it was reordered and delivered via the headquarters in South Germany instead of asking the warehouse in the Netherlands. And purchasing of transport services did not take account economies of scale. Each country engaged its own freight forwarders and thus contracted subcritical lot sizes. For this reason, the development of a cross-border control philosophy was decided in order to leverage appropriate synergies and to lead the group to the next level of optimization. A synergetic control philosophy was seen as a precursor to a virtual, network-based organization that enables new technologies. Based on standardized processes, they worked toward a goal of "digital supply chain readiness".

Approach: The initiative was developed and implemented in four steps: In the first step, a blueprint of the future control philosophy was drafted and then refined. In the second step, the synergistic philosophy of control was not generally advocated, but rather decided separately for each function. Synergies were calculated in the form of global business cases, so that disadvantages were taken into account in individual countries but were not decisive for the further course of action. In the third step, the old and new control philosophies were run in parallel in the form of a pilot, on the one hand to avoid risks, on the other hand to incorporate experience and to secure the acceptance by a successful pilot. The fourth step provided for the area–covering rollout and the termination of the previous country-dominated control. This was supported by appropriate training and communication.

Results and digital supply chain relevance: As a result of the initiative, efficiency increases of between 7 and 13 percent of the specific cost were achieved for the functional areas concerned. The future viability of the company was also significantly improved by means of now-scalable structures. The "digital supply chain readiness" was established.

Success factors: Three factors were crucial for the implementation of the new control philosophy. First, the management of the company had to be convinced of the need for further development. Managers responsible for the countries were concerned about the loss of influence and an associated loss of personal power. Due to the global business cases and a supporting change management, which took into account MBOs or incentives, this factor was taken into account. Team spirit was strengthened by the definition of a new "win-win" mindset, which required a higher openness and cooperation of executives and employees. Secondly, a transnationally integrated IT landscape was crucial for the efficient implementation of the new philosophy. For this reason, additional IT projects were set up on the basis of the already well-developed infrastructure. This provided a suitable integration platform for making the future control mechanisms happen. Thirdly, it was crucial that the new control philosophy was holistically conceived. In addition to the questions of control parameters and responsibility, the supply chain governance, organization, process landscape and management principles were developed consistently with each other.

1.2   Mindset, openness, orientation and attitude

Practically, the values of supply chain management always result in concrete behaviour and, vice versa, real behaviour forms values over time. This is why actual discussions of such values ideally lead to a challenge of this kind of practical behaviour or the determination of associated desired practices. Concrete examples and case studies on how to behave in specific situations are typically more helpful than abstract definitions of values, norms, cultures and so forth. This does not mean that case studies replace such definitions, but a pure declaration of the philosophy of the supply chain management is not good enough to coherently implement it. You will rarely find an organization that hasn't created some kind of short list of its values with regard to the supply chain. If you compare such lists between companies, you will be surprised how much they all look the same. I cannot think of a company that doesn't support team work, for example. But, how does the company specifically want the supply chain team to work together when it comes to bottlenecks in production or overpromises of sales? This is why a practical discussion of *concrete behaviour and practices* is key to make supply chain values happen and form one, consistent supply chain culture (again, see Figure 1.1). Having said that, the desired behaviour and values associated can be grouped in four areas (in general Pümpin/Kobi/Wütherich 1985).

The *goal mindset* reflects the contribution of supply chain management to the harmonization of interests of internal and external addressees of the enterprise. It involves the selection of stakeholder groups for which a benefit foundation is to be created. And it expresses the assessment of the general relationship between the economic goals of supply chains and its social responsibility. Two extreme positions of supply chain practice can be distinguished, the shareholder and the stakeholder approaches (Dylick 1992; Nork 1992; Schaltegger/Sturm 1992 and others).

The idea that the responsibility of supply chain management is reduced to purely economic goals, for example, the minimization of logistics costs, represents the shareholder approach. Non-economic concerns such as ecological and social target dimensions are understood in the course of this view only as final constraints. Conclusively, consideration of public concerns is usually limited to compliance with legal requirements. Such an opportunistic extreme of the goal mindset of the supply chain management meets especially with the pursuit of the *shareholders* after short-term realization of success.

However, the consistent policy pursuit of the shareholder approach, which is essentially limited to interest groups in the task environment of the company, is not sufficient for a higher impact of supply chains by the demands of public stakeholders. Such an increase in concern would be attributable to the fact that certain deficiencies, such as ecological scarcity, are not sufficiently reflected in the market players' behaviour nor by corresponding legal requirements. In such a situation, the supply chain management has to justify the consequences of its action in environmental and social terms. Without the assurance of sufficient social benefits, for example, by avoiding traffic jams or packaging waste, supply chain management would question the admissibility of entrepreneurial activity and thus jeopardize the existence of the company. This committed form of a pluralistic orientation of the political logistical goals characterizes the ideal picture of a *stakeholder approach* (Ackoff 1977; Freemann 1984), in which, apart from those interested in the economic services of the supply chain, there are other societal stakeholders.

The entrepreneurial vision, which can certainly be specified for supply chain management (Göpfert 1999), is closely linked to the required goal mindset. In this case, the supply chain vision contains the original idea of what social benefit is to be created, and thus constitutes a kind of guiding star for the supply chain. At the same time, visions are thus reminiscent of scenarios, but differ from them in that they are usually conveyed without an alternative and are based on incomparably more subjective foundations. The formulation of supply chain visions therefore requires a deep understanding of the market and its employees as well as the relevant stakeholders (e.g. Bertodo 1990; Hätscher 1992). To the extent that supply chain management overcomes established contexts of perception, it is also possible to speak of a "transcending vision" (Kirsch 1992). For example, the *vision of a digital supply chain* itself can pave the way for a quantum leap in the improvement of supply chain management and a pioneering role in Germany's successful positioning as a "laboratory for the world". The transcendent nature of such a vision is deliberately provocative, and therefore encourages employees to think outside the box.

In addition to the vision, the goal mindset of supply chain management depends on the extent to which it meets the concerns of its stakeholders at all, which means especially of its *openness*. The openness of supply chain management describes its internal or external orientation and its ease of change, whereby ideally the following two behavioural poles are typically to be identified (in general Bleicher 1995): The dominance of an inboard structure in the minds of supply chain managers characterizes one end of the openness spectrum, which is called *introversion*. External relations with other corporate divisions, but also with regard to upstream and downstream value creation stages, are not taken into account in the ways of thinking and behaving. As a result of such a cultural pattern, no one within the supply chain really feels responsible for logistically relevant problems of, for example, suppliers, customers and R&D employees. The isolating attitude then leads to the loss of the overall understanding of supply chain services. Added to this is a change-hostile attitude towards supply chains. Suggestions for improvement are reluctant. Corresponding measures are perceived as unpleasant because they disturb the usual "run". As a result, they are only half-hearted. In addition, a corresponding initiative is missing entirely.

On the other side of the openness spectrum, there are externally networked and open ways of thinking and behaving, which are referred to as the *extraversion* of supply chain management. Its high sensitivity ensures that changes in the needs of others are perceived and implemented in their own actions. In this respect, one can speak of an intensively practiced service and total cost thinking of supply chain management towards in-house and external customers as well as against third parties, which concerns both the supply and the disposal side. In addition to the behavioural anchoring of service and cost-related quality aspects, the extrovert culture pattern is expressed in a pronounced employee, customer and competitive thinking on the one hand and social and environmental protection thinking on the other. Essential components of such an open self-conception of supply chains are also thinking in material cycles, which is also referred to as recycling principle (Vester 1980b) and thinking in flows (Weber/Kummer 1994). The latter is substantiated, for example, by the internalization of the following supply chain principles, which take account of process orientation in the narrower sense (Goldratt 1984; Klaus 1993):

- The production flow, not the capacity, has to be adjusted.
- The utilization of a non-bottleneck capacity is not self-determined but predetermined by a different size in the overall process.
- The provided and used capacity is not synonymous.
- A lost hour of the bottleneck is a lost hour of the system. An hour gained from a non-bottleneck is comparatively meaningless.

- Bottlenecks determine stocks and run.
- Planning premises must always be checked simultaneously.
- Throughput times are target size not design parameters.
- Flows are all the more efficient the fewer "media breaks" in the supply chain occur.
- Flows are all the more efficient the sooner fault prevention instead of retrofitting takes place.
- Flows are all the more effective the higher the match between customer desire, product and process.

Furthermore, the change-friendly self-image of extrovert supply chain employees promotes the adoption of improvements in the sense of both evolutionary kaizen processes (Imai 1993) and revolutionary innovations. In contrast to the rather opportunistic introversion, extroverted thinking and behaviour are better prepared to promote the affirmation of dynamism and complexity. For this reason, they are to a certain extent also a prerequisite for the implementation of digital supply chains and change-oriented management structures per se. In the context of digitalization, openness also means that the relevant technologies can communicate with each other and ensure data continuity (Vogel-Heuser 2014; Büttner, 2014).

In addition to openness, the *temporal orientation* of supply chain management also influences the orientation of general political goals. The temporal orientation describes its position on a spectrum between past and future imprinting (in general Bleicher 1994): The history of the past is attributed to supply chain employees who look back on the successes and laws of the past. By doing so, they seek for security. In this respect, the cultural image is characterized by a *spiritual gilding of the past*, thus reflecting a rather lethargic, opportunistic attitude. Instead of the possible, it focuses on the status quo of the so-called old hands of supply chain management, which invokes their wealth of experience. However, it is overlooked that past experience in complex supply chain systems often does not provide much assistance. In such situations, it is less the "monolithic traditionalist with the completed life experience [who is in demand and] who blocks the offspring with his own pioneer past, . . . but the flexible partner whose projections are convincing" (Höhler 1992, translated). This is especially true for the implementation of a digital supply chain. Despite the potential dangers discussed earlier, moments shaped by the past will always play a role in the minds of managers. Among other things, the supply chain culture is the product of the company's development so far.

In contrast to the past-oriented image of the culture, the *future mood* reflects a pattern of behaviour characterized by the fact that supply chain managers commit themselves to possible rules of the future, by anticipating them, by influencing them by correspondingly innovative means or by robust steps (Haussmann 1978). The great importance of shaping the future and focusing on innovation in particular results from the fact that with high complexity only an excess of positive behaviours provides the necessary mental flexibility in the minds of supply chain employees. More of the possible over the real promotes the creativity of supply chain management and is also the source of innovation (Höhler 1992). In this sense, digital supply chain management always means innovation and requires shaping the future.

Despite the opportunities that come with an innovation-oriented attitude, the future imprint of supply chains can certainly also open up danger areas. The loss of tradition associated with an overemphasis on future changes can lead to erosion of company culture. It can lead to uncertainty among supply chain employees in the performance of strategic and operational tasks. Orientation standards are missing when old thinking patterns are adopted but new ones are not yet established. In addition, the development momentum can make supply chain management feel tempo-pressure, and therefore eliminate stakeholder involvement in the decision-making process. The exaggerated shaping of the future then leads to an impairment of the openness of supply chain management, jeopardizing its ability to develop (Höhler 1992).

Since every political goal-setting process requires a normative framework, the *attitude of conflict resolution* is a central value of supply chain management. The possible conflict solution modes can also be removed on a spectrum (in general Bleicher 1995): On the one hand, supply chain management can tend to have regulations which unilaterally represent the interests of only one reference group. In this case, the responsible supply chain managers tend to uncompromisingly enforce the alleged "corporate interest", if necessary through appropriate tactical and opportunistic behaviour. Such a form of conflict resolution, however, permanently discredits the trust of supply chain management, which is needed to fulfil its interdepartmental coordination function and the associated relationship maintenance. This creates unfavourable conditions for the realization of strategic and operative tasks. Such a conflict-promoting framework is therefore called *confrontation*.

As part of a conflict-resolution mode counterbalancing confrontation, supply chain management is committed to finding a balance between the pluralistic interests in accordance with its cross-sectional function. Other areas as well as subordinate employees are given a say. This type of conflict prevention is called *consensus building*. As part of a collaborative dialogue, a consensus will then be found between the various in-house and external stakeholders. The path of consensus thus takes into account the requirements of a future-oriented and open supply chain culture, insofar as it does not lead to uncertainty among those excluded and a view that such changes are a threat (Kanter 1993). For this reason, consensus building also fits in with the network character of digital supply chains.

Realistically, supply chain management will always have to position itself between confrontation on the one hand and consensus building on the other. For one thing, conflicts resulting from diverging interests of supply chain managers towards its stakeholders can never be completely ruled out. On the other hand, they can be regarded as a performance-enhancing factor for supply chains up to a critical level. Functional consequences arise when ideas are stimulated, tensions are relaxed, clear relationships are created or one's own positions are reconsidered (Kast/Rosenzweig 1985; Nork 1992).

The profiling of supply chain management on the basis of these normative soft factors is often given too little consideration in practice. Ensuring that such soft factors in the sense of *change management* are consistent can be the crucial success factor.

The change profiles relating to the mindset, openness, orientation and attitude of supply chain management suggest a distinction can be made between a rather *stability-oriented-opportunistic* and change-oriented-obligated system formation. The former results in a past-oriented and introverted supply chain culture; it corresponds to the shareholder approach and a confrontational conflict resolution mode. The supply chain management is so far barely able to represent (in a given period of time a large number of) various interests, to take into account the rules of the future, to perceive changes in the needs, etc. The resulting level of complexity of the normative management level of the supply chain system is correspondingly low. Otherwise, the latter, the *change-oriented system formation*, implies a high degree of system complexity of the normative.

The supply chain (meta-)management has to establish a fit among the elements of the supply chain culture as well as between this and its other over- and subordinate systems. The redefinition of the supply chain philosophy, which is relevant in this context, may well be understood pragmatically in the sense of a *culture follows strategy*. It forms a necessary condition for the development and maintenance of success potential through strategic supply chain management. The situation analysis of the information system forms the starting point for the strategic planning of supply chains.

2   Supply chain information

The supply chain information system identifies a structured set of all activities for provision of information, especially for the collection and evaluation of information about current events and relevant facts with regards to the flow of goods. Since the information system is part of the management system, the other executive subsystems, such as organization, planning and control, are the *addressees* of the information system. Information can be interpreted as knowledge needed for the primary coordination of its addressees. In addition to this customary definition of information in the sense of *purposeful knowledge* (Wittmann 1959), Weber and Kummer add experience to the scope of the information system. In this way they address a rather undirected broadening of the knowledge base of a supply chain, which should by no means be confused with the production of so-called numerical cemeteries, but rather with the determination of adaptation constraints and innovative possibilities of supply chain management (Weber/Kummer 1994). The latter understanding is very relevant in connection with the possibilities offered by digital supply chains. It also shows that collecting huge amounts of information, or *big data*, and the associated comprehensive data storage facilities, often referred to as *data lakes*, do not necessarily provide value per se, but require use cases and specific direction to generate value. But let's start at the very beginning. What is new about supply chain information in an increasingly complex environment?

2.1   Complexity, information and coordination

As has been noted, the complete recording of all information relevant to the flow of goods in highly complex contexts, and digital supply chains in particular, is not possible. Strategic tasks of supply chain management are influenced by highly dynamic external influencing factors in addition to the complexity resulting from the cross-sectional function of supply chain management. Therefore, strategic tasks in particular are characterized by high *uncertainty*. In addition, a number of operational tasks are challenged by disruptors, that is, by factors that have not completely been anticipated. For example, disruptors question the traditional MRP planning for make-to-order supply chains. Consequently, the *controllability* of such strategic and operational issues is limited.

From an information theory perspective, the relationship between the complexity and coordination of a supply chain is as follows (in particular Malik 1993).

The work of Ashby (1965, 1970, 1971) and Conant (1968) on information transmission has shown that any coordination of a well-defined fact requires a certain minimum amount of information. Without the transmission of this minimum amount of information, therefore, the solution of a coordination problem is not possible. The *transmission capacity* thus becomes a measure of the coordination capability. The required transmission capacity depends on both the complexity of the data input and the output. Take the example of a transmission model composed of m transmitter variables X and n receiver variables Y as well as an information system F transforming the input into an output. If p is the number of all possible input states and q is the number of all possible output states, $p = q = 2^{1000}$ results for every 1000 binary input and output variables. The number of all transmissions, the p input in q output conditions, is then qp. It requires a minimum transmission capacity of the information system of about 10^{300} bits. It becomes clear that the required transformation capacity of the information system is primarily determined by the *input-side complexity*, which represents p.

On the other hand, Bremermann (1962, 1965) demonstrates on the basis of findings from quantum physics that a system consisting of matter can process information only up to a certain limit. He concludes that this is a maximum of mc^2/h [bit/sec] with m = mass of the system, c = speed of light and h = Planck's constant. The formula leads to a top limit of the physically possible information processing in the amount of $2 \star 10^{47}$ bit/g/sec, which is also called *Bremermann's limit*.

In this context, *Malik* notes that although the Bremermann limit seems very large, it is actually very small when it comes to capturing very complex systems. For example, in the forefront of strategic supply chain planning, which includes n binary design variables, the complete interaction of the elements of the considered system foresees $2n$ possible states to capture. If, for example, one assumes that there are 7 goods groups in a supply chain division that can be distributed in 6 countries to 3 target groups, each with 3 different service levels, supply chain management has to take into account 378 variables, and thus 10^{113} options. Although it may be objectionable that certain options be ignored in the run-up to supply chain planning because they are obviously leaving, the elimination of certain opportunities must be taken into account and is associated with a certain amount of information. In addition, the acquisition problem becomes significantly more extensive if one considers that the supply chain area also relates to other branches of the company. In particular, the coordination tasks of supply chain management require amounts of information that are often no longer representable in the light of Bremermann's limit. As a rule, the amounts of information to be included are at least so great that the design of the information system is of eminent importance. However, this situation, that is, the link between limited transmission capacity and limited coordination, does not seem to be well-known to many executives. The inadequate consideration of these information-theoretical laws thus leads to a more *arbitrary choice* of a more or less plausible strategy from a very large number of equally possible alternatives. It "resembles a drive through a ramified river delta, although one is unaware that one is even in a delta" (Malik 1993, translated). And it is equivalent to the denial of system complexity.

Against the background of these information-theoretical basics, it becomes clear, on the one hand, why it is often not possible to completely capture all relevant detailed information on goods flow. On the other hand, it can be seen that the lever for an adequate design of the information system is on the data input side. Instead of the detailed depiction of all goods flow–related facts, the *recognition of patterns* should occur. This means capturing the order of the system under consideration. Unlike in the earlier example of the planning problem with regard to supply chain division, it can be assumed that in reality there is usually no complete interaction. In other words, even in complex systems, "not everything is connected to everything on a regular basis, but just 'a lot with a lot'". However, this statement must not give rise to the assumption that the Bremermann limit would not be relevant. In addition to this quantitative aspect, qualitative features of system complexity seem to be of particular interest. It raises the question of how or how much is connected. The order thus contains rules resulting from the interplay of behaviours and processes within the supply chain and surrounding system. It favours and constrains certain behaviours of the system, expressing what makes up the system as a whole and, at the same time, allowing us to grasp system complexity. Here, order can be understood both statically in the form of a combination of substructures to a whole as well as dynamically in the sense of a certain system behaviour over time. Above all, the relatively young interdisciplinary science of *synergetics* (Haken/Haken-Krell 1989) deals with the recognition of dynamic states of order. All in all, pattern recognition becomes the prerequisite for coping with complexity (for this and in the following Ulrich/Probst 1991; Weick 1969). It is the core component of digital supply chains. And it is capable of closing the already mentioned so-called knowing–seeing gap.

Using the example of *football*, which also represents a highly complex system, pattern recognition is particularly evident in the perception of rules and tactical moves. A detailed analysis, such as a slow motion of a shot on goal, here contributes little to the understanding of the game as a whole. Even if the comparison between a football match and a supply chain may be considered conditionally permissible – the rules of football are still widespread – it does illustrate what is important in pattern recognition. The supply chain manager, who sees himself as a sports layman with ever-new disciplines, has to familiarize himself with the changing rules of the system. Patterns of supply chain systems can be expressed, for example, by the ordering behaviour of customers, in order changes, delivery service requirements, ecological damage or load levels of transport capacities.

The fact that complex supply chains can only be modelled and not analysed in detail may lead one to conclude that since "everything is so complex" that no *deterministic statements* about how the system operates are possible, and therefore it is no longer manageable. In this connection, Hayek distinguishes two types of deterministic statements: Thus, this statement can mean

> which class of circumstances determine a particular kind of phenomena, without us determining the individual circumstances that decide which Individual case from the predicted class of patterns will be able to specify individually. Therefore, we can justifiably claim that a particular phenomenon is determined by known [. . . forces] and at the same time admit that we do not know exactly how it came about. Further, asserting that we can explain the principle that a particular mechanism works invalidate the fact that we are not able to say exactly what it will produce at a particular space-time.
>
> (von Hayek 1972, translated)

Thus, even in complex systems of supply chains deterministic statements are possible – in the sense of Hayek.

2.2 Pattern recognition

By focusing on strategically relevant information, the level of complexity to be captured increases relative to information required for the operative business (Scholz 1987). In the course of forming the information system for strategic supply chain management, it is therefore more important to prioritize information instruments and methods that take into account the pattern recognition process. In this context, we can describe the spectrum characterizing supply chains between pattern recognition and detailed analysis in particular by two dimensions, the *scope and format of data* (Figure 2.1).

The data volume or information content expresses the extent to which the way of information collection is closed or open. The closed procedure means that the data is collected according to predetermined criteria and obtained from known sources. Such information retrieval often corresponds to "hard" data, which means with a high degree of data in quantitative form. The problem to be mapped here is relatively well structured and can therefore be detected relatively well in its quantity and value framework. Although quantitative closed-loop data often promise information–economic advantages, in the majority of cases such data are history oriented, and therefore at best allow for an unobjectionable extrapolation of the past. Their information content is comparably low. They characterize the detailed analysis in the form of a *stability-oriented information system*. For the number and variety of data that can be processed in such systems (in a given period of time), the complexity of the information system of a supply chain is weak. Examples of these kinds of information systems are traditional business intelligence (BI), total cost of ownership (TCO), ABC analyses and confirmative statistics, amongst others.

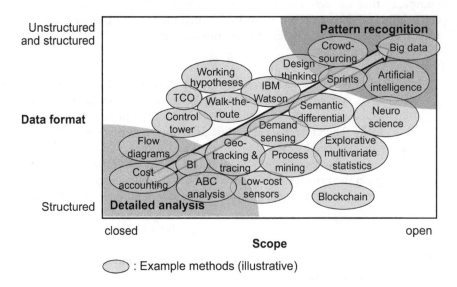

Figure 2.1 Change profile of supply chain information

Qualitative-open information differs from quantitative-closed information, and therefore requires a different form of analysis. Qualitative-open information results from the freedom of the information system to consciously absorb new sources and data. Such information is more prospective and, above all, takes into account pattern recognition and the already mentioned need to advance the accumulation of experience for supply chain management. The information content is high; the qualitative character of the information is expressed in particular by the consideration of so-called theoretical constructs, such as customer satisfaction, which can be measured multidimensionally by indicators, recorded as semantic differentials or described verbally (Borkowsky 1994; Mann 1995). Qualification therefore does not exclude the use of quantitative data. The openness or scope of the information recorded is also reflected in this context by the involvement of the later-affected persons, who can ensure both the use of the entire know-how available in a company, as well as the acceptance of the acquired data (Weber/Kummer 1994). In addition, this approach most likely promises to capture the essential features of a complex supply chain. In this respect, it describes a *change-oriented information system*. Example methods or tools that represent such kind of information systems are design thinking, sprints, crowd sourcing and artificial intelligence, amongst others. With respect to design thinking, a number of different interpretations of this method exist, so it is worthwhile to take a closer look. Well known in this context is IBM Watson, which traditionally focuses on unstructured data, i.e. text, and thus can be a good complement in a change-oriented information system.

In addition to the variables explained here, it goes without saying that further characteristics for the description of the information system can be mentioned.

For example, the *relevance of the information* for the decisions of supply chain management is of high importance, which suggests that useful information, rather than data cemeteries, is provided. Further, not insignificant requirements also form the *objectivity* of the acquired data; that is, their *profitability, reliability, validity and completeness*. However, these features of data with regard to its form and scope express, in particular, the ability of an information system to capture the complexity of supply chain–related variables. In addition to an allocation of the information system as a whole, individual instruments or tools, such as flowcharts and ABC analyses, can be positioned in the change profile shown in Figure 2.1.

In practice, many companies are currently developing their portfolio of information tools in order to support their digitalization strategy and leverage the value of data. The *lessons learned* of such exercises suggest that typically the tool selection has to be performed in a use case–specific mode. The traditional way of selecting tools suggests one preferred vendor per field of appliance, for example, for AI tools. However, this does not leverage the full potential of such tools. Even within one appliance field the tools differ and show individual strengths or weaknesses based on the single use case to be analysed. A *multi-vendor strategy* thus has to refer to a pay per use–based subscription model rather than time-based licences. The vendor portfolio has included a large and an increasing number of vendors over the past years and evolves dynamically over time.

Moreover, the scope of relevant information shifts from G&A functions towards operations, in other words, from *IT to OT*, and many IT organizations are not very experienced with the latter. This means they need to be set up in a cross-functional fashion to secure sufficient supply chain as well as IT competencies. By necessity, the setup of a supply chain information system is interdisciplinary.

2.3 Big data, predictive analytics and sensors

In supply chain management practice, the need for pattern recognition has already had many effects. This development is supported by the improved technological possibilities in three ways.

Firstly, the digital *storage and processing capability* of large data volumes has become possible and has been growing strongly since the year 2000, which is when the expression "big data" emerged (Hilbert/Lopez 2011). The processing of large amounts of data has long been possible via mainframe computers, but in recent years it has also become possible with smaller computer capacities, in some cases virtually via cloud computing and, from an economic point of view, very economically. The data volumes, which from a supply chain point of view can be relevant here, basically refer to process-related data, customer data and supplier data, as well as employee data and data from other stakeholders or environmental sources. They require a certain degree of accuracy, for example, in the minute range for just-in-time delivery, which in turn drives the data volume.

Having said that, it is not just the volume of data that can be stored, but also the opportunity of bringing the data together and understanding how they relate to each other. In particular, the combination of relevant data can create value because it allows the identification and understanding of the underlying value drivers. As a prerequisite, the relevant database has to be integrated, which means that there is a technological platform that enables combined analyses. This platform is called the *data lake*. The data lake ideally grows over time as supply chain management learns about big data and progresses in digitalizing its supply chain. Ideally, more and more use case are implemented, data assets are integrated and value is generated along the journey towards a digital supply chain.

Secondly, the improved and more economical capacity of computing power has significantly improved the ability of *predictive data analytics*. These new possibilities of data analytics are the core of any pattern recognition process insofar as the intelligence of corresponding algorithms decisively determines the quality of identified patterns and design recommendations to be derived. Such algorithms are procedural instructions that allow for the decentralization of decisions. Ten Hompel (2013, translated) says insofar: "We can give the machines a bit of thinking – but shall keep the plug in our hands". Next to artificial intelligence, multivariate analysis methods such as factor, variance, cluster and other analyses, as well as simulations with incremental improvements (Bousonville 2009 speaks of evolutionary algorithms), can help to identify and apply corresponding behaviours of supply chains.

Modern IT tools for the field of predictive analysis are already able to comprehensively support the supply chain management, in particular to perform:

- Demand forecasts
- Environmental analyses of traffic jams, pollution, etc.
- Social media and market research
- Customer relationship management
- Data management and validation
- Improvements to the product and service portfolio
- Network planning and optimization, including transport routing
- Resource and capacity management
- Crowd logistics
- Compliance management
- Assessment of supply chain risks
- Financial and investment planning

Decisive for the beneficial use of such IT tools are, above all, the selection of the right *algorithms*, the availability of relevant data and sufficient expertise in the supply chain context. Some marketing initiatives try to give the impression that there is a salutary algorithm that can solve all problems. Experience has shown, however, that in the field of probability analyses, a large number of algorithms are typically available for one and the same type of analysis. And again, it is not about the comprehensive consideration of as much data as possible, but about the integration of the relevant sources. Particularly relevant are those data that potentially serve as a determinant (underlying driver) of a target variable, such as capacity utilization, delivery flexibility or throughput time. Not least for this reason, it is also necessary, in addition to a sufficient analytical expertise, to integrate sufficient supply chain expertise.

While in the US auction platforms already exist for the development of the best algorithms, this market in Europe is still in the process of being developed. It should also be assumed that such algorithms require certification, which means quality assurance by third parties. In addition to the development of algorithms for the operational steering of object flows, algorithms for the design and development of supply chain systems as a whole will play an increasing role. Since the latter relate to the coordination of supply chain management and are closely linked to controlling tasks, we can also speak of *meta-algorithms* here. They take care for the development and selection of the right algorithms. Bauernhansl (2014) speaks similarly in this context of "system of systems", which refers to the autonomous development and design using the plug-and-produce capabilities of systems.

Thirdly, the decentralized use of IT in supply chains also benefits from the reduced storage capacity in combination with significantly more economically viable use of *sensors*. This trend enables the decentralized control of the smallest units, for example, of transport means, packaging, industrial trucks, etc. Cost-effective sensors are usually seen in concert with other technologies, such as the mobile and wearable computing. Their potential use in supply chains is broad and can for example (Kückelhaus et al. 2013):

- Influence user behaviour on a personal and business level.
- Integrate customers as an active partner in the order process.
- Promote the use of Auto-ID technologies in businesses and customers.
- Improve personal work through the use of wearables.
- Support the Bring Your Own Device (BYOD) trend.
- Provide a man–machine interface for (self-)control.
- Enable the smooth actual-time tracking of shipments.
- Make a corresponding control of supply chains possible.

The different sensor types can be directly assigned to the "6-R" of supply chain management, for example, in the right place with GPS/WLAN/GSM cell, in the right quality with temperature sensor/depth image scanner, etc. Additionally, there are also sensors that do not measure but automatically perform certain actions in a decentralized fashion.

The rapid technical development of sensor technology is mainly to be described in three dimensions (Tuttle 2015):

- *Energy efficiency*: The energy consumption of the sensors is very low, for example, in the lower microampere area of button cells. It will continue to reduce even further in the future in order to be able to integrate even more functions per sensor.

- *Connectivity*: The sensors are characterized by different connection technologies, such as WiFi, Bluetooth, ZigBee and Thread, amongst others. Each technology is characterized by its own strengths and weaknesses, such as range, IP capability, energy efficiency and network capability.
- *Integration*: Sensors combine numerous functions, such as memory, processor, receiver, energy management, etc.

Of course, the combination of the three approaches mentioned – big data, data analytics and sensors (or cyberphysical) – offers corresponding possibilities for pattern recognition in supply chain management.

2.4   Master data and contextualization

In the context of the perception of complexity, a distinction should be made between endogenous and exogenous complexity. In other words, there is homemade complexity and externally determined complexity. In practice, *homemade complexity* often arises from master data that is not consolidated and unified. For example, the bill of materials and customer data are heterogeneously structured and documented due to external growth in the past. In addition, the parts lists in the various functional areas (procurement, production, etc.) and sites differ, for example, the material number in SAP. This unnecessarily creates additional complexity and potential problems. For example, different material numbers at different sites make it difficult to balance both capacities as well as material. Homemade complexity can be countered by consolidating master data management, *cleansing* master data and streamlining the portfolio of products, parts, production assets, customers and suppliers. Ideally, companies start such data cleansing activities while working on their supply chain of the future. Otherwise, they risk to approach digitalization too late from a market and competitive perspective.

Next to cleansing, modern big data architectures suggest that the *contextualization* of data helps to make such data comparable and possible to consolidate. Of course, contextualization only helps to harmonize nomenclature, whereas data cleansing addresses redundant and wrong data. If the data are cleansed, however, contextualization is a pragmatic way to consolidate different sources in a meaningful way, rather than developing data lakes as one source of truth over years. Data lakes are relatively easy to implement if they are close to the ERP landscape, like in the SAP HANA environment. However, in the operations sphere and all its different systems, a contextualization approach often is more realistic today. This may change over time, given that existing IoT platforms in operations and supply chain management in particular all strive for standardizing use cases and consolidating the associated data.

Many companies also do not adequately assess the complexity of their offering portfolio and related costs or contribution margins. The current portfolio thus is not questioned. To what extent individual products are profitable is not well-known, because the cost calculation offers no information about it. The allocation of cost (via cost centres) to products and service providers is not realistically represented by an appropriate cost–driver logic. Instead, important information is lost through averaging. Understanding actual supply chain cost via *de-averaging* and based on relevant cost drivers is therefore a prerequisite for determining the right degree of complexity in a commercially viable fashion.

The consolidation of the product and parts portfolio also requires integration of the *bill of materials* of various functional areas. Moreover, the development of *configurable products* through standardization, parameterization and modularization allows flexibility at the same (or lower) cost. Appropriate IT support through suitable software solutions and using classification standards such as eCl@ss or others is the basis for a consistent management of the material management data in this case.

Efficient handling of internal complexity is anything but trivial in praxis. The following use case shows which types of material management can be used here. They are the prerequisite for the effective examination of external challenges and digital supply chains in particular.

Project example: integrated materials management

Initial situation: An FMCG company had significantly broadened its product range over the years. Due to increasingly individualized consumer behaviour, it had also differentiated the product range in order to maintain its competitiveness. An as-is assessment showed that the contribution margins of the various products were extremely different and partly negative when taking total cost into account. Incidentally, the number of products offered was simply out of control, which was illustrated by a comparison with selected competitors. Also, at the level of semi-finished products and raw materials, there was a very high level of complexity. In many cases, the introduction of new stock/shelf-keeping units equaled the introduction of new inventory.

Objective: In order to reorganize the complexity of the offering portfolio, the company set up a program. The aim was to consolidate the supply ("above the skin") by streamlining the portfolio. The company also wanted to study the semi-finished products and raw materials ("below the skin") in order to more efficiently manage, as far as possible, the complexity within the production and supply chain. On the basis of common classification standards, integrated bill of materials (BOM) concepts would be implemented, which were equally taken into account in procurement, production and distribution.

Approach: The program was executed in four steps. In the first step, the complexity costs and corresponding complexity and value drivers were determined. The complexity drivers were not limited to the actual product performance, but also included secondary services such as special packaging and shelf maintenance. The analysis of contribution margins taking into account the complexity costs revealed the potential for improvement in the supply portfolio. The analysis of the complexity drivers showed possibilities to develop integrated parts lists. In the second step, the products were prioritized. The focus was on their current contributions to success and identifiable potential for improvement. On this basis, pilots were set up for an effective materials management in the third step. The relevant measures were very comprehensive because they took into account both complexity-reducing and value-adding starting points. The task of the pilots was to demonstrate the feasibility of the methodology and to generate momentum for further implementation. At the same time, work was carried out on processes for the permanent anchoring of future materials management. The implementation of the latter together with a company-wide rollout were the subject of the fourth step.

Results and digital supply chain relevance: As a result of the program, the pilot product range could be reduced by more than 20 percent and the value could be increased by similar price measures. This laid the basis for a successful rollout over the other product areas with a potential of comparable magnitude. In addition, the defined processes of the improved materials management, for example, for pricing and customer segmentation, can be implemented in a self-controlled manner in the sense of a digital supply chain.

Success factors: Three factors were decisive for the successful implementation of the material-efficiency program. Firstly, it was important to recognize that comprehensive complexity reduction was not the only goal. In intensive discussions with the executives of the company, it became clear that the company was currently living on the complexity of its customer requirements and that responding to individualized customer requests through new offerings is a core competence. In many cases, therefore, it had to be about paying the higher complexity appropriately. Secondly, it was crucial for the acceptance and effectiveness of the program that the company not limit itself to product articles, but also scrutinize the corresponding semi-finished products and raw materials. As a result, the discussion was extended from the level of portfolio management to the bill of materials level. In other words, not only the "what" was at stake, but also the "how". Thirdly, it was important to realistically manage the expectations of those involved. The further development of BOMs is usually a medium- to long-term endeavour, so the program aimed in many areas at anchoring suitable processes instead of the future BOM itself. Over and beyond quick wins at the product-portfolio level, a continuous improvement process was initiated.

3 Supply chain planning

3.1 Target setting

Supply chain planning is a process of "qualitative, quantitative and temporal determination of future goals, means and . . . processes for the design and control of the operational supply chain management system, including systematic, information-processing . . . and social interaction processes" (Bircher 1989, translated). In a sense, a crystallization point of all planning activities is the target system. It is the result of strategic and tactical, rather than operational, supply chain planning. And it is always an integral part of the target system of the company. The effort spent on the target setting of supply chain management compared to other divisions is derived from its attractiveness (Weber/Kummer 1994). In a resilient perspective, the target system of digital supply chain has to be structured as follows.

The change of supply chains that is expressed by the target system can essentially be determined on the basis of its dimensioning and target level (Figure 3.1). As already explained, supply chain problems are usually characterized by multi-dimensions, which means they are defined with respect to their economic, technological, environmental and social implications. Companies, which in extreme cases limit themselves to only one, usually the economic dimension, disregard the high dynamics that can arise precisely from the other dimensions. Such a comparatively isolating approach tends to be accompanied by a focus on efficiency standards. Supply chain costs are then often used as input for measuring efficiency. In addition to the monetary costs, delivery time can be understood as an input variable. It leads to a time-based efficiency measurement (Jacoby 1994; Pfohl 1994). Efficiency is to be ascribed to operational supply chain management because it directs supply chain processes in existing structures and tries to optimally position itself, graphically speaking, on a given cost-service–level function. It thus primarily pursues *stability goals* that represent stability-oriented structural patterns of the supply chain target system.

The challenge of stability goals and their efficiency focus is that due to the missing multi-dimensioned approach these goals often lack differentiation and connectivity to demand patterns. For example, so-called Runners are characterized by stable demand and high volumes, as opposed to Noisers, which

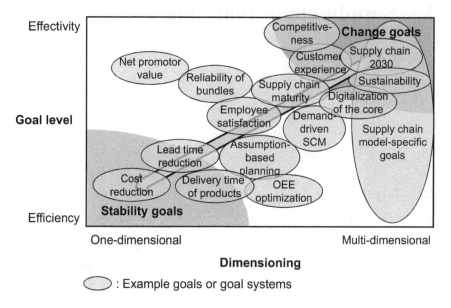

Figure 3.1 Change profile of supply chain targets

include rush orders and highly customized products. The consideration of *supply chain models*, and thus a differentiated steering logic, is missing. In this case generic goals suggest that all products can follow the same logic and that the supply chain can be managed as one, typically via demand forecasts and respective inventories. This ignores, however, that typically the demand of Noisers is hard to forecast and that the management of the supply chain seeks differentiation. Supply chain goals, therefore, need to consider these changes in a complex world.

The stability goals are opposed by *change goals*. On the basis of their multi-dimensional facility, they address the dynamization of the economic, technological, ecological and social environment and interior world of supply chains and set new standards in terms of effectiveness. Graphically, the setting of change goals can be visualized as the replenishment of the cost–service–function of a supply chain, and possibly also as its curvature, equalization, etc. (Göpfert/Wehberg 1995). The objectives of competitiveness and sustainability, which are at the heart of digital supply chains, are also goals of change in this sense. Change goals also consider the different supply chain models where necessary to respond to more customized product portfolios and the change of customer behaviour.

One problem that arises in the structuring of the supply chain target system is the complexity of possible goals and *target relationships*, which results above all from the great opportunities for behaviour and design of supply chain processes. In other words, working out supply chain goals is a complex problem in itself (generally Adam 1983). For example, different supply chain models can overlap as far as they route back to the same semi-finished products and raw materials along the bill of materials. And efficiency levels depend on investments in supply chain infrastructure or eco partners, for instance. At least the following target relationships have to be distinguished, which may be complementary, indifferent and conflictual (Göpfert 1992):

• Intra-functional relationships within the objectives of the supply chain function (e.g. in the so-called magic triangle between supply chain costs, service and stocks)
• Interfunctional target relationships between logistics and other operational functional areas (e.g. logistics-oriented production versus production-oriented logistics)
• Temporal relations (short- and long-term goals)
• Relationships between company goals and individual goals of the employees (e.g. personal claim of the manager and goals of the logistics)

Key indicators offer the opportunity here to condense the facts of the complex reality that can be measured directly or via indicators: Search grids can provide structuring assistance in the context of an inductive key figure formation. It should be noted that the corresponding key performance indicators (KPIs) must be aligned with the process-oriented philosophy of supply chain management (Helfrich 1989; Pfohl 1994).

A suitable structuring instrument is the *target cube* of supply chains shown in Figure 3.2. It suggests distinguishing between a *potential, process, and result perspective* and connects them with the profiling variables of change and supply

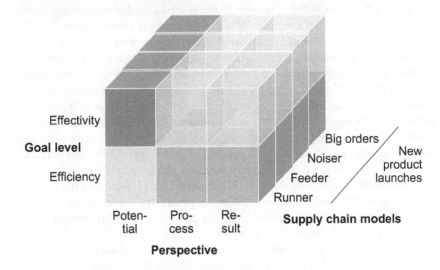

Figure 3.2 Target cube of supply chain management

chain models in particular. Basically, all fields of the displayed cube can contain attractive target content. By way of example, from a process-oriented point of view, the effectiveness variable "process quality" (actual to target number of process interruptions, etc.) and the efficiency variable "process productivity" (km per trip, handling operations per hour, etc.) can be cited. It becomes clear that the effectiveness and potential perspective is subject to transformation and projects associated, while realizing that efficiency results have to be addressed in a continuous improvement mode to a certain extent. If necessary, key figures from other areas of the company, such as production, procurement and disposal, must also be included in the supply chain target system. For example, supply chain management cannot improve performance if strategic sourcing suffers from a lack of market power and insufficient delivery by suppliers. In addition, the operating equipment effectiveness on the shop floor can heavily influence supply chains when unplanned shutdowns reduce the available capacity.

Last but not least, supply chain model–specific targets have to reflect the nature of different demand patterns, and thus steering mechanisms. In most cases it is pointless, for example, to set inventory targets for Noisers beyond process stocks. A lot of target KPIs and reporting systems miss this kind of differentiation, which is one of the key route cases for the *seeing–knowing gap* discussed earlier in this volume. Supply chain management typically has the data to differentiate between supply chain models but they don't put the figures together in a way that generates insight to know what is going on.

Another common problem for the development of relevant goals is that the scope of supply chain management, and thus the associated cost, is defined too narrowly. The recording of supply chain costs in practice is by no means trivial. Often, only those costs that result from the tasks of the logistics and export department are added. However, holistic recording of supply chain costs, in the sense of a process-oriented approach, is the prerequisite for optimizing supply chains holistically on the cost side. When logging supply chain costs holistically, the supply chain practitioner is surprised in one case or another by the amount of these costs. Depending on the industry, *supply chain costs* can in many cases account for 15 to 20 percent of total value-added costs. In the nomenclature question of the definition of supply chain costs, note that only the costs of those activities that can be influenced by supply chain management (as a function) are included in the supply chain costs. At the same time, it is vital that management controls the entire supply chain in an end-to-end fashion. Capacity planning, for example, is part of the cycle of production planning and detailed scheduling, but it is also essential to sales and operations planning, and the balancing of capacities in particular. For example, Bauernhansl (2014) estimates the *efficiency potential* of digital supply chains at 30 to 40 percent of the inventory costs or 10 to 20 percent of the supply chain costs and even 60 to 70 percent of the complexity costs, the definition of which may vary considerably.

In the context of a cost-efficiency discussion for digital supply chains, it is vital to understand what transaction costs are. We can differentiate between process and *transaction costs* on the cost side. The concept of transaction costs builds on the approach of Williamson (1985, 1991), which conceptually processes the presumption of Coase (1937): "there is a cost of using the price mechanism". Consequently, transaction costs can be understood as the "costs of market coordination". While the number of new transactions in the course of digital supply chains is increasing, the level of specific transaction costs, which means the cost per transaction, decreases due to the use of new technologies. This makes it possible to assemble new, individual processes for supply chains, in the extreme cases with a lot size $N = 1$, which means the service for each delivery is individualized and customized.

In practice, *benchmarking* is a popular way to derive goals. Although many businesses have had bad experiences with benchmarking exercises because they were not performed properly, it can be helpful to compare different performance indicators between companies and businesses. It is important to consider that supply chain networks typically have different structures, for example, geographical footprints, technology and product portfolios. An apple-to-apple comparison has to take this into account. Actually, the comparison of structural characteristics can be even more insightful than comparing performance indicators. Sometimes, it is even better to avoid the expression "benchmarking" for exactly that reason. From the point of view of the resilient understanding of supply chains, however, it can offer starting points for developing new ideas from outside for the further development of digital supply chains.

Project example: benchmarking of supply chain

Initial situation: Over the years, a company in the service sector always concentrated on its service know-how and corresponding offer. Secondary services, such as supply chain management, were rather neglected because corporate management did not consider them to be particularly important to the company's success. In their view, the services would not be "delivered" but would be provided by personnel and equipment. Supply chain processes only played a role in the maintenance and servicing of plants, and thus were of secondary concern.

Objective: Due to high pressure on margins, there was a growing need to examine all possible approaches to increase cost-efficiency and margin. It was determined that supply chain processes would also be benchmarked. The results of the benchmarking process were included in the target agreement process and implemented by the line managers.

Approach: Benchmarking was carried out using a four-step process. In the first step, the scope of benchmarking was defined in terms of the criteria to be included, peer companies and the target level. Great emphasis was placed on a clear nomenclature. Depending on the availability of the reference data, a complementary primary survey of peer companies could be considered, which could be obtained for participation in the benchmarking process. In addition to a comparison with external companies, an internal comparison between locations was also carried out. In order to avoid delimitation problems, a process framework was used for the relevant supply chain processes.

The second step of the benchmarking process involved collecting the data from pre-structured entry sheets. The survey at the various locations was accompanied on site to ensure uniform understanding. In addition, the additional information relevant for comparability was collected. For example, stocks of spare parts could only be compared to the extent that their age and location were comparable. At the same time, it was important in this context to know which maintenance strategy underpinned the performance data in order to be able to discuss suitable measures later.

In the third step, the comparability of the data was ensured by means of a suitable normalization. The data was used to perform the company and location comparisons. As a result, efficiency and effectiveness gaps were identified, which provided information on the potential for improvement in the supply chain.

The fourth step then included discussions with those responsible to discuss the benchmarking outcomes and to adopt targets and next steps.

Results and digital supply chain relevance: As a result of the benchmarking, the company identified those areas that would generate a greater than 10 percent improvement, which corresponded to a higher double-digit million euro amount. In addition, a number of areas were identified where the company should take better account of the service expectations of the market. Next to the earnings effects, benchmarking provided the opportunity to compare supply chain management with other companies in terms of content. The identified differences in efficiency and effectiveness indicators signalled different supply chain practices, including possible starting points in the sense of digitalization.

Success factors: Three factors were of decisive importance for the success of benchmarking. Firstly, it was crucial that the supply chain processes and associated resource consumption were holistically covered by the process perspective. Secondly, the detailed coordination and transparency of the approach and methodology with those responsible was important. The so-called buy-in of the management often is not self-evident, especially in times of many "praised" benchmarks. Many companies have gained extensive experience in benchmarking across a range of areas in recent years and know that the validity and acceptability of the results are crucially dependent on the approach and methodology. "Jumping in" to a benchmarking exercise with the view of "we'll see what comes out" is generally not advisable. Third, the methodology used, that is, a clearly defined nomenclature and consistent normalization, were critical to the success of supply chain benchmarking.

3.2 Basic supply chain strategies

The implementation of the supply chain goals, which are initially defined in the target system, is achieved through strategic planning. However, the target planning also depends on the possible strategies or their feasibility. *Strategy* (*strategos*, Greek = "army leader") is still often understood as a kind of martial arts or army leadership. It then easily leads to the view that competitors as well as consumers should be outsmarted, indeed defeated. Only if one loses can the other win. However, such an understanding of the term has increasingly been replaced by the insight that competition between companies is not war. Rather, the task of the company has to be seen as improving solutions to customer problems and providing benefits to society in general. Strategies in this sense serve to build up and maintain such potential benefits. Such an understanding corresponds to the self-referential character of complex supply chain systems, takes into account the demands of stakeholders and enables the coevolution of the enterprise and the surrounding system (Mann 1995).

With regard to supply chain management, basic and functional strategies can be differentiated. *Functional strategies* address the specific contents of the individual supply chain subfunctions, for example, transport, packaging, etc. They are decided in a rather decentralized mode. Prospectively, this can take place autonomously, even in an automated way and in exchange with other cyber-physical systems. Bauernhansl (2014) also speaks of "shop-floor-near control loops". According to ten Hompel, "If additional services are required, . . . the CPS . . . addresses business objects and services in its cloud. The result of business objects and services and thus the desired process is created on demand" (ten Hompel 2013, translated). As much as the development of supply chain systems is modelled in a self-organized manner or via so-called meta-algorithms, the planning process has to be cascaded or even completely decentralized.

Basic strategies, on the other hand, relate to those structures of a supply chain that are defined across all subfunctions and connect with the business strategy. With regard to the possibilities derived from these structures, one can also speak of cross-sectional potentials. Important cross-sectional potentials arise above all from the targeted competitive advantage as well as the applied supply chain models and learning strategy. Basic supply chain strategies have to be planned according to the situation, and thus have to be individual and specific. On the other hand, they can be summarized through relevant patterns.

One of the most common misunderstandings is to believe that basic strategies in the course of digital supply chains will initially not change so much. It is assumed that digitalization just impacts the customer journey and offers some use cases regarding supply chain functions. This is, however, typically not correct, because the potential of digital supply chains is not limited to the application of new technology within the supply chain. It also has to deal with higher complexity caused by digitalization, for example, in terms of an individualized product portfolio, and thus new supply chain models and capabilities are required. Moreover, the customer experience does not stop at receiving a customer order. Delivering products provides a range of contact points with customers, and thus outbound logistics are part of such a journey. Last but not least, customers need to ask for supply chain–relevant features in a digital environment, for example, transparency through tracking and tracing.

3.2.1   Competitive advantage

It has already been established that supply chain management should make a contribution to the competitiveness of the company. It can be the central core capability that determines the competitive edge. The role that supply chains can play in the overall competition depends on its attractiveness with regard to cost reduction and differentiation potentials. The competition strategy of supply chain management is thus defined by the question of whether the goal is the minimization of supply chain–relevant costs or the maximization of the relevant customer value (Porter 1986 and in addition Darr 1992; Delfmann 1990; Jünemann 1989; Poth 1991; Schiffers 1994; Weber/Kummer 1994, etc.).

In a graphical representation – with the delivery service on the abscissa and the supply chain costs on the ordinate – the former *cost leadership* strategy means an attempt to shift the supply chain cost-service curve downwards (Göpfert/ Wehberg 1995). By influencing relevant cost drivers, the lowest possible cost level with sufficient service level is sought. The latter *differentiation* strategy, on the other hand, represents the endeavour to shift the cost-service function of logistics to the right. The consideration of the competitive advantage to be achieved is completed by the option of processing the entire market with a uniform logistics standard or segmenting it into several niches to be served individually, whereby the *niche strategy* tends to correspond to the striving for differentiation. Because the more manageable the served market, the sooner it is possible to respond to the individual service needs of customers. Digital business and business models often correspond to segmentation and niche because the use of new technologies makes the cost of such a differentiated market processing manageable. In this context, Anderson (2007) speaks of "long tail" and a 98-percent rule that replaces the previous 80:20 rule. The extent of the complexity of the supply chain planning system brought about by the competitive strategy then increases. Figure 3.3 shows a corresponding change profile of possible competition strategies in supply chain management. It shows the polarization of supply chain patterns of behaviour in the form of more stability-oriented cost dominance on the one hand and change-oriented benefit dominance on the other.

A differentiation or niche strategy has to build on customer needs and address them explicitly. Clay, Mashall and Glynn (2017) have elaborated such needs in a changing world considering new, digital technologies. Their research has been summarized by a description of Dawn, a 25-year-old woman representing

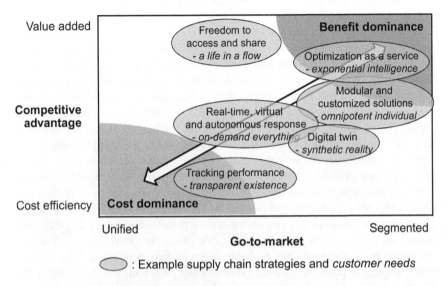

Figure 3.3 Change profile of the competitive strategy of supply chain management (needs by Clay/Mashall/Glynn 2017)

the typical customer behaviour of the future; let's call her *Dawn Digital*. Dawn Digital is characterized by the following behaviours, amongst others:

- She doesn't know how to drive; however, she's driving all the time.
- She's never been to a doctor, but she visits her doctor every week.
- She never logs on, but she is indeed always online.
- She's always shopping, however, she's never in line.
- She's never ever been "lost".
- Her T-shirt is connected to the web.
- Her tattoo unlocks her car.
- Her superior is a robot.

This behaviour is no science fiction, nor is it even a particularly extreme perspective on technological influence. It's more a sketch of a not too far away future full of disruption. Digital technology won't just change the customer experience; it will also change how the world works and supply chains operate. It will change "how people connect, create, escape, accomplish, work, unwind, understand, stand out, fit in, get smart, get well, get money and simply live" (Clay/Mashall/Glynn 2017). Key questions from a differentiation perspective are, conclusively:

- What does supply chain management need to do differently to meet the needs of the customer of the future?
- How will the value proposition and supply chain model need to change?

- How do we stay relevant to Dawn, and what can supply chain management do to support this?

Selected customer needs and supply chain propositions to respond to it are shown in Figure 3.3. The question of whether the competitive behaviour of supply chain management is more stable or change oriented certainly does not depend solely on the desired competitive advantage and the form of market development itself, as also shown in Figure 3.3. Rather, the concrete change in supply chains must always be viewed against the background of its further basic strategic considerations. In particular, the consequences for supply chains deriving from a market-growth/market-share portfolio determine their exact degree of complexity (Klimke 1983). Thus, so-called *dogs*, in which supply chains try to minimize inventories and distribution costs in particular, are more likely to be associated with cost-dominated patterns of behaviour. The endeavour to design the service processes as economically efficient as possible implies stability-oriented management structures. In contrast, the role of supply chains in so-called *stars* are, according to its principle, probably more benefit dominated. The favourable competitive position makes it easier to keep pace with the dynamics of the competitive environment in the form of change-oriented behavioural patterns.

Competitive positions are often defined in the company at the product or service level because, in the first place, the positioning question is not about the competitiveness of the company as a whole, but always about its offerings in particular. In individual cases, this may mean that the supply chain of a company is highly differentiated according to customer segments, product areas and regions, but this does not change the basic considerations regarding the competitive strategy of supply chain management. In other cases, supply chain management is not considered at all, because, traditionally, a very *product-focused mindset* and happy-engineering culture does not recognize the potential of supply chain management. This, however, is changing the faster products are being commoditized and digital strategies are seeking for support in operations. Thus, secondary services like supply chain management are becoming a competitive factor and appreciated by the businesses of a company, gaining recognition even outside the supply chain management department.

Supply chain management as a secondary service of companies thus is the differentiating factor in many markets with almost interchangeable or commoditized products. The following project example shows the contribution that digital supply chains can make to customer loyalty.

Project example: smart customer retention

Initial situation: In the course of a customer survey, a manufacturing company determined that its customers considered the product range to be almost completely interchangeable with its competitors. According to the survey, one of the main reasons why customers were loyal to the company was the good service it provided. In the face of increasing customer turnover, the company faced the challenge of recognizing impending customer shifts as early as possible in order to be able to take countermeasures, as needed. The importance of customer loyalty was due in particular to the high acquisition costs for winning new customers. It was significantly more valuable for the company to retain existing customers than to attract new customers.

Objective: The company specifically aimed to halt the increase in the turnover of relevant customers within the next 12 months and halve fluctuation within two years. Impending losses of valued customers should be identified in good time by the use of big data and predictive analytics in order to be able to implement countermeasures in individual cases. If acquisition efforts remain unchanged, this should significantly increase growth over the next two years.

Approach: The company started a four-step process. In the first step, comprehensive data from 14 categories was collated in one database. This included the operational data of service provision (service quality, value-added services, sales and marketing activities, etc.); the master data of the customer company (seat, size, sector, etc.); personal data of the purchasing-relevant customer employees (hobbies, marital status, career level, etc.); customer satisfaction with the product range and service of the company (attitude, recommendation behaviour, willingness to change, etc.); their ordering, acceptance and complaint behaviour (sales, lot size, order times, etc.); the market conditions in the respective customer segment (price pressure, service relevance, etc.); competitive behaviour (campaigns, innovation, etc.) and corresponding changes in these factors over time. In the second step, a change index based on static pattern prediction methods was introduced, classifying customers by customer value and a net loyalty index (NLI), which essentially expresses the probability of exchange. High-value customers and NLI were statistically demarcated. In the third step the focus was on deriving appropriate countermeasures. For example, the service level was increased, additional value-added services were offered and a feedback call was held on-site, etc. in order to counteract a change in the respective customer and to better understand potential reasons for customer loss. The effectiveness of these customer loyalty measures based on the respective customer profile was also included in the analysis. In the fourth step, the newly established customer loyalty process was anchored in the line organization. If possible, the interfaces to the data sources (CRM, social media, etc.) were IT-technically mapped in order to avoid media breaks or system interfaces. An incentive system for sales and service employees was set up to foster their participation in improving the data and early warning indicators were taken into account.

Results and digital relevance: As a result, 74 percent of the customers who were considering a change of supplier were identified. This means that the second type of mistake – i.e. willing customers who were not identified early – was therefore 26 percent. The error of the first kind, by contrast – the false identification of loyal customers without the intention of switching – was 14 percent. Both errors could be further reduced over time. In order to derive suitable countermeasures, the main factors of a higher willingness to change were identified. In particular, 24 percent of the supply chain service determined the loyalty of customers. The company's goals of increasing customer loyalty and growth have been achieved.

Success factors: Decisive factors for the successful implementation of the project were above all the comprehensive consideration of customer-relevant data and the possibilities of statistical procedures on the pattern prediction and the consideration of supply chain service as a differentiation factor in the company's competition.

Internet of supply chain services

Digital technology allows for individualization within the supply chain, for example through service differentiation according to different customer segments. This supports the dominance of benefits. Digital supply chains additionally offer the opportunity to offer completely new value-added services and to further develop the business model of the company in a hybrid (virtual/real) way. Insofar as such services are represented via cyberphysical systems on the Internet, it is also possible to speak of an Internet of Services, here the *Internet of supply chain services.*

A synonym for new services is the mobile software application (i.e. app), which is a software application with access to mobile devices such as a tablet PC or smartphone. It is less about the app itself, but about having certain information available at all times, making specific decisions at any time or being able to link selected processes anywhere. These include, for example, the ordering of so-called intelligent products per se, the actual-time transparency regarding the delivery and status of customs clearance, the subsequent change of a service level and the control of outsourced activities. The possibilities offered by Logistics 4.0, especially in customer service, will play a major role. Here, the now cost-effective use of sensors allows the economical implementation of so-called predictive maintenance concepts, which can be connected to the spare parts logistics. The use of cyberphysical systems then allows machines to virtually order their own spare parts, as needed, and prevent media breaks. Such new logistics services can deliver significant added value from the customer's perspective.

The role of an in-house service provider may also be internal services, such as the provision of a control cockpit to track workload utilization and other logistics metrics. This can also help to increase the benefit for the internal customer, assisting him in achieving his goals. In addition, the provision of IT services for supply chains marks a possibility of the Internet of Services.

As an example of the possibilities of digital supply chains to develop new services and to exploit the networking potential, the following case of application is outlined.

Project example: crowd logistics

Initial situation: A logistics service provider in the field of courier, express and parcel services (CEP) saw digitization as a strategic opportunity. The company established a scouting team to identify new services with business potential. A starting point for this was the available transaction data of mobile phone users, which are marketed by mobile operators.

Objective: The aim of the initiative was to define and implement services based on available transaction data in order to profitably develop the core business. Also, the company wanted to present an image to customers as being a provider of innovative digital services.

Approach: The initiative was structured in four steps. In the first step, a study was used to narrow down the services in question, detailing them in terms of process, developing an appropriate IT application (an app) and designing a business case. The CEP service provider wanted to integrate mobile users for delivery in the last mile in the area. With broad involvement of the population in certain areas, the last mile could largely be covered in this way by third parties, which are already on the ground and have certain patterns of movement. This approach was referred to as "crowd logistics". In special cases, the company hoped that the addressee could pick up the package if it could be organized efficiently based on the movement data. In this case the addressee became a service provider for himself, in a way becoming a "prosumer" (producer and consumer). In the second step, the feasibility was checked. In order to respect data protection, the mobile operators provided the movement data only in anonymous form. This asked for special requirements on the selection of the participants for the crowd logistics, because only certain types of movement patterns were of interest for the mapping of the last mile. The subscription process was designed to ensure that it was appropriately selected. The pilot in the third step gave a more realistic picture and showed where adjustments were needed. In the fourth step, the new services were rolled out across the different regions.

Results and 4.0 relevance: In addition to the positive positioning through the creative service idea, the new service offered savings potential in the process costs of the last mile in the double-digit percentage range. This already took into account that the subscribers received a premium for each delivery accepted. Crowd logistics proved valuable in urban areas because there were enough digital traces to reconcile the collective behaviour of subscribers with the needs of supply chain management. It proved to be efficient in structurally weak areas because the out-of-service costs of the CEP service provider could be reduced to a few shipments.

Success factors: Decisive factors in the implementation of the new service idea included compliance with data protection requirements and the user-friendliness of the IT application. In order to develop the idea itself, it was crucial to have an ongoing overview of correspondingly available data and new business models of relevant market participants, in this case the mobile service providers. Without a corresponding scouting on the market, the CEP service provider would have missed this opportunity.

3.2.2   Sales & operations planning

Many companies have one approach to manage their supply chain. In many instances, service levels are managed via stocks. To meet market requirements and leverage the full potential of digitalization, however, it is typically not good enough to design one overarching supply chain. There is no one-size-fits-all approach when it comes to steering mechanisms, target inventories, lead times, service levels, reporting, pricing and so forth. Different demand patterns ask for different supply chains with different characteristics and associated design principles. This is what we call *supply chain models*. A supply chain model is an operating system to develop, design and manage a supply chain in line with the specific demands and other requirements.

Based on how stable or dynamic the demand for a specific product is, we can distinguish five different types of supply chain models (Figure 3.4):

- *Runners* show high annual volumes with stable demand characteristics. Runners often represent a baseload because they determine a major share of the utilization of the supply chain infrastructure. Runners are relatively easy to handle from a supply chain management point of view because the can be easily forecasted and don't cause surprises.
- *Noisers* are ordered in smaller lot sizes and have high volatility. The demand for Noiser products is thus difficult or even impossible to forecast. Noisers typically represent rather customized and niche products. They require thorough management due to their relatively high process cost compared to Runners.
- *Feeders* are ordered in smaller lots than Runners but are still reasonably sized and have less volatile demand than Noisers. Therefore, Feeders can be better forecasted. They are called "Feeders" because they typically provide the opportunity for increasing the utilization of production assets by "feeding" in between other lots within the production planning and scheduling.
- *Big Orders* combine the characteristics of Runners and Noisers in a way because they represent large single lot sizes that are ordered once in a while. Because Big Orders do not show a steady inflow they are not easy to predict, and they challenge delivery as well as production infrastructure due to the high volume.
- *New Product Launches* represent any new offerings that are being introduced to new or existing customers. In order to realize a proper time-to-market and scale-up of new offerings, supply chain management must determine the steering mechanisms of such as early as possible. New Product Launches can be Runners, Feeders, Noisers or Big Orders. The flip side of New Product Launches is portfolio de-proliferation, which can challenge supply chain management in a similar way than managing the time-to-market.

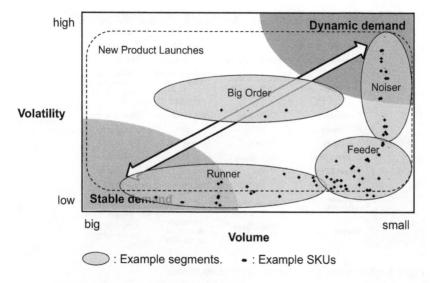

Figure 3.4 Change profile of supply chain models

The impact of supply chain models is significant. However, segmenting products for supply chain models is simple. You can even do this segmentation for supply chain models in Excel, based on an excerpt of the relevant ERP data, as shown in the following example:

- *Average*: grand total/# of data point (# of weeks)
- *Standard deviation*: STDEV.P(aa:zz)
- *Coefficient of variation (CV)*: StdDev/Average
- *Runner-Feeder-Noiser*: =IF(CV<=0,75;"R";IF(CV<=1,33;"F";"N"))

Importantly, the definition of supply chain models refers to the *demand characteristics of external markets*. There is no use in analyzing the structure of internal production orders as a basis for building supply chain models. Sometimes, supply chain managers refer to the demand structure of their internal customers if there is a lot of intercompany delivery and the responsibility is limited to single sites or production steps only. Even worse is if internal silos represent a multi-step production process at different sites with distributed responsibilities and lacking overall alignment. In this case, the internal decision making easily creates its own internal complexity far away from market behaviour. This, however, turns it around; this is not the way supply chain models or their associated design principles should be determined. Internal orders and respective lot sizes are subject to the design of supply chains consistent with pre-defined models, not vice versa.

Once the right supply chain model for a product is defined, supply chain management can attach key design principles to determine how to handle it.

- EXAMPLE -	Item	Runner	Feeder	Noiser	New Products
Production	**Monthly volume**	XXX units	YYY units	ZZZZ units	Target KPIs dependent on expected demand and thus SC model, incl. ramp-up
	Average lot size	optimum	variable	variable	
	Scheduling	Make-to-delivery	Make-to-stock	Make-to-order	
Supply chain	**Flexibility**	Demand stable, flexibility thus not important	Monthly demand predictable, Limited flexibility required	No detailed planning, placeholder capacity	
	Punctuality	Daily basis	Daily to weekly	Weekly or more	
	FC accuracy	xx%	>yy%	-	
	Reliability	xx%	≥yy%	<zz%	
	Delivery time	Continuous	y days	ATP based	
	Target DOH	xx	yy	zz	
	Target cost	- M EUR and -XXX FTE (vs. baseline 2016)			
Procurement	**Supplier reliability**	x% service	y% service	ATP based	
Sales	**Margin**	Secure base profitability	Increase/ smoothen profitability	Opportunistic Noiser margins	

Figure 3.5 Key design principles of supply chain models

Of course, *key design principles* and parameters have to be set individually for each business and company. However, supply chains do show repeating patterns, as shown in Figure 3.5, that supply chain management can refer to in order to avoid reinventing the wheel again and again. In line with the end-to-end perspective of digital supply chains, all relevant functions need to be involved when determining the design principles in order to define a common ground as to how to operate. For example, it is vital that the high process cost of Noisers and their make-to-order procedures are considered within the pricing approach of the sales organization. The lot sizes of Noisers are small and thus the changeover costs typically are high. In addition, procurement must secure the necessary flexibility at suppliers in terms of their available-to-promise (ATP) involvement for such. For each supply chain model, coherent principles must facilitate cross-functional alignment rather than seeking manual coordination on a case-by-case basis.

Following the typical design principals for the relevant supply chain models, traditional forecasting of the demand of single products really works with selected models only, like Feeders. Other supply chain models, such as those for Noisers, are facilitated by other approaches, for example, forecasting of the demand of placeholder capacity, which means forecasting on a product group level, that determines buckets for capacity utilization of a single production asset.

In seeking alignment and consensus as to demand and supply, organizations run a *sales & operations planning (S&OP)* exercise. Many S&OP processes suffer from the attempt to handle all products the same way without considering the different nature of each model. While the approach of planning and forecasting is specific for each supply chain model, i.e. its method, tools and content,

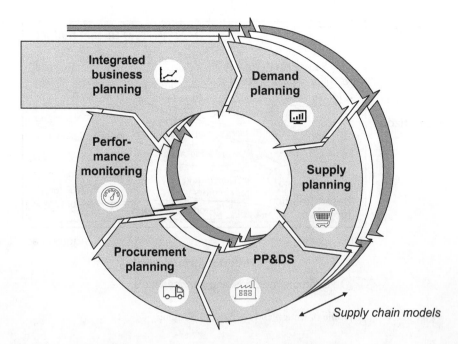

Figure 3.6 Sales & operations planning (S&OP) for digital supply chains

the formal responsibilities of S&OP can be similar or even the same. Many companies, though, do have specialized S&OP managers for each supply chain model. Figure 3.6 shows a typical S&OP process, including its differentiation for respective models.

The quality of the S&OP is determined by the following key success factors, which ask that planning and forecasting be:

- Cross-functionally integrated (strategy, sales, procurement, finance, etc.).
- Bi-directional (multi-loop alignment between demand and supply).
- Cross-site (balancing capacities and material).
- Multi-dimensional (volumes, revenues, margins).
- System and alert based, thus managing by exception (not manually).
- Continuously improved (regular review and refinement).
- Independently governed (e.g. neither by sales nor by production).
- Supply chain model specific (e.g. ATP for Noisers).

Predictive analytics can help to enhance forecasts and get more value out of data. The results can be fed into respective S&OP systems, for example, SAP IBP or Demand Solution. Over and beyond shaping relevant parameters of the system itself, artificial intelligence then helps to identify adjustment needs, for

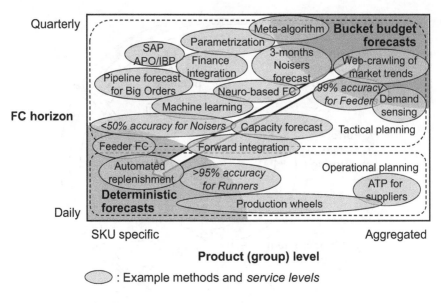

Figure 3.7 Change profile of tactical and operational planning

example, by regular reviews of market factors based on web-crawling appliances. On this basis, it can support developing planning algorithms in line with environmental changes, automatically. In this situation, so called meta-algorithms help to increase the degree of automatization and to further reduce management-by-exception efforts initiated by alerts. Figure 3.7 visualizes the change profile of relevant planning methods, selected use cases and service levels associated with key supply chain models.

In addition to the aforementioned basic patterns of competitive behaviour and corresponding supply chain models, another concept assumes that competitive advantages are based on the unique assets of companies, especially their knowledge and know-how. With a few unique capabilities of the company, the so-called core competences, competitive advantages are established (D'Aveni 1995). Supply chain management can certainly become a core competence (e.g. Sauerbrey 1991). In this context, it represents the result of learning processes. We will therefore discuss the learning construct in more detail next.

3.2.3   Learning

Organizational learning

The supply chain competence of a company can be a major factor in its competitive position. However, many companies have yet to realize that they lack competencies is this area. In other words, there is a *shortage of supply chain expertise*, both in quantitative terms, i.e. the number of relevant employees, as well as in terms of quality, i.e. the depth and scope of specific supply chain expertise. Many companies limit themselves to the development and maintenance of their competences. They channel the skills of their employees and organization as a whole mainly on product-relevant knowledge. For example, many manufacturing companies love to do happy engineering and highly sophisticated product development. In the past, supply chain management was viewed as simply delivery, "truck driving" or even "pallet pushing". At the same time, there is a growing awareness that as products become more and more homogeneous any secondary services such as supply chain management can be decisive, as can the corresponding skills and appropriate learning. This applies all the more to the character of digital supply chains. A company that limits its digitalization strategy to the customer journey will fail. It also needs the "motor room" in place, which means digital supply chains are key facilitators for respective strategies. Here, supply chain management becomes business relevant, creates impact and makes a difference towards customers.

Let's talk a bit about learning. Learning means multiplying knowledge in the broadest sense (Probst/Büchel 1994). It is the central prerequisite for the autonomy of a system as well as for its survivability in general. A self-contained learning theory does not exist thus far. Rather, learning-theoretical explanatory approaches are to be differentiated. Some focus on emotional-activating determinants and work with stimulus-response patterns, such as classical emotional conditioning. Others are based on cognitive-rational considerations dealing with complex issues in the sense of an insightful illuminate learning (Meffert 1992). *Hierarchical learning* structures build on the idea that learning complex issues first requires the handling of simpler content. Due to the complexity of supply chains on the one hand and the primarily rational behaviour of such management on the other hand, the cognitively rational explanatory approaches are especially relevant in the following.

Furthermore, individual learning should be separated from *organizational learning* in supply chain management (Probst 1994; Probst/Büchel 1994): Individual learning includes the intrapersonal processing of supply chain employees, which are related to knowledge building. By contrast, organizational learning encompasses the knowledge base of the supply chain system as a whole, not just as the sum of individual learning activities. It expresses the interactions between the members of the supply chain; in particular, it represents its independent record and the (re-)accessibility of knowledge (supplementing Vester 1994). According to this, an independent quality is to be attributed to organizational learning. On the other hand, individual learning in supply chains and the organizational learning of supply chains do have a *shared reality*. This shared reality consists of the needs, attitudes and values of several system members. Organizational learning is also referred to as the process of changing "cognitive maps" or "social reality constructs". It is defined, as it were, by the intersection of the many-layered contexts of supply chain employees. To a certain extent, the motors of learning are the convergences and divergences in the contexts or realities. The *art of learning* is to maintain a balance between convergences and divergences (Cohen/Levinthal 1990; Fiol 1993).

Problem-solving skills

Learning can be understood in a quantitative and qualitative dimension. Before presenting some of the key factors that determine the extent of learning (quantitative dimension) in the following point, the first step is to look at the different ways of learning (qualitative dimension). Learning is not the same as *learning*. Supply chain management, like corporate management in general, knows three ways: learning solutions, learning problem-solving skills, and meta-learning (similar, but generally Argyris/Schön 1978).

Learning solutions is the efficient adaptation to given goals in relatively stable environments. It includes the correction of existing implicit patterns of behaviour or the unconscious knowledge base of supply chain management. Such learning is expressed, for example, by experience in packaging and handling processes as well as by exercise gains in route planning. Failure to achieve the right goals gives the impetus for learning processes. The latter goes hand in hand with the confirmation, and in part also with the refinement of the knowledge base of a supply chain. For example, when drones learn from each other to optimize transport routes, this affects solution learning. The latter is an optimization lever that should not be underestimated in the interests of supply chain efficiency.

Compared to the learning of solutions, the *learning of problem-solving skills* refers to the further development of the conscious knowledge base of supply chain management. The expediency of the otherwise fixed, seemingly inviolable formal goals of supply chain management is called into question. New priorities are set and competences expanded. The learning of problem-solving abilities includes the self-development of such new competences, for example, in the form of the development of meta-algorithms, that is to say rules of behaviour for adapting existing or developing new algorithms.

The learning of problem-solving skills is also accompanied by a reorientation in normative terms. Problem-solving skills cannot simply be "slipped over" to management. They require a corresponding conviction, insight into their usefulness, even meaningfulness. This very fact, the lack of benefit or meaning, is at the same time also the "driving force" of this kind of learning.

For example, a company may feel compelled to segment its customers and differentiate the delivery service by priority of those segments. Building such segmentation skills may be driven by the belief that equal treatment of all clients, irrespective of their strategic importance and profitability, does not make sense. In that case, the company and supply chain in particular are applying new problem-solving capabilities to effectively serve its customers. Likewise, the evolution of the supply chain in terms of digitalization requires new problem-solving abilities. Many potential solutions are not yet known or widely used due to the pacemaker nature of cyberphysical technologies. The stronger self-control of some supply chain processes, for example, in manufacturing, requires a higher (problem-solving) competence.

Different *levels of competence* can be distinguished. Against the background of the logistical nature inherent in supply chain management, a largely uncoordinated form of task fulfilment characterizes the lowest level of competence. This level of problem-solving ability can be referred to as "pre-supply chain management". In a second stage, "supply chain–interested parties" begin to deal for the first time with the coordination idea of supply chain management. For example, pilot studies and proof-of-concepts provide the formal framework here. However, their efforts remain at the conceptual level due to their overall low problem-solving abilities. Island solutions are still the rule. On the other hand, "advanced supply chains" succeed in enforcing a holistic concept, which at the level of "supply chain professionals" has developed into competitive advantages. Finally, at the highest level of competence, which is referred to as "post-supply chain management", the respective concept lives on all levels of the hierarchy. Explicit consideration of the resulting coordination tasks is no longer required. Supply chain management becomes the self-understanding of corporate management (Weber/Kummer 1994).

Companies that are still dealing with the basics of supply chain management will probably be overwhelmed by even more complex forms of digitalization and "lose" their employees. Due to their highly innovative character, the organization of digital supply chains requires a high level of competence. Hence, supply chain professionals or post-supply chain specialists are needed. The learning of problem-solving skills is not just a one-off; rather, it is a recurrent, revolving process that involves improved *learning of learning*, or meta-learning. This becomes evident when one realizes that in the course of learning, one probably does not acquire the supply chain competence par excellence. Instead, one learns in relation to many different facts. The devil is in the details. In addition, it can be assumed that problem-solving abilities acquired in a dynamic environment will in a sense age. Permanent learning is the result.

To sum up, combining these two types of learning can be contrasted with two polar types, the competence-oriented learning strategy and the solution-oriented learning strategy of supply chains or supply chain management, respectively (Figure 3.8). The former corresponded to change-oriented, the latter with stability-oriented supply chain structures. Because the number of possible manifestations of the knowledge base of supply chains increases with increasing intensity of competence-oriented learning, this increases the degree of complexity of the supply chain planning system caused by the learning strategy.

Diffusion

The theory of diffusion and adoption attempts to describe, explain and shape the acceptance and dissemination of knowledge in social groups (hereinafter referred to as Backhaus 1990; Meffert 1986). The question of the learning

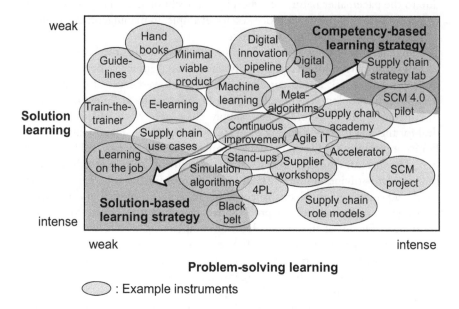

Figure 3.8 Change profile of organizational learning within supply chains

drivers and obstacles of (digital) supply chains is thus directed towards the adoption and diffusion of such know-how. In this context, adoption models try to answer the question of whether managers accept innovations in the field of supply chains, and on which the acceptance of these innovations depends. Sociologically oriented diffusion research is then concerned with the dissemination of innovations over time, understood as the sum of all adoption processes. The status of research on the *diffusion drivers* of supply chains is currently considered to be low (but Göpfert/Wehberg 1996), and thus an overview of hypothetical diffusion drivers and barriers must be limited. It is possible to distinguish know-how versus adopter-specific influencing variables. Among the know-how–specific factors are the drivers and obstacles to learning that arise from the peculiarities of the respective problem-solving abilities. According to experience, this includes factors such as the relative advantage, the compatibility, the complexity as well as the testability of the competency innovation:

- *Relative advantage* describes the benefits that an innovation offers compared to its alternatives. The competitive and social benefits of digital supply chains have already been discussed several times. According to this, the opportunities associated with such a build-up of competencies depend, above all, on the attractiveness of supply chain management and digital supply chains in particular. Many manufacturing companies, for example, that discuss digitalization do have pre-mature supply chains and thus face significant potential of doing both. They can benefit significantly from developing their supply chain management as well as executing their digitalization strategy.

- *Compatibility* is the ability to integrate into the existing. New problem-solving abilities can be introduced all the more promisingly if they modify what has been done so far, and thus rely on existing structures instead of completely knocking them over in order to then proclaim their rebuilding. The development competence is compatible insofar as it corrects the previous approaches of supply chain management in the direction of a resilient perception of already existing tasks and does not aim to create completely new supply chain specific functions.

  In the case of digital supply chains and related technology, the compatibility of the referenced systems often is still inadequate. This applies less to the ERP systems, in which a few large providers already ensure a high degree of compatibility. In the field of production planning and control, however, the provider landscape of corresponding CIM or *MES* systems is comparatively fragmented (similar to Soder 2014). In some cases, suitable standards that guarantee compatibility between systems are missing. For this reason, the latter are currently being discussed intensively under the heading *de facto standards* in the Industry 4.0 community.

  In addition to the IT infrastructure, Nyhuis et al. (2008) show the criteria for the adaptability of *robotics* systems, which is also still in its early stages (but Steegmüller/Zürn 2014). In addition, there are issues of data security, reaction time and energy-saving. For *data security* considerations, a European open cloud (cloud) is ideally needed on the basis of unified requirements and responses in actual time (i.e. in the millisecond range). Taking into account Moore's law (Moore 1965) for regularly doubling the performance of computer chips, digital supply chains also need *energy-saving* solutions in view of the high IT capacity requirements in terms of a green IT. All this influences the compatibility of digital supply chains.

- In addition to compatibility, the extent of the difficulties that supply chain management will face in addressing new problem-solving abilities will also be driven by the *complexity* of skill innovation. Since the development competence as to digital supply chains is to be attributed a high degree of innovation, and even has a paradigmatic character, the uncertainty of the management caused by the diffusion process can be correspondingly huge. New paradigms struggle for recognition for a long time at the beginning of their life cycle before their potential is widely recognized and their diffusion accelerated (Kuhn 1967). In the context of the learning processes, it must therefore be ensured that the innovations to be processed remain manageable for the management. Learning in "small steps" is more useful here than the "big bang". Considerable resistance can otherwise result.

The corresponding transformational journeys have to be organized in a smart way. It's not good enough to get to know the elephant. but you need to slice him properly in order to succeed. Therefore, the discussion how to introduce, pilot and *roll out digital supply chains* is of highest importance. Considering that the S&OP process and the associated supply chain models are at the heart of digital supply chains, it can be reasonable to structure the journey for sites, for example. The S&OP includes the PPDS process on site just because capacity planning is subject to both. Accordingly, PPDS principles have to be reviewed in light of mass customization and portfolio shifts. This is why capacity planning can be a focus point and needs to be developed, site specifically, in order to make a rollout of the digital supply chain a success.

- Finally, the *testability* of a new competence marks the option for management to minimize fear of contact by "trying it out". A digital twin in terms of simulation games and practical examples on cyberphysical systems supports the awareness of management. Learning-by-doing with means of proof-of-concepts as well as pilots promotes a higher understanding of what a digital supply chain is. The profound cultural changes that accompany them indicate, however, that the learning of such problem-solving skills is a rather lengthy process. This is why it is even more important to follow an agile approach of continuous improvement rather than one-off waterfall initiatives.

The *adopter-specific parameters* describe the characteristics of the supply chain (management) itself that determine the learning behaviour. They are of central importance insofar as learning is largely a self-organizing process and thus not alienated by the adopters. Basically, subjects to learning can include both supply chain managers as well as logistics machines that learn. Favourable framework conditions, for example, in the form of a "learn-shop digital supply chain", can be created and give impulses. Both the competence-oriented and the solution-oriented learning of supply chains, as already mentioned, are primarily determined by the respective contexts of their system members. The divergences or convergences between the contexts thus become a central *learning driver*. The causes of divergences can, for example, lie in the different training of supply chain employees, partly in engineering and partly in business management. It can be assumed that the relationship between context *divergences* and the extent of learning suggests a bell-shaped course. If the learning behaviour is increased towards divergent contexts, from a certain point on the discrepancies become so great that they lead to counterproductive conflicts. They then hinder learning rather than promote it (similar to Kirsch 1976). Other adopter-specific learning drivers include *risk appetite* (Probst 1987) and *innovation orientation* (this is accompanied by an appropriate future development) in supply chain management as well as *perceived environmental complexity* and the resulting misfit.

In addition to the latter intra-personal factors, other interpersonal behavioural determinants also influence the learning of logistics. So-called *opinion leaders* occupy a central position in the communication structure of supply chain management, and thus have multiplicative effects on the diffusion process. They fulfil a risk-reduction task for supply chains when setting benchmarks. Because of their high influence, they usually function as power and professional promoters (Witte 1977). On the other hand, *taboos*, or so-called non-discussables, significantly impede the learning process (Probst 1987).

The supply chain academy is ideal for anchoring the learning process in the company and digital supply chain in particular. The following use case illustrates its use in practice:

Project example: supply chain academy

Initial situation: A manufacturing company recognized that numerous opportunities for further development of the business had their origins in the supply chain. However, respective skills were limited in terms of quality and quantity because of the traditional focus on manufacturing and sales. An attempt to recruit individual supply chain executives via recruitment consultants was partially successful. However, such an approach could not cover the demand in this area of the organization with regards to quantity. The company found that external training on supply chain management was generic because company-specific issues were not adequately addressed. It lacked the "barn odor".

Objective: Company management decided to set up a supply chain academy in order to build up the required competences in-house, to anchor the topic of supply chain management internally and to be able to specifically address the corresponding possibilities for improvement. The aim of the academy was to train some 150 supply chain experts over the next three years.

Approach: The supply chain academy was set up in three steps: First, a company-specific training program was developed that took into account the company's competence requirements. To support the e-learning training, web-based training modules were developed or adapted. A target group of employees to be included was identified for each business area and academy-specific degrees were defined, for example, the "advanced supply chain professional" and "supply chain professional". In the second step, the supply chain academy training program was piloted. Based on the pilot, possible improvements to the training content and procedures were identified and incorporated. In the third step, the supply chain academy was rolled out company-wide.

Results and digital relevance: Due to the high level of acceptance among the employees, the company's internal demand for training measures was higher than the demand, so that the supply chain academy was able to exceed the training goals. For the future, the company also saw itself well prepared for the learning content of digital supply chains due to the now established systematic development platform for its employees.

Success factors: Two factors were particularly critical for success. First, the training requirements were closely aligned with the company-specific requirements, which made it possible to directly apply the competences conveyed. In doing so, the company found the right balance of training content between the imparted technical solutions and strategic competencies for problem solving. Secondly, attendance at the supply chain academy was perceived by the employees as a form of professional development due to the awarded degrees, so that the personal motivation was very high.

Learning, planning and competition strategy revealed the most important basic strategies of supply chain management. The functional strategies of logistics now have to be explained.

3.3   Functional strategies

The task of supply chains is basically the management of spatio-temporal processes as well as the related transformations. Defined processes cause such transformations (Pfohl/Stölzle 1992; Zöllner 1990; Göpfert/Wehberg 1995). For example, separation processes affect a transformation with regard to the quality of the goods. Warehousing facilitates the transformation of time, and so forth. These supply chain processes mainly relate to the flow of materials, goods, residues and spare parts, as well as to the flow of information and to the design of supply chain potential. While the steering and development tasks of supply chains have a greater relation to their management system, the remaining processes are primarily directed to the execution level (similar to Pfohl 1990). The various processes build on each other. Certain processes include others or presuppose them. Supply chain development, for example, encompasses all other areas of work, as it aims at the integrated qualification of all supply chain structures against the background of a dynamic overall understanding (Göpfert/Wehberg 1995).

The intermingling of the different types of transformation expresses the system thinking of supply chain management. A design area influencing all variables is the configuration of the supply chain. The configuration strategy also defines much of the management's competitive room for manoeuvre. For example, 24-hour customer service is unlikely to be possible without an adequately decentralized spare parts logistics system. The configuration is also a particularly attractive subject of the S&OP, as well as a learning strategy of a supply chain. For instance, it determines the balancing potential of capacities and materials between sites.

3.3.1   Configuration

Networks of higher order

The configuration strategy of a supply chain characterizes the spatial arrangement of supply chain activities in their overall view. It goes beyond the mere warehouse problem, as it is not confined to the location of individual transhipment locations. However, the exact content design of the transhipment points, such as the equipment, conveyors, etc., plays a subordinate role (see, for fine-selection of individual micro-locations, for example, Gaebe 1981; Lüder/ Küpper 1983, and the warehouse Pfohl 1990).

If the theory of the general location factors according to Weber (1922) is taken up, a resource, work, consumption and transport-oriented configuration strategy can be differentiated. The configuration in each case is based on the relevance of cost factors and associated resources, such as labour, consumption, logistics, etc. (Schäfer 1980; Stahl 1994). In the following, the focus is on the *transport-oriented configuration* strategy. Of course, this does not wish to exclude the other factors altogether. Such a perspective, however, seems justifiable, as – in the context of competition considerations – it is in more and more instances the transport that causes particularly high costs and resource consumption. Thus, a transport orientation in the configuration of operational systems becomes more and more important in the future. In a way, digitalization can also reinforce this trend if the desired flexibility in the supply chain leads to higher transport volumes and resource consumption, and if the networks are not planned effectively.

In the course of digital supply chains, the configuration is much more flexible and distributed. The configuration is constantly in flux, in the sense of process orientation in the broader sense. Not the configuration as a whole, but individual objects (e.g. pallets, means of transport) undergo *continuous service improvements* (e.g. routes, cross-docking sites) in the course of a trial-and-error process. These are used as learning processes for the rest of the "swarm" so that the other objects are passed. Anderson (2007) also points out that digitization is slowly reversing the "dictation of location" for the availability of products and replacing them in principle with *markets without borders*. He speaks in particular of decreasing transaction costs, increasing transparency of offers and the growing omnipresence (ubiquity) of goods. Digital supply chains essentially support this development, and it is already observable today. For example, you can see this thanks to the rapidly growing market for courier and express services (CEP) due to e-commerce. It results in the trend of more delicate and flexible supply chain systems. And the discussed customer needs of Dawn Digital (Clay/Mashall/ Glynn 2017) do not leave any doubt that these trends apply to the broad portfolio of products as well as services in terms of mainstream consumption.

The form of the supply chain depends in this sense above all on two quantities: the number of nodes and their connections (for this and in the following Wehberg 1994). The *number of nodes* results from the amount of bearings in vertical and horizontal terms. In terms of vertical, this affects the number of storage levels, such as factory, central, regional and distribution warehouses. With regard to the horizontal, the number of bearings per stage is meant. In contrast, the *number of connections* involves the question of which nodes are to be connected to one another. A distinction must be made between vertical connections between different levels of storage and of horizontal connections between the bearings of a stage. The former should be realized, among other things, when skipping a storage level for service reasons, for example, especially for delivery time, or seems appropriate from a cost point of view. The latter, for example, create the conditions for achieving equalization effects if they enable the transfer of safety stocks from one regional warehouse to another, even at short notice.

The combination of the above criteria leads to two types of configurations: hub-spoke systems and change-oriented grid systems. The *hub-spoke systems* are centralized indirect connectivity arrangements, and thus are associated with stability-oriented supply chain structures. In contrast, *change-oriented grid systems* are decentralized configurations with direct connections on the other side (Figure 3.9). The high level of change in grid systems results from the fact that the number and variety of possible supply chain relationships is comparatively high. In particular, the complexity of these types of systems requires a high degree of supply chain planning. The positioning between the two extremes can be done as a *multi-hub system*.

Historically grown supply chains often approach the grid system as they evolve. The increasing branching of the network then becomes more concrete, similar to complex river systems. An initially unstructured networking is often the result. In such a situation, among other things, the performance-related arrangement of supply chain activities can justify longer processing times, higher working capital and limited transparency, as well as the danger of strong fluctuations or instabilities. Vester (1980b) refers to this form of development as *density stress*; that is, the supply chain is disturbed when density stress occurs. The development, similar to a carcinoma, leads to disordered *chaos* if the supply chain is not re-structured in good time by forming, if necessary, segment-specific, largely self-organizing subsystems or corresponding guardrails. Such a

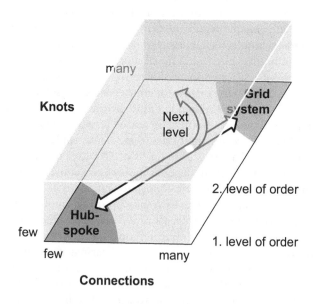

Figure 3.9 Change profile of the supply chain configuration

structured networking of highly complex systems is accompanied by the leap in *supply chain configuration to a higher level of order*, as illustrated in Figure 3.9. The connections within the subsystems are numerous. In contrast, the exchange between them is limited to comparatively few but intensive connections. The differences between unstructured and structured networking are becoming obvious (Gomez/Probst 1987; Wildemann 1994). In this sense, a digital supply chain aims for a higher order, which means highly complex but structured networks. Guardrails for network development can be used in this context. For example, such guardrails can be:

- Regional site clusters or regions that ask for special treatment.
- Listed freight forwarders or warehouse operators with distinguished performance levels.
- Prioritized customers or a list of dedicated clients that has been promised a special service level.
- Certain products that rely on a dedicated supply chain network structure in order to keep its brand promises.
- Selected time frames such as holidays or weekends that operate differently.
- Generally, customized supply chain models and the associated operating rules.

The self-optimization of supply chain operations, for example, through algorithms, then moves within the limits of such crash barriers. Talking S&OP, the system will ask for management intervention as soon as assumptions are not met. Based on respective alerts, the supply chain is then based on a management by exception, accordingly.

Incidentally, the higher order of configuration takes into account the trend and the necessity of keeping the division of labour of a value-added system connected by a supply chain as closely as possible (Hesse 1993). The frequently propagated trend towards internationalization is critical here (Vester 1995). Next to the spatial order itself, the configuration of value-added activities thus has to be taken into account, which means cross-site integration. Both areas are closely linked. Therefore, the decision to integrate is to be seen against the background of the following goals (Liebmann 1991; Pfohl 1990, 1994):

- Minimization of transport costs on one side and storage costs (storage house and storage) on the other side.
- Realization of synergy effects and specialization advantages.
- Achieving an effective supply chain service (especially delivery time and flexibility).
- Tax optimization of international value-added networks.

Strategies such as *geography postponement* (Bowersox/Closs/Helferich 1986), *bundling* and (de-)centralization can play an important role. It should also be noted that the subsequent success of a company's dis-integration strategy depends largely on coordination with the value-added partner who performs the service. If the coordination of the two succeeds, Porter (1986) also speaks of *quasi-integration.*

As an example of the integration possibilities between industry and trade, the following use case serves to optimize the goods receipt.

Project example: goods receipt

Initial situation: Over the course of many years, a food retailing company had been pursuing a steady growth path first in Germany and later increasingly in European countries and, ultimately, worldwide. Every year, numerous new stores were opened and connected to the supply chain network. In doing so, the company relied on regional distribution warehouses. These offered two advantages in terms of distribution to the individual market locations. First, it allowed the company to avoid the acceptance of dozens of third-party deliveries from the various manufacturers in the markets. Secondly, the provision of a broad article portfolio in the distribution warehouse – matched as closely as possible to the regionally varying consumption preferences of the customers – enabled a short-term reaction to demand-related reordering of a market. Most days, one to two "tailor-made" deliveries of one market per day could be ensured.

Objective: Over time, sales growth inevitably led to increasing inventory levels in ever-larger distribution warehouses. In the run-up to Christmas, for example, it was always possible to use this as an instrument in purchasing. In parallel with this volume growth, information technology also continued to evolve, and the company consistently opted for greater automation of its internal processes – from warehousing and picking to rolling stock inventory. Only with regard to the delivery of the goods from suppliers – either with their own vehicle fleet or by means of their assigned freight forwarder – there was no satisfactory progress in efficiency over the years. At the end of the 2000s, productivity in this important step even declined, and management had to react.

Approach: In the course of an investigation, it soon became clear that the company itself could not solve this problem on its own. The different suppliers encountered different requirements for the company's competitors with regard to the loading of their goods, different product categories with different limits (e.g. food vs. non-food, cool vs. dry) and often different delivery points for these categories within the warehouse (e.g. "Fruit always gate 7" or "Non-food only on Tuesdays"). The warehouse operators increasingly installed "fully automated" goods-receipts processes which had to be operated manually by the delivering drivers which took considerable time before. A set of measures were put in place to facilitate disposition and delivery for all participating market partners.

Results and digital relevance: Downtime of the delivering forwarders was reduced from up to 4 hours to an average of 2.5 hours. At the same time, the companies involved reduced employee misconduct and damage of items during delivery, which resulted in additional cost reductions. The example also illustrates that an evolutionary, largely autonomous approach in several iterations and integration of upstream value-added stages can provide a good result, while the previous, isolated attempts of the retailer were previously inconclusive.

Success factors: A key success factor was the intercompany coordination of the interface, so that the partners involved in the supply chain did not cause additional process breaks due to individual optimization. The advantages of automated warehouse processes have been consistently demonstrated. The use of supporting IT, e.g. by a mobile accessible application for loading ramp management, also proved to be critical to success for the self-controlling approach.

City logistics

With regard to the interface between industry and trade, receiver-side bundling would be advantageous in many cases. In this context, city logistics is one example for doing so. The *origin* of the concept of city logistics comes from the need to minimize the environmental impact of urban traffic by *bundling transports* in and around cities and conurbations, as well as through intelligent networking, and to increase traffic efficiency and efficiency in general. The retail trade in the inner cities in particular has only a few storage options. The result is high transport frequencies with often low utilization levels of road vehicles. Roads and loading capacities in city centres are limited. Delivery windows are usually limited to a few morning hours. Residents protest deliveries during the night. Retailers do not desire an extension of deliveries to the afternoon hours, because it is feared that supplier traffic hinders customer traffic. A corresponding cooperation between the carriers affected by this bottleneck promises improvements here, although at this point the line between cooperative and competitive relations should also be very narrow. However, the high degree of heterogeneity of the generally small-volume freight flows, and in particular the previous bundling strategies (e.g. refrigerated, value-added, tank vehicles, services such as shelf management), do not always meet the goals of city logistics concepts and requires intensive coordination. In this context, digital supply chains offer new opportunities to organize intelligent logistics for the city. Closely related to the construction of such a city logistics is the establishment of freight transport and distribution centres at the periphery of the city. Originally, city logistics focused the *inbound* flow of retailers, accordingly.

Now, a next level of city logistics builds even stronger on autonomous transports and direct deliveries. Customers don't go into the city so much for shopping anymore but for entertainment and socializing, if at all. Retailers and city shops have to meet these developing needs to stay attractive. At the same time, they have to strengthen their Internet presence, facilitate multi-channel contacts to end customers and connect these with their on-site offering in the outlet. A retail shop in the future will be more of a showroom, event space and social platform than a supermarket or simple shop. Storage and shelf space are becoming less important because products can be shown virtually but in an application context. The delivery can be direct from distribution centres to customers. For example, shops that are selling kitchens are not presenting cookers anymore, but rather performing cookery courses and adventures or associated *experience worlds*. While building on the same network principles as the traditional concept, city logistics of the future will consider more service aspects, focus on *outbound* logistics and be much more individualized for customers rather than customized to retailers only.

Many retailers think about this kind of city logistics such that they try to determine the best service provider and the one-and-only transport network for the future. In an evolutionary perspective, however, there is no one-size-fits-all, nor is there an A-candidate of one top model. Rather, there is an ongoing evolution of several transport concepts, and thus several networks being part of the *retailer's eco-partner system*. A range of city logistics networks are being piloted, tested and scaled where viable and continuously improved. For example, crowdsourcing solutions for city logistics are evolving in many cities, and there is a lot of creativity to market/enter city logistics as a new crowdsourcing service provider.

Willingness to integrate

The extent to which potential benefits can actually be realized depends on the willingness of the value-added partners to support and implement the supply chain network patterns they have devised. Despite the high potential for success, the willingness of supply chain management to integrate – that is, the extent to which the value-added partners agree to undertake or to give up certain functions of the overall supply chain – can vary greatly. Survey results on willingness to integrate, however, show that there is a high level of interest in integration (Göpfert/Wehberg 1995). However, note that *expressed readiness* may not correspond to actual readiness.

Many factors influence an industry's willingness to integrate. One factor impacting an industry's integration strategy is the extent of partners' willingness to compromise in terms of delivery time (Göpfert/Wehberg 1995): The non-storability of supply chain processes (Rendez 1992), which means the synchronicity of service provision and use, requires that logistics capacities are available to meet peak demand. The desired delivery time should always be met. Such a form of capacity planning, however, may entail competitive disadvantages if the capital commitment costs caused by uneven utilization are too high. Despite the fact that logistics services per se are not storable, the external factor, for example, the product to be sent, can be stored. A temporal *balance between supply and demand* of logistical capacities and thus the smoothing of utilization peaks becomes possible. However, such an integration strategy on the part of the industry (it assumes warehousing tasks) presupposes an appropriate willingness to compromise the trade and subsequent value-creation stages. In addition, a digital supply chain solves the need for scalable capacities and flexibility by outsourcing logistics services in a network to external third parties, as required.

Tax optimization

Finally, the integration considerations of an international value creation network must take into account *tax and customs law*. The first considerations are typically summarized under the category "Tax optimized supply chain management". In the past, international tax law made it necessary for the physical flow of goods to be as deep as possible in the country in which the company wanted to tax. In practice, this requirement sometimes led to goods being transhipped in one country only to profit from the tax benefits of that country. In contrast, tax law nowadays looks at the causal value creation; that is, it is not as important where certain value-added activities are carried out. Rather, it is crucial who coordinates the value-added activities. For example, if a company's supply chain team is based in Singapore and gains 5 percent efficiency gains along the value and supply chain each year, these profits typically can be taxed in Singapore. The tax law thus fulfils the actual idea of supply chain management as a coordination task. However, given the potential loss of image in the case of public discussions of alleged tax evasion, many companies are reluctant to exploit these opportunities under tax law. In reality, this legitimate scope for tax law will probably play a role, above all, for globally active companies.

3.3.2 Transport

Mode and means of transport

The transport function marks the space bridging of goods (in the following Jünemann 1989; Pfohl 1990). With regard to the choice of mode of transport, it is important to build transport chains in such a way that the specific advantages of each mode are relevant. The advantages can be described above all on the basis of the criteria of transport speed and costs, as well as the environmental friendliness and networkability of the mode of transport. Of course, in terms of the systemic thinking of supply chain management, they are always to be seen in connection with the cost and service consequences of other areas. The weighting of decision-making criteria for the *choice of transport vehicle* is industry specific, if not company specific. Digital supply chains then map appropriate decisions of the mode of transport choice via suitable algorithms.

While, for simplicity, both the speed and the transport costs per tonne-kilometre increase from inland navigation and shipping via rail and road to air freight, the corresponding energy consumption, and thus the environmental impact, tends to increase in this order. Of course, any cost advantages will only come into play if the corresponding minimum ranges are guaranteed and if the costs of transhipment can be neglected compared with transport costs. The speed of the carrier is not the same as the delivery or disposal time. Furthermore, the *networking abilities* of inland shipping, classic airfreight and rail are comparatively low. It depends on factors such as the locations of air, sea and inland ports, the course of inland waters and the rail network. In contrast, the main advantage of truck or road transport is usually its pronounced ability to form networks. It is thus highly suitable to meet individual transport needs in the area. Prospectively in the course of digital supply chains, intelligent, and thus self-controlling, vehicles or truck drones will increase the strength of this mode of transport. The automobile industry currently expects corresponding offers until about the year 2025. Analogously, ten Hompel (2014, translated) describes the following image of the future for internal transport: "swarms of autonomous vehicles take over . . . transport. The arrangement of workstations can now be changed at any time. The vehicles learn from each other. Their software agents negotiate orders and rights of way and constantly swap locations for new stations or warehouses."

Current examples of the first self-steering vehicles are the Ray Park robot from Serva Transport Systems, Indego 1000 lawnmowers from Bosch, Container Shuttle from Altenwerder Hafen, F015 prototype from Mercedes, autonomous forklifts from Aberle and Still and the Bubble Car from Google. *Autonomous driving* can be considered as a mature technology; its development towards being market standard mainly depends on regulation and acceptance. Intra-plant and highway applications are pilot areas, but autonomous transports are not limited to these.

It becomes clear that with innovation efforts the *traditional boundaries* between modes of transport will shift significantly. Innovations such as maglev trains and intelligent drones for the roads and, in the future, also aviation, promise to be able to redefine the performance characteristics for the respective modes of transport (ten Hompel 2014). Cost structures may also shift, such as inland shipping due to increasing fees for the use of artificial waterways. Moreover, other mega trends such as global warming impact transport modes as well. For example, the river Rhine in Germany is increasingly associated with transport risks for inland shipping, given the volatile water levels due to climate extremes.

The inclusion of different modes of transport in the form of the modal split for a transport chain takes the form of *combined transport*. A symbiosis of the different modes of transport means that all those involved in the transport process benefit from each other precisely because of their differences (Vester 1995). In contrast to the "broken traffic", there is no change of transport container during cargo handling in combined traffic. Its main aim is to combine modes of transport that are particularly suitable for the area with modes of transport whose advantages are used on the line. As basic forms of combined transport, hip-pack transport can be distinguished from container traffic. With piggyback transport one means of transport transports another. Examples of combined road–rail transport are the loading of entire swap bodies, the so-called rolling country road, where complete road–rail trains are transported by rail, and the roll-on, roll-off waterway. In the case of container traffic, containers, for example, ISO containers and lattice box pallets, are used to streamline the handling of the cargo (especially for the trucking of airfreight, Göpfert 1994).

In addition to combined transport, which means the successive switching of carriers, it may also be appropriate to provide different modes of transport in the form of different supply chain segments next to each other. The combined use of centralized and decentralized transport networks with appropriate modes of transport can then help to reduce transport costs while increasing supply chain services (Herron 1968).

The choice of *means of transport*, meaning the equipment of the fleet, is directly related to the decision for a particular mode of transport. In doing so, the choice of means of transport will always be measured by the quality of the selected vehicle, which generally reflects the degree of fulfilment of certain requirements imposed by certain stakeholder groups of logistics, primarily consumers (on the quality term Pfohl 1992). Above all, the following five criteria determine the quality of the means of transport:

- Transport security
- Technical equipment
- Human factors
- Drive technology
- Fuel

In the course of digital supply chains, decisions are made autonomously, like the products themselves decide on their packaging, the packaging on their transport containers, the transport containers on the means of transport, and the latter on the transport route. Everyone involved has access to the relevant information via a cloud. The future *transport organization* thus is recursive, semi-autonomous, redundant and self-referential. Transport management in this case is focusing on managing exceptions as well as determining the right (meta-)algorithms that facilitate the learning of this kind of autonomous decision-making. In the future there will hardly be any truck drivers or transport planners. But there are supply chain experts that design the transport system by applying both their deep expertise in transport management as well as the associated technology.

Integrated transport strategy

Depending on the modal split and the quality of the means of transport, two extreme basic patterns of transport can be summarized: integrated and isolated (Figure 3.10). The *integrated transport strategy* enforces multi-modal transport chains within the framework of change-oriented logistics structures on a high-quality level of intelligent means of transport. The combination of transport modes and the consideration of quality requirements of certain stakeholder groups leads to potentially multi-layered state forms of the system of transport

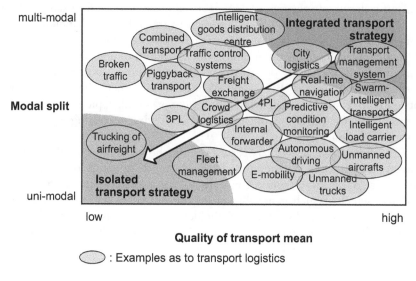

multi-modal

Modal split

uni-modal

low   high

Quality of transport mean

⬭ : Examples as to transport logistics

Figure 3.10 Change profile of the transport strategy

logistics. Integrated transport corresponds to the characteristics of digital supply chains insofar as it best promises to meet its flexibility requirements on the transport side. It is only through the use of cyberphysical systems that a far-reaching networking of means of transport (vehicles, transport participants) and traffic infrastructure is made possible and allows, for example, traffic accidents to be prevented and environmental protection to be improved. This means that the systems communicate permanently with each other, for example, in actual time, information about the weather, the traffic situation or the availability of traffic infrastructure. Cyberphysical systems play a central role, especially in electro-mobility, as they enable efficient battery and charge management (acatech 2011). The *isolated transport strategy*, in contrast, is limited to uni-modal transport with moderate means of transport quality. It takes place in more stability-oriented structures of logistics management.

The following project example shows the importance of the quality of the means of transport and how to ensure it.

Project example: internal forwarding

Initial situation: At the production sites of an international company in the raw materials industry, the supply and disposal activities of the production and maintenance facilities at the respective locations had grown over the course of time and were independently managed. In particular, the internal transport of raw materials, auxiliary materials and operating supplies to the departments as well as the disposal of recyclables and residues were the responsibility of the companies at each individual site. Over time, all the production sites had purchased their own transport equipment optimized for the specific requirements, trained production and maintenance personnel for these activities and integrated the transport organization into the processes of the respective facility. As a result, the energy effects of planning and carrying out transport activities at one location could not be systematically exploited due to decentralized control, and the transport services of the locations could no longer be compared with one another. In addition, potential could not be achieved by standardizing the equipment. There was a lack of sufficient transparency regarding transports, transport requirements and the corresponding use of resources.

Objective: Company management no longer found this situation to be acceptable, especially because a comparison with other international companies in the raw materials industry had shown that other companies had centrally organized their internal transport activities with great success. The company therefore set itself the goal of increasing its cost-cutting potential.

Approach: The conversion of the decentralized organization of internal transports to the central organization was implemented in four phases. First, all transport services provided by the respective units of the locations were recorded as part of an as-is survey. A concept was then developed as to how an "internal freight forwarder" should provide the transport services of the respective location in the future. The core of the concept was the use of cross-location transport management software, which was to ensure the transparent recording of transport requirements, the processing of transports and the invoicing of transport services according to the polluter-pays principle. In the next phase, the feasibility of the project was demonstrated on the basis of a pilot location, and then the concept was rolled out to the other locations. Once the concept was implemented, the transport equipment could be standardized and the transport personnel specialized in further optimization steps. Outsourcing freight-forwarding tasks was conceivable in the medium term.

Results and digital relevance: Implementation of the internal freight-forwarding project increased efficiency from 18 to 23 percent, depending on the location. In particular, the current transparency of transport requirements reduced the proportion of empty runs and achieved synergy effects in the bundling of transports to production and maintenance operations. Bi-directional transports between the warehouse and the respective area were replaced by transport networks. In addition, the equipment has been standardized, and the life span of the respective equipment has been extended considerably. The project is a good example of the potential of avoiding homemade complexity in transport equipment, how it can be harmonized through standardization, how complexity can be better managed and how it can contribute to more (internal) customer orientation and flexibility in transport logistics. The support of the internal freight forwarder by modern transport management software and a prospective platform enabled a stronger self-organization of the control in the sense of a digital supply chain in the medium term and the scalable integration of external transport companies as required. It also simplified the use of electro-mobility through networked battery and charging management.

Success factors: It was crucial for the success of the project that support from company management was available in every phase. In addition, the fears of those responsible for production and maintenance that the switch to central control of internal transports could have a negative impact on the performance of their operations was countered by their early inclusion in the planning of the project. In particular, great importance was attached to the selection of the pilot location. In the optimization phase following implementation of the concept, the consistent measurement of KPIs with the resulting derivation of savings potential was decisive for increasing efficiency.

Freight transport centres are a core component of bi- and multi-modal transport chains and are increasingly being assigned a leading role. In the following, they will therefore be dealt with separately and briefly.

Freight transport centres

The concept of the freight transport centre (in German: GVZ) includes the consolidation of different modes of transport at a conveniently located hub of the logistics system (e.g. Hesse 1993; Wiedemann 1993). Freight transport centres generally take on the function of a *goods distribution centre* (German: GVtZ), especially in connection with city logistics concepts, which forms the interface between local and long-distance traffic (Kracke et al. 1994). The central advantage of such freight transport and distribution centres is that they lead to a *linearization* of the transport connections when additional source and destination points are included in a supply chain system. While in situations without such nodes an exponential increase of traffic connections can be observed, the number of connections – in the case of such transhipment facilities – behaves proportionally to the number of new source and destination points to be included. Although at first glance the impression may appear to arise, freight transport and distribution centres are by no means necessarily linked to a hub-spoke logistics strategy. They can, for example, justify such a configuration at the first-order level of the supply chain. At the second level, however, supply chains can be structured in the form of a grid system.

De-materialization and 3D printing

The more efficient design of transport flows must be separated from their substitution by the increased use of only information flows. Transport avoidance takes the place of transport control. This so-called *de-materialization* of logistics processes offers great potential for increasing efficiency (e.g. Schmidt-Bleek 1994). Intangible transport can replace material transport. Examples include teleconferencing and teleworking, in which company employees work at home on their PCs (Höller 1994). The combination of "Home" and "Office" then becomes the so-called Hoffice, so that occupational traffic is avoided.

Another example is *3D printing*, also known as additive manufacturing. In this process, three-dimensional workpieces are built up in layers (e.g. Gebhardt 2002; Fastermann 2012). Production is computer-controlled from one or more solid or liquid materials according to predefined dimensions. During production, physical or chemical hardening and melting processes take place. Typical materials for 3D printing are plastics, synthetic resins, ceramics and metals. The most important techniques of 3D printing are:

- Selective laser melting and electron beam melting for metals.
- Selective laser sintering for polymers, metals and ceramics.
- Stereolithography and digital light processing for liquid synthetic resins.
- Polyjet modelling and fused deposition modelling for plastics and partially resins.

Combined printing processes working with different materials are increasingly being used. Important advantages over conventional manufacturing processes lead to an increasing spread of 3D printing also in series production. Compared to the injection moulding process, it has the advantage, among others, of eliminating the costly production and changing of moulds. Some very complex moulds can be produced with 3D printing that cannot be produced via classical manufacturing processes. Compared to material-removing techniques such as turning, cutting and drilling, 3D printing has the advantage of eliminating material loss. In many cases, 3D printing is also more energetically advantageous because the material is produced directly in the required dimensions. Last but not least, 3D printing allows significantly faster development times through prototyping.

The possibility of setting up 3D printers in a more demand-oriented or more decentralized manner offers considerable de-materialization potential for transport logistics and can influence all stages of the value chain. However, due to the – depending on the technology – sometimes considerable machine costs, the overall manufacturing and logistics costs must be optimized. For manufacturers and logistics service providers, this offers opportunities to introduce new value-added services and business models. For example, so-called *fabbing shops* offer 3D printing as a stand-alone service, similar to copy shops. And system manufacturers can, for example, move backwards in the direction of parts suppliers if they print important parts themselves. With increasing learning and scale effects at the printers themselves and their production, the opportunities to optimize value chains on the basis of additive manufacturing and to develop new business models will grow, especially in the maintenance, service and spare parts business. The possibility of an economical production of *batch size N = 1* corresponds not least to the flexibility concept of digital supply chains. The efficiency effects of each de-materialization, however, depend on the exact pattern of technology use and must be evaluated concretely in each individual case.

Many companies outsource their transport logistics to logistics service providers or forwarders. The strategic purchase of such transports often offers considerable potential because the complexity associated with the transport services is not handled effectively. The following project case shows the possibilities of simulations and outlines the self-organized purchasing process in the course of digital supply chains.

Project example: purchasing of transport services

Initial situation: In the past, a company in the manufacturing segment had outsourced its distribution logistics to various service providers. In order to simplify the allocation process, the purchasing manager defined five regions, and "top dog" forwarder was selected for each. In addition, there were historically grown business relationships with over a dozen forwarding agents. The purchasing manager justified this approach by stating that it was not possible to compare around 50 forwarders on around 200 individual routes, especially as many providers made their prices for selected routes dependent on paired traffic elsewhere. In addition, they had had good experiences with many forwarders and did not want to take the risk of changing suppliers. In a rather random comparison of freight rates, however, the company found that the selected forwarders did not necessarily always offer competitive rates when comparing individual routes.

Objective: The company sought to review the purchasing process for distribution logistics (full truckload) and, where possible, achieve further savings. The service was to remain unaffected, which means the company did not want to achieve any savings by worsening the service level.

Approach: In the course of strategic purchasing, a digital RfP process (Request for Proposal) was set up and the addressable purchasing volume defined. More than 50 service providers were asked to submit offers. The basis was around 200 routes of the distribution network, in line with the company's strategy. The specification of premises for pricing or links in the form of paired transports was permitted. Around two thirds of the invited forwarders submitted bids, with at least three proposals for each route in order to ensure a market comparison. Against this background, the coverage of the routes and consignments was over 99 percent in each case. On the basis of the bids submitted, alternative allocation scenarios were calculated using simulation procedures. For example, the proportion of long-established and proven forwarders played a role. The preferred scenario provided the basis for negotiating the offers with the selected forwarding agents.

Results: The company was able to realize savings of 11 percent on transport costs. One third of these savings were due to intermodal transport, and thus supported the company's sustainability strategy. However, more than half of the freight forwarders had to be replaced because the offers of the providers who had been active so far were disappointing in some cases or even not available for many routes. All in all, the number of integrated forwarders could be reduced from 17 to 12.

Success factors and digital relevance: Key to the project's success was the development of allocation scenarios and the corresponding simulation algorithms. This made it possible to take paired traffic and the strengths of individual providers into account. While the simulation and awarding of contracts in the outlined case study were controlled centrally by the project team, the algorithms provide a basis for steering towards the overall optimum again and again in the course of future, self-organized negotiation processes between decentralized units. In this respect, the case study also stands for the use of intelligent procurement rules for transport services in the digital supply chain.

Packaging logistics is closely related to the use of transport logistics in general. Exemplary packaging strategies are therefore presented in the following.

3.3.3 Packaging

Functions of packaging

Packaging is the separable wrapping of a good, the packaged good (Koppelmann 1979). The functions of packaging are manifold (hereinafter Jansen 1987). Ultimately, they reflect a requirement profile that is placed on them primarily by logistics and marketing, and in which supply chain management must bring about a suitable compromise. The *marketing-induced requirements* of packaging include the sales function (e.g. its function as an information carrier and differentiation instrument), as well as the use function (e.g. how the packaging can be closed). The *logistic-induced requirements* include transport ("underrideable, non-slip"), storage ("stackable, manageable") and protective ("impermeable") functions. The starting points of a logistics-compatible packaging design are logically primarily directed towards transport packaging (Baumgarten 1972), while the starting points of a marketing-compatible design are more likely to be product packaging.

Note that the use of *transport packaging* is at least partially substitutive to the emergence of product packaging. For example, elaborate product packaging designed to protect the product can be made more economical in terms of material consumption by adequately designing load carriers. Moreover, in individual cases it is even possible to completely dispense with industrial product packaging if, for example, consumers use their own household packaging for milk or butter (which is not always harmless for reasons of food law). The same applies to some packaging designs initiated for marketing reasons, such as high-gloss packaging (Luttmer 1993). The disposal of transport packaging is also more a matter of logistics control than of product packaging. In Germany for example, many companies have already solved the problem of the disposal of product packaging by participating in the Dual System Germany (DSD). According to § 6 of the German Packaging Ordinance, industry and trade are obliged to take back transport, repackaging and consumer packaging and to recycle it. Alternatively, they can participate in the DSD, which guarantees regular collection and achieves certain material-specific collection rates.

This does not mean that marketing-induced requirements no longer play a role against the background of competitive considerations. *Product packaging* can support the positioning of a product as a brand offering. And the importance of marketing packaging requirements for logistics can also be seen when, for example, special attention is paid to the ease of disposal of product packaging within the scope of the application functions. Moreover, certain marketing-induced requirements cannot be ruled out, for example, for reasons of food law. This is true although the trend of making products smarter with means of digital technology can reduce the requirements towards product packaging to a certain extent. For example, information require-ments can also be met via suitable information terminals or mobile devices that access the Universal Product Codes (UPC) or Quick Response (QR) codes of the products.

At the end of the day it is not an either/or question, but rather one of a pos-sible shift in the focus of logistics with regard to the fulfilment of its functions. Conversely, the close linkage of the marketing and logistics-induced tasks of packaging also places certain demands on the design of the packaged goods or on the product policy of marketing.

Standardization and postponement

The formation of logistic units, *unitization* (Pfohl 1990), is closely related to the logistic design of packaging. Both from an ecological and an economic point of view, it is helpful to combine individual packaged goods into larger units when storing, handling and transporting goods. Ideally, the transport, storage, ordering and loading units, etc., should be the same (Bahke 1976; Böttger 1991). The summary of larger sales units, for example, the "Ocr-Pack" and the use of pallet loads as secondary placements, can also have a sales-enhancing effect. As a rule, logistics units are set up within the framework of appropri-ate standardization and make it necessary to coordinate companies at different stages of the value chain. The harmonization of several packagings in the form of *modularization* – as a special form of standardization – is necessary when two or more companies with different packaging sizes work together in parallel in a transport chain. Examples of standardized units in packaging logistics are pallets and containers (Michaletz 1994).

Closely related to the standardization of packaging materials is the standard-ization of the packaged goods themselves. In particular, the links between the packaging system and the company's postponement strategy, here assembly postponement (Bowersox/Closs/Helferich 1986), must be considered. *Assembly postponement* aims to integrate those value-added activities that differentiate the products into the logistics chain as far as possible. This endeavour is in line with the desire to use certain packaging standards across large parts of the supply chain. On the other hand, the marketing-induced differentiation measures, albeit "late", conflict with the standardization efforts of supply chain management. Different products often require different packaging. And the ongoing individu-alization of products as a result of many digitalization strategies makes the need of balancing between standardization and differentiation even more relevant.

Flow-oriented packaging strategy

In summary, the typical and basic patterns of packaging logistics can be pre-sented on a spectrum with the following two poles: *Flow-orientated packaging* strategies attempt to realize logistical requirements in the form of value-added stages of comprehensive standards. Horizontal cooperation enables the stan-dardization, modularization and networking of intelligent packaging materials, especially in the areas of transport, handling and storage. The coordination of the packaging logistics of the company under consideration with the other sup-ply chain functions makes it clear that the flow-oriented strategy corresponds with change-oriented structures and a digital supply chain in particular. In many cases it is only possible through cooperation with upstream, downstream and secondary logistics stages. In particular, the assembly postponement often associated with the flow-oriented strategy ultimately creates the prerequisite for a higher degree of complexity of the entire system, which becomes obvious, for example, in the form of the high product variety that can be handled by supply chain management. In contrast, *marketing-dominated packaging* strategies aim to implement corresponding differentiation efforts, especially in the area of product packaging. The dominance of marketing can lead to the fact that logistical requirements are often seen as a restriction and not as an opportunity. External relations, which speak for a flow-oriented design of the packaging system, remain largely unconsidered. Corresponding strategies are therefore based on stability-oriented logistics structures (Figure 3.11).

In individual cases it seems quite conceivable that in the medium term the development of product packaging that has just been presented may become obsolete. Even though the complete obsolescence of packaging will seldom be depictable, considerations aimed at *zero packaging* can provide creative impulses for packaging avoidance and thus prevent too much packaging, so-called overpacking, by limiting it to what is functionally necessary. Such efforts to achieve savings can, of course, be exaggerated if, for example, the stackability of transport packaging is sacrificed in favour of thinner packaging materials or the protective function is abandoned (Frerich-Sagurna 1993; Luttmer 1993).

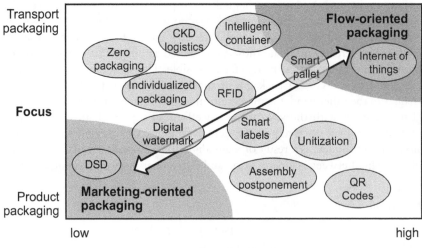

Figure 3.11 Change profile of packaging logistics

RFID and the Internet of Things

In the sense of flow-oriented packaging strategies, it may be appropriate to support the control of flows of goods at the level of the individual packaged good through the use of suitable information and communication technologies. Transponders or control chips can be attached to the individual transport and product packaging to enable transparency or even decentralized control.

Radio frequency identification (RFID), for example, offers transparency and traceability by automatically reading out certain product information off the packaging that is then uniquely identifiable via radio waves. It can be understood as a preliminary stage to the use of cyberphysical systems. However, such identification of objects can also be carried out using barcodes or 2D codes.

> In the field of goods transport logistics, RFID has established itself as a passive technology for identification, localization and status determination. Up to now, however, these systems have only been able to determine the positions of goods comparatively inaccurately and to update their status only very rarely. The use of cyberphysical systems in supply chains with intelligent, active objects offers opportunities for new applications, such as continuous position tracking and status queries in real time, and opens up new possibilities for planning and controlling deliveries.
>
> (acatech 2011, translated)

Devices such as *sensors and actuators* extend the functionality by the registration of states or the execution of actions. Through the use of cyberphysical systems, the "RFID-based Internet of Things . . . gets eyes, ears, arms and legs" (ten Hompel 2014, translated).

Cyberphysical systems embed software technology in the packaging and connect it by means of a communication platform in an Internet-like structure. This technology is discussed with the *Internet of Things* because it links the real objects, here the packaging, with a virtual image, and thus gives them the opportunity to control themselves. Initial applications of such packaging systems include the intelligent smaRTI range, the intelligently networked DyCoNet container and intelligent inBin containers (ten Hompel 2013, 2014). The term "Internet of Things" goes back to Kevin Ashton in 1999. The goal of the Internet of Things is to close the gap of information between the real and virtual world. It is a core component of digital supply chains because it enables decentralized control of highly complex supply chain networks.

If packaging cannot be avoided, appropriate disposal is required. However, before the strategies of disposal logistics are discussed, the behaviour patterns of warehouse and information logistics are presented.

3.3.4 Warehousing

Warehouse functions

Warehousing logistics contains all the information relevant to the amount of warehouse stock. *Stock* levels can be understood as the buffer between input and output of two downstream supply chain processes, which arise as soon as the two processes differ in time (Tempelmeier 1983). They always arise, for example, when more economical batch sizes are to be used in production, procurement and logistics. Furthermore, they arise when, for example, speculations are made about the scarcity of certain goods, whereby the scarcity can result both from economic (procurement prices) and ecological (scarcity of natural resources) correlations (Pfohl 1990).

Overall, inventories can be traced back to two central factors: First, they are the result of the *lack of synchronization* of quality flows, more precisely of the output of one river and the input of the other. Even when management is fully informed, technical and organizational inconsistencies often stand in the way of a complete coordination of the processes, in addition to the economic reasons just mentioned. In this context, stock levels are partly intended, but are generally understood as an expression of insufficient process orientation in the narrower sense (behaviour in the system). In this form they are the exact part of everything "flowing", which at first makes their existence appear unsatisfactory (similar to Kroeber-Riel 1966). In particular, they stand in the way of short processing times. On the other hand, stocks are partly to be seen as *slack*, i.e. as the result of a lack of controllability of supply chain processes. They are then the result of uncertainties in mostly downstream and upstream process stages and the result of more or less existing process orientation in the broader sense (behaviour of the system). Corresponding imbalances can be attributed to demand booms, traffic jams, smog bans and machine failures, for example. Last but not least, inventories in the form of queues can also be economical. In this context Erlang (1909) lays the foundation for a *theory of queuing* which was further developed in the 20th century in the course of operations research. In summary, warehousing tasks are always a function of the system complexity of supply chains.

Brook-bed model

Against the background of the complexity management of supply chains, the tasks of warehousing can be illustrated using the so-called brook-bed model (similar to Kummer 1992; Stahlmann 1988). In many companies the insufficient process orientation is obscured by stocks. Since the patterns according to which the supply chain behaves are not recognized and also the most extensive synchronization of the processes fails, one helps oneself by compensating the lack of supply chain competence by comparatively high stocks and the associated storage costs. Not the actual problem, the lack of knowledge of the system behaviour or the processes running in logistics, but only its symptoms, namely uncoordinated and unforeseen stock calls, are dealt with. In real terms, however, the high level of confirmation only intensifies the problems arising from the inadequate process structure. Thus, high inventories are accompanied by long processing times, which lead to further planning horizons and thus to even greater uncertainty (e.g. Wildemann 1994). In this context we can also speak of an *ambivalent control loop* for storage.

In such a situation, it is above all the reduction of the stock level that shows the bottlenecks and discrepancies. In the course of the inventory reduction, it also becomes clear which inventory level can be attributed to a lack of synchronization of the processes and thus can usually be reduced and which share can be attributed to uncertainties regarding the system behaviour. The goal must then be to determine the type of "un" order. Typical *sources of disturbance* in the supply chain have to be identified in order to be able to initiate its process-oriented handling. Behavioural patterns for logistics and warehousing in particular must be conceived which counteract the disruptive factors identified in an appropriate manner and, above all, reduce the dispersion of stocks attributable to them. Inventory reduction thus functions as a means of perceiving complexity. At the same time, inventory reduction presumably raises a multitude of conflicts between different areas of the company, which were previously covered by the high inventory level and the associated complexity negation or "rape". It can thus be used as a conflict driver, so to speak.

These remarks made clear the position of the warehousing function in the course of the horizontal, which means along the supply chain, and the resulting functions (also Thonemann 2010). However, the warehousing tasks are also geared to the goods program to be served by supply chain management. For cost reasons, their differentiation in the form of differentiated *selective warehousing* may seem expedient. As is well known, the essential selection criteria for warehousing are the demand structure of the goods (RSU) and the ratio between the quantity of the goods to be stored as well as the sales and procurement volume attributable to it, ABC (Grochla 1978, and continuing Bowersox/Smykay/LaLonde 1968; Stahlmann 1988). These are being summarized by supply chain models, accordingly. The use of cyberphysical systems in the sense of a digital supply chain can be helpful because it helps to recognize relevant behaviour patterns of (semi-)finished products and to sharpen them over time. This leads to a *dynamic understanding of selective warehousing* which builds on alerts or early warning signals to adjust stock levels, where possible. Algorithms thus are flexibly adjusted with means of meta-algorithms.

Too much differentiation in warehousing according to the goods it holds can, however, lead to the savings it achieves, for example, through lower capital commitment costs and insurance premiums, being overcompensated by the additional expense of the now more complex disposition. In this context, *automatic data processing and self-control* in the sense of a digital supply chain can be decisive for the economic use of a differentiated strategy. In this respect, selective warehousing always requires a comparison with rather undifferentiated, flat-rate warehousing. The more or less differentiated control of warehouse stocks is one of the basics of complexity management of supply chains and digital supply chains in particular. Depending on the sector and size of the company, some of them find it difficult to manage selective warehousing, dynamically, because they lack a robust approach and methodological knowledge. Let's therefore discuss a project example for a basic optimization approach.

Project example: inventory optimization

Initial situation and objectives: A company in the manufacturing industry with a global production network and worldwide supply relationships between locations found that its working capital was comparatively high on the basis of the published annual financial statements of its main competitors. The company was not conclusive as to the extent to which the figures were due to structural differences between the companies and as to how the causes were distributed among the areas of outstanding receivables, liabilities or inventories. In addition, the share of quick orders increased, leading to significant disruptions in the supply chain, especially in production. For this reason, the company launched several projects, including inventory optimization.

Approach: The inventory optimization project was divided into four phases. In the first phase, the current supply chain relationships in the production network as well as inbound and outbound logistics were structured in the sense of baselining and the basic inventory data collected. In the second phase, the products were segmented from a supply chain perspective (volume, niche and occasional products) so that, for example, products with a high volume and uniform demand were combined. As an alternative to the current division of labour between production sites, new scenarios were developed, such as the concentration of all occasional products with low volume and volatile demand on selected production sites and roads. On this basis, new target inventories were determined both by internal benchmarking per product segment (top down) and by analytical extrapolation of target inventories (bottom up).

The third phase focused on the adjustment of inventories, with the company holding transitional buffer stocks in certain product areas as a safety measure. Parallel to the adjustment of the confirmation to the determined target level, selected suppliers and customers were addressed with regard to their willingness to take over certain stocks on their part or, if covered by the company, to take this into account in pricing. In the fourth phase, the now optimized approach to inventory optimization was permanently anchored as a process and responsibility was transferred back to the line in order to prevent the optimization effects from being unsustainable as a one-off exercise.

Results and digital relevance: Inventories were reduced by more than 12 percent on average and by up to 85 percent in selected product areas. By introducing proper segmentation and integrating customers and suppliers, inventory management processes were referenced and expanded. The resulting improved controllability of the value-added chain offers the possibility of anchoring self-control mechanisms in the sense of a digital supply chain using suitable algorithms. If demand patterns change or new products have to be added, inventory management itself can be further and continuously optimized in this case.

Success factors: The following three factors were decisive for the success of the project: First, the holistic optimization took into account the alternative division of labour between the production sites. Secondly, the robust methodology combined the top-down view in the form of internal benchmarking with the bottom-up view in extrapolation. Thirdly, the permanent anchoring of inventory optimization as a self-organized process in the company enabled the implementation of sustainable inventory reduction.

In addition to the decision facts of the warehousing logistics mentioned here, the so-called just-in-time will be examined in more detail in the following.

Just-in-time

Just-in-time (JIT) is a delivery concept that originated in Japan. It is understood in the sense of a timely delivery. It is often equated with Kanban, but in addition to the product area it also refers to procurement – *JIT procurement* – and distribution – *JIT distribution*. The exact timing of the supply is not an end in itself. Rather, it requires classification into the supply chain and corporate goals. Just-in-time is therefore concerned with achieving a high level of reliability and delivery flexibility and reducing the capital commitment costs caused by warehousing. It thus makes a contribution to the company's *market orientation*. On the other hand, Just-in-time must be applied along the entire supply chain if it is to achieve the goals just mentioned. Due to the broad significance of this concept, the just-in-time (planning) philosophy is also spoken of, which generally attempts to increase added value through the punctual delivery of objects, especially goods, and the associated design concepts. Such a JIT philosophy is an expression of a high level of competence in supply chain management as well as a high level of integration of intra- and interorganizational processes. It is supported by a digital supply chain, which means in particular by the use of cyberphysical systems with their possibilities of self-control. At the same time, it requires a minimum extraversion of supply chain management.

The JIT philosophy has also been criticized many times in the past because fundamental *disadvantages* are associated with it. In this context, the following are cited above all:

- JIT delivery by rail or inland waterway is not possible because the throughput times on these modes of transport are often too long and the reliability and flexibility are often inadequate (Vester 1995).
- Due to the smaller transport lots in the course of the JIT, the transport frequency and thus the total traffic volume increases (Blamauer 1992). The proportion of empty return journeys is increasing. Also the shift from a little heavy to many small vans is, despite the initially higher utilization of the individual vehicle, at least from an ecological point of view, rather a disadvantage and leads to the fact that the road is converted into a "main warehouse" (Atteslander 1987). In addition, transport safety is reduced due to the often adopted "fire brigade function" of JIT in the event of failures in delivery (Thaler 1990).
- The advantageous implementation of JIT is increasingly countered by the so-called transport time syndrome (Reese 1993; Zäpfel 1989). Due to the increase in disruptive factors, delays occur for the first time. As a result, in addition to the usual call-off quantities, which are calculated on the basis of usual calculations, further orders are placed in order not to disrupt the flow of value added. This type of behaviour can then lead to longer delivery times and once again earlier call-offs of deliveries as a result of the increased transport volume that this tends to entail. The advantages of JIT can therefore be overcompensated.
- In addition, there are supposed disadvantages that result from the departmental thinking of some practitioners and are partly characterized by comparatively emotional and generalizing arguments (e.g. Hahn 1991).

However, these criticisms of JIT are relativized when one realizes that:

- The problems of multi-modality are by no means due to the JIT system itself. On the contrary, the lack of reliability and flexibility of the railways is a temporary problem, without the use of this mode of transport also appearing suitable for JIT. In the course of the multi-modal design of the JIT transport chains, freight transport and distribution centres can then also be integrated and corresponding bundling effects achieved (Fischer 1993; Reese 1993). The long transport times of rail and inland waterway transport do not contradict the JIT philosophy. High transport times and punctual deliveries do not fundamentally contradict each other (Hesse 1993). Empirical results show that a large number of companies can also live with higher delivery times in the course of JIT than the 24 hours already established in many places (Göpfert/Wehberg 1995).
- The JIT discussion is often based on a too narrow understanding of the term. Transport frequencies, lots and degrees of capacity utilization are then put at disposal ceteris paribus. It is not recognized that a holistic introduction of the JIT philosophy along the entire supply chain does not treat the production, storage and transshipment locations of those involved as a constant. Rather, the introduction of so-called JIT warehouses, which means buffer warehouses close to the transport sinks, and the establishment of value-added partners, for example, nearby suppliers and manufacturers, make it possible to adapt the overall configuration and also avoid the disadvantages of the transport time syndrome described earlier (Spelthahn/Schlossberger/Steger 1993). However, the former solution, the JIT warehouse, contradicts the JIT philosophy to the extent that the latter is aimed precisely at avoiding warehousing (Zibell 1989).

Overall, therefore, it is not possible to make any generally valid statements about the *advantages* of the JIT philosophy. It depends on the individual case-specific design of the concept idea. In individual cases, a "before-time" (BT) could therefore prove to be more advantageous, which means the deliberate admission of intermediate storage. An exaggerated emulation of the JIT idea is also hindered by the fact that it requires a certain minimum control over the supply chain, which can often be called into question due to corresponding disruptive factors.

Integrated warehousing

The summary of these behaviour patterns leads to two extreme system strategies of warehouse logistics, as shown in Figure 3.12. A distinction must be made between *isolated warehousing* and integrated warehousing. Due to uncertainties, management's lack of process orientation or other factors, isolated warehousing is forced to maintain comparatively high inventories. The differentiation of warehousing with regard to certain selection criteria is dispensed with. JIT principles are not applied. The degree of system complexity is therefore comparatively low.

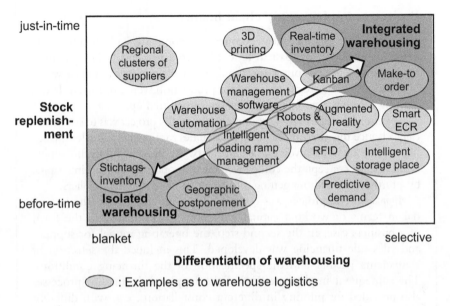

just-in-time

Stock
replenish-
ment

before-time

blanket   selective

Differentiation of warehousing

⬭ : Examples as to warehouse logistics

Figure 3.12 Change profile of the warehousing strategy

In toto, isolated warehousing logistics corresponds to stability-oriented structures. In contrast, *integrated warehousing* impresses with a high degree of differentiation of the goods to be served by it in the form of selective warehousing. Wherever possible and advantageous, process chains are coordinated just-in-time within the framework of changing logistics structures. The integrated warehousing can also be supported by the possibilities of digitalization in the form of cyberphysical and self-controlling systems, as a basis for selective warehouse management and JIT. Intelligent, self-controlling threats, for example, carry out storage and retrieval processes as well as inventory management decentrally.

The close connection between JIT and selective warehousing or BT and flat-rate warehousing is due, among other things, to the fact that only in the rarest of cases is the entire goods program of a value-added system just-in-time-capable (Zeilinger 1987). JIT-capable are in particular AR goods. The high supply chain competence, which is a prerequisite for selective warehousing, also supports the establishment of JIT, and vice versa. In this respect, JIT and selective warehousing together form the core components of integrated warehousing. Furthermore, driving an integrated warehousing strategy requires precise knowledge of the demand structure as well as qualified information logistics in general.

The complexity of the warehousing strategy is mainly derived from the possible conflicts of objectives such as delivery reliability and capital commitment. In addition to classic inventory optimization, the supply chain finance concept can offer additional target contributions. The following project case illustrates the concept.

Project example: supply chain finance

Initial situation: An electrical engineering company had already made extensive efforts in the past to reduce its working capital. The payment conditions on the customer and supplier side were exhausted. The warehouse logistics and stocks required for production were optimized. It was looking for new ways to further reduce capital tied up.

Objective: Against this background, the aim of the project was to systematically advance the interim financing of liabilities to suppliers and sales financing to customers by involving a third party. By implementing this supply chain finance concept, the company wanted to optimize its working capital by a further step without getting into target conflicts with its suppliers.

Approach: The project was completed in four steps. First, the potential in terms of working capital reduction was estimated in the form of a business case. In the second step, the operating model for supplier and sales-side financing was developed. This included the selection of a financing partner and the specification of the financing conditions. The subsequent implementation of the supply chain finance processes also provided for piloting in different constellations, e.g. with different invoice and delivery addresses and IT integration of the value-added partners. Finally, the supplier- and customer-wide market launch was prepared and implemented.

Results and digital relevance: By introducing the supply chain finance concept, it was possible to shorten the payment term vis-à-vis suppliers by almost 30 percent and reduce receivables from customers by around 25 percent. The project example also showed the potential of networking different value creation partners in the course of a digital supply chain, for example, when supply chain finance is used as an intelligent service or via an app in individual cases.

Success factors: The success of the project depended crucially on the acceptance of the new supply chain finance offer on the part of suppliers and customers. On the supplier side, it was important to correctly assess the company's market power in the respective product group. On the customer side, the new supply chain finance offer could be positioned as a customer-friendly value-added service, which was conducive to acceptance.

3.3.5   *Information logistics*

Information logistics comprises the information services of administration and disposition, i.e. the processes connected with order processing and the tasks serving overall operational control (similar to Augustin 1990). These two areas will be examined separately in the following, before the basic patterns of information logistics will be addressed.

Administrative logistics

Order processing characterizes all activities for the passing on and treatment of customer orders, including the internal orders initiated thereby as well as information and communication procedures (Pfohl 1972, the same 1990; Türks 1972).
In principle, every order is processed on the basis of information that anticipates
the flow of goods (time orders), accompanies it (handling regulations for hazardous goods, consignment notes for hazardous waste, delivery notes) and follows
it (control information, invoicing). However, these are shown in a limited *substitutive relationship* to each other. For example, linking order processing makes
it easier to implement more anticipatory information flows instead of lagging
information flows. It concerns intra-organizational interfaces as well as interorganizational interfaces and can be achieved, for example, by standardized order
forms that are made available to customers. The introduction of electronic data
processing systems as well as the establishment of *EDI* interfaces – in particular
the ISO standard 9735 "Edifact" (Electronic Data Interchange for Administration, Commerce and Transport) – is also a suitable solution to enable remote
data transmission (RDT). In the context of new digital supply chain technologies, new standards are also being developed, for example, for the use of a cloud
to control object flows or based on blockchain to proof origin. Such forms of
linking help to avoid manual work as well as duplication of work. The reliability
of the information associated with integration then makes it possible to dispense
with ex-post controls in particular. On the other hand, the lack of a link results
in more lagging information and longer processing times. If one considers in this
context that the order *processing time* is a major factor in advance of the delivery
time, which can in practice amount to up to 75 percent, the importance of linking administrative processes for the delivery service becomes clear.

Order centres and merchandise management systems

If the order processing processes are bundled not only in terms of IT but
also spatially, this is also referred to as *order centres*, i.e. shared service centres
for the administrative processes of supply chains. Such spatial integration
makes sense above all if the processing processes require a certain amount of
manual processing despite IT integration via cloud computing, robots, etc.,
and if spatial grouping allows a more efficient work organization because,
for example, statistical balancing effects can be realized in capacity utilization. The structure of order centres is also superior if the technology used
is distributed IT systems that support decentralized work in the form of a
virtual order centre.

Ten Hompel (2014, translated) summarizes the interplay of bundled order
processing and decentralized cyberphysical systems as follows:

> Above all, there is a cloud-based administration on which the economic
> goals and strategies are implemented. Here, customer orders are processed
> in a conventional way, orders are triggered, and finances are managed. But

when it comes to real-time, application-specific processing, when things get moving, the multi-agent controls of the cyberphysical systems take over the work – the CPS of the intelligent cists, shelves and vehicles.

Computer-aided *merchandise management systems* (e.g. Zentes 1994) are to be mentioned for the retail sector. The use of these systems in conjunction with customer cards such as the Payback card, for example, provides retailers with significantly greater transparency regarding buyer behaviour, because behaviour patterns can be traced in a customer-oriented manner. In addition, acatech (2011) emphasizes that intelligent and networked objects are used especially in retail. Increasingly, the "digital product memory of objects" is also being used to optimize processes, especially in supply chain management. The objects adapt to digital business processes as required and communicate. This makes it possible, for example, to track orders via the web.

Multi-channel management, CX and foresighted planning

Multi-channel management is particularly important for administrative logistics, i.e. the use of various communication and sales channels for information and order processing using the Internet or Internet-like structures. Multi-channel management requires real-time information in order to synchronize the various channels. It provides benefits to order processing, but can also offer advantages for advertising, pricing and distribution of products (Heinemann 2012).

Studies show that consumers are increasingly looking for and buying information on the Internet because the possibilities for comparison are better on the Internet than in retail and ordering is easier. Pricing on the basis of suitable algorithms in real time and with the aid of search engines allows suppliers to always make the most cost-effective offer. And the virtual delivery of products, for example, software, can replace conventional distribution channels such as the dispatch of software via CD-ROM via an express service provider.

The discussion of multi-channel management is not limited to retailers but is also relevant to manufacturing companies that can sell and deliver via various channels. In this context, it is important to mention that the *customer experience (CX)* is not limited to the steps of the ordering process. Customer experience includes everything that creates a point of view for customers, and thus includes delivery and service aspects as well as general marketing or recommendations by friends and family networks. Many companies have limited their CX efforts to the design of the company's website, which does not address the full potential. Typically, supply chain management is heaving a significant influence on the customer journey in this sense and is part of a corresponding experience.

In order to process orders ahead of time, companies can use *predictive planning* to anticipate future orders using statistical forecasting procedures and control their internal processes on the basis of this forecast. Predicting purchasing behaviour also makes it possible to proactively approach individual customers if it is assumed that they are likely to buy at a certain point in time, i.e. pick up an order. Foresighted planning makes sense if the statistical quality of the forecast is so high that its costs and the costs of a possible later correction of the forecast, i.e. of the internal order backlog, are more than compensated for by the time advantage of the anticipatory approach. The *quality of the prediction* depends on its statistical validity, reliability and objectivity. For this reason, these companies use customer cards, for example, to monitor individual customer purchasing behaviour, purchase customer information from third parties and develop suitable profiles of the behaviour pattern. This is because the quality of the data increases when different data sources are combined. In addition to the anticipation of orders, the methods of predictive data analysis can also be applied to individual circumstances of the disposition, for example, to the anticipation of traffic jams, order changes, inventory differences, etc.

As mentioned earlier, a core element of information logistics is the S&OP process (sales & operations planning). The use of large amounts of data (big data) and predictive analytics offer possibilities to raise the S&OP process to a higher quality level, which is illustrated in the following case.

Project example: predictive S&OP

Initial situation: A retail company for clothing and sporting goods was exposed to extremely cyclical fashion trends with only very short product life cycles. Vertically integrated competitors reinforced this trend with increasingly short development cycles of only a few weeks in some cases. The frequent introduction of new collections led to life cycles and shopping cycles in some segments approaching each other almost completely. Overall, this increased the risk of misjudging demand for certain items, leading either to overstocking or to lost sales because the company was unable to meet demand. For 54 percent of the articles, the deviation from actual sales was more than 25 percent. Demand planning thus became a key success factor, with conventional forecasting methods increasingly considered inadequate.

Objective: The aim of the project was to improve forecasting reliability using innovative planning methods. By setting up a forward-looking S&OP process, overstocking and lost sales were to be reduced. The company aimed to achieve a forecast accuracy of more than 95 percent in the medium term, with a maximum of 5 percent lost sales.

Approach: The project was completed in three steps. In the first step, a data cube was set up. Relevant secondary data was collected, as well as additional primary data via newly created consumer panels. The latter exercise was necessary above all because the company used both multivariate statistics and prognosis parameters based on behavioural science when selecting the methods. The forecasting approach distinguished, among other things, between an affective, conative and cognitive dimension, whereby the latter could be measured, for example, by Bayesian statistics, which measures the degree of personal conviction. In the second step, the data was examined for exemplary regularities in order to apply any identified statistical correlations to the pattern prediction. Among other things, variously parameterized and explorative factor, cluster, regression, variance and discriminant analyses were used. Randomly selected data samples from the past were used to check the reliability of forecasts and compared with actual sales. An iterative approach ensured the gradual improvement of the forecast results. In the third step, the new planning methodology and the revised planning process were transferred to regular operation. The responsible employees were extensively trained for this and the reporting was revised. The consumer panels that had been set up were maintained on a permanent basis, and were later used for other market research tasks as well.

Results and digital relevance: The short-term increase in planning reliability was accompanied by earnings increases in the double-digit million euro range. The company expected further potential in the medium term as a result of the continuous further development of the methodology.

Success factors: The project had three success-critical factors in particular. First of all, the proper application of multivariate statistical methods for pattern recognition and prediction was a decisive factor for increasing the forecast quality and implementing the improvements. Secondly, a sufficient data depth and width was required to place the analyses on a sufficient basis. Data integration was accordingly important. And thirdly, the active inclusion of behavioural aspects of consumers in the course of primary data collection was critical to success in order to ensure the necessary customer perspective.

Dispositive logistics

Production planning and detailed steering (PPDS) can be understood as the germ cell of disposition (Kern 1992). Relevant steering instruments aim at supporting the development of a joint disposition for production, procurement and distribution logistics (Diruf 1994). Traditionally, such instruments try to establish plan-directed flows of goods at the beginning of the value-added process as far as possible in the course of a flow-oriented design of operational processes. The *de-coupling point* defines the step of the value chain that attaches anonymous products to customer orders. In line with the integration concept of supply chains, it can make sense to shift such a de-coupling point to the end of the value chain, if possible.

Against the background of PPDS, the control concepts of logistics can now be arranged according to the type of complexity management. Conventional PPDS systems like the MRP are characterized by a step-by-step processing of planning and control steps. Schedule, capacity, sequence planning etc. are successively run through. However, this linear form of disposition often leads

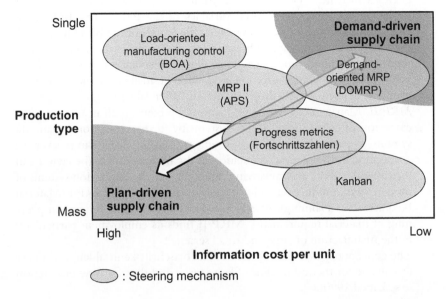

Figure 3.13 Selected methods of process control (based on Warnecke/Kühnle/Bischoff 1994 and complemented by Wehberg 2015)

to a denial of process complexity due to its closed system of unlinked subtasks and can thus fall victim to the trivialization trap or *controllability illusion* already mentioned. Newer concepts therefore try to master this problem in a different way, namely by modifying or extending the conventional methodology. But also newer concepts such as MRP II often do face difficulties to manage the complexity properly. While the processing of different planning steps is better integrated, the execution of such planning is still challenged by high market dynamics. For example, rush orders and change requests make the planning partly obsolete during the production freeze. This is why digital supply chains often need a new, demand-oriented paradigm that supports the complexity of digital supply chains.

The *production type* answers the question of whether there is workshop and flow production or individual, series and mass production. The type of production is a central complexity driver of production logistics and it is closely related to the more recent control concepts. In the following, we want to classify the most relevant control concepts, accordingly (Figure 3.13):

• The *load-oriented manufacturing control (BOA)* is based on the recognition of the high importance of the average order backlog of production systems as well as of individual workstations in particular for the average throughput time of orders, weighted by order size. The system behaviour, i.e. the representation of the lead time as a function of the stocks, is expressed in so-called operation curves, which are to be determined system and operation specifically. Order intake thus becomes the central variables of the PPDS. The BOA then distinguishes between three parameters: the length of the planning period, the width of the pre-emptive horizon and the height of the load barrier. It represents a form of progressive scheduling. It is suitable above all for individual production, but also for the production of small series, and is therefore primarily applied to workshop production (Wiendahl 1987).

- *MRP II* (Management Resource Planning) presents itself in its core as an extension of conventional PPDS systems by further operational planning systems, in particular primary requirement planning. It tries in this way to correspond to the process orientation in the narrower sense (behaviours in the system) and the accompanying integration of the disposition systems of procurement, production and distribution. It is based on MRP I (Material Requirements Planning), which is dedicated to the scheduling and planning of material requirements. MRP II finds its employment particularly in the manufacture of large and small series.
- The concept of *progress metrics* (so-called Fortschrittskennzahlen) is primarily suitable for the production of large series and thus for flow production (e.g. Zibell 1990).
- The *Kanban* concept is also based on the relationships between the average order backlog on the one hand and the lead time on the other. It deviates, however, from the conventional PPDS procedures by structuring the goods flows in the form of intermeshed control loops. The pulling principle replaces the pushing principle. If a certain demand exists in a production and value-added stage, it is covered from a buffer store. The replacement order, which is required to maintain the buffer stock, is given to the preliminary stages by an information carrier, the so-called kanban. This triggers a sequence of demand chains, based on the primary requirement, in which the flow of information is opposed to the flow of goods. The Kanban concept is therefore clearly characterized by the JIT philosophy. On the other hand, it takes into account the basic idea of self-organization to a great extent. The Kanban concept finds its application primarily in series and mass production. It offers an appropriate basis for flow production in particular (especially Wildemann 1983).
- And others, for example, so-called chaotic material flow systems (Wölker/Holzhauer 1995).

These classic steering concepts must be rethought and further developed in light of digital supply chains. In addition, the increasing importance of conserving natural resources places new demands on the management of the value chain and production in particular:

- *Demand Oriented MRP (DOMRP)* logic, therefore, combines proven push mechanisms with pull principles where relevant. By doing so, it combines S&OP based with lean management capabilities while considering heterogeneous supply chain models. For DOMRP, it is vital to understand that an end-to-end supply chain needs to make sure that the principles of a digital supply chain and the PPDS in particular are consistent with each other. Corresponding steering logics and design principles such as self-organization and generalization thus have to be considered on the shop floor, and vice versa. Moreover, PPDS algorithms have to be distinguished for each step of production. Often, two different (semi-)finished products share the same input material or product of the preceding step, which can lead to so-called upgrades, Feeders and Noisers (RFN upgrades), as a consequence (Figure 3.14). The planning part of DOMRP has to be seen dynamically, so that predictions have to be further developed dynamically with means of meta-algorithms and corresponding alerts. Also, the RFN segmentation is a continuous effort.

DOMRP has not been comprehensively considered by standard software like SAP, but is expected to be incorporated as part of the innovation pipeline of such vendors. This basically includes the segmentation of supply chain models, the consideration of proper PPDS mechanisms in terms of an adjusted production wheel, optimization procedures, as well as dashboards, amongst others (Figure 3.15).

Ant algorithm

The use of cyberphysical systems in manufacturing can offer the possibility of self-control and the associated *flexibilization* of large series in the direction of a batch size $N = 1$ (see Figure 3.10 again). The de-coupling point of a digital supply chain is ideally shifted further forward in the value chain. Digital supply chains aim at combining the cost structure of large series with the flexibility of small series. The favourable cost structure can be made possible by the lower

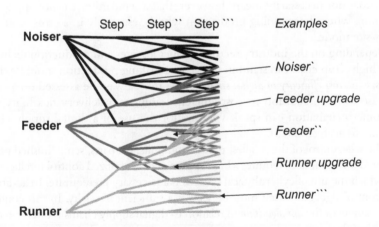

Figure 3.14 RFN upgrades within the bill of material

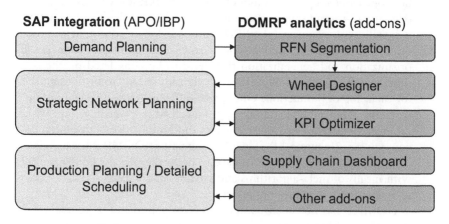

Figure 3.15 SAP add-ons for DOMRP

specific costs of information logistics, i.e. above all the lower disposition and IT costs per service unit. Bauernhansl (2014, translated) states:

> The ramp-up as a set-up process for the entire factory is becoming an everyday occurrence. . . . We still work according to the Taylorist principle of division of labour: belt and tact are the core, the pulse beat of the pyramid of value creation. This will no longer work in the future. Since we also define the production quantity and flexibility with the definition of the cycle and limit the number of variants and variant flexibility with the linking of the value-added steps.

This does not necessarily mean, however, that a standard tact is not applicable anymore when determining production wheels, especially in a cross-asset and cross-site mode.

Depending on the industry sector, product features and production technology, high setup costs can stand in the way of making production more flexible, so that the *cost efficiency of digital supply chains* must always be assessed on a case-by-case basis. In addition to cost efficiency, improved delivery flexibility and customer orientation can speak volumes for the use of a digital supply chain (similar to acatech 2015).

The self-control of the smallest production units, i.e. parts, semi-finished products and final products, requires a high degree of decentralized control intelligence, for which the use of cyberphysical systems is a necessary prerequisite. In addition, the control algorithm itself must be seen as a sufficient necessity. In this context, the example of the *ant algorithm* in relation to digital supply chains is often cited to underline the crucial importance of the correct mathematical representation of the behaviour of highly complex systems (Bousonville 2009). In the search for food, individual ants excrete pheromone along their path. Other ants are more likely to choose a path with a higher pheromone concentration. This approach of ants can be described as swarm intelligence: A higher performance (here the search for the shortest route) is achieved by the interaction of many simple actors who can only contribute a part to the overall solution. The interaction of the smallest production units in the course of a digital supply chain will have to function comparably (Hirsch-Kreinsen/Weyer 2014).

The following project case by Schlick et al. (2014) emphasizes the importance of system integration for self-control in manufacturing using the example of paper-based operational and IT-based medium-term production planning. The focus is on the synchronization of both planning processes.

Project example: escalation management

Initial situation: A medium-sized company used a PPDS to plan production orders. This supported the IT-related mapping of the timing of orders in the course of the overall planning. At the level of individual production steps the company worked with planning boards which, according to the principles of lean production, made it possible to organize production on the basis of a paper-based card system. The approach was therefore characterized by a media discontinuity between the IT-supported medium-term planning horizon and the paper-supported operative planning horizon. Both planning horizons were manually adjusted with a lot of effort.

Against this background, the management of escalations was also hampered by media disruptions. "Media disruptions occur because information about the reason why an order cannot currently be produced is insufficiently documented. . . . This also results in a longer machine downtime. In addition, the media break prevents statistical evaluation and thus a return of knowledge regarding the causes of the problem" (Schlick et al. 2014).

Objective: In order to avoid such media disruptions, to increase transparency and to be able to make decisions quickly, the company aimed to ensure that the relevant order, machine and line-related data are available and processed appropriately at all times. "In order to be able to react quickly and accurately in the event of an escalation of problems during order processing, people must be put in the centre of attention when creating an escalation, entering information and retrieving information" (Schlick et al. 2014).

Approach: The company chose a three-step approach. In the first step, the planning board was digitized to eliminate the media disruption. Employees at the planning level were given the opportunity to access the current status of the digital planning board system via various terminal devices. The visualization of the production orders was structured in tabular form, for example, sorted according to individual production lines and using colour codes. Depending on the role of the user, different views could be set, for example, daily planning, machine occupancy, planning for a specific line, etc. The user was able to select the most suitable viewpoint for the job. The second step involved the development of a program function that would enable the production employee to directly document the processing of orders and, if necessary, to identify problems. "Order and (. . ., machine data can . . .) be entered by scanning optical markers on order papers or on processing machines. In a third, longer-term step, the information collected on delays in order processing and their causes is transferred to a continuous improvement process" (Schlick et al. 2014).

Result and digital relevance: The benefits of system integration lay primarily in the improvement of the organizational process for order processing and could therefore only be quantified to a limited extent. In the short term, the simpler escalation of problems in the production process was the top priority. The digitization of the escalation process during order processing makes it possible to use statistical methods to recognize patterns in the behaviour of machines and equipment. In the medium term, this will enable decision-makers to eliminate specific causes of escalation and continuously improve the planning process. The corresponding pattern recognition, as a core component of a digital supply chain, then shows results.

Success factors: A decisive factor for the successful implementation of such a project is typically the willingness of the managing and operative employees of the company to invest in the IT processes of production, even though a large part of the benefit can only be gained in the medium term through corresponding learning gains on the basis of statistical evaluations. Furthermore, sufficient transparency and knowledge of the planning processes in production are critical for success, which in turn requires the close involvement of those involved in planning.

Green manufacturing

Due to the increasing importance of conserving natural resources, production control concepts will in the future have to take greater account of *energy cost efficiency* in the form of "green manufacturing". The energy cost efficiency of a company basically comprises two areas of improvement; namely, improvements on the supply and demand side. The latter are also referred to as demand management. Supply-side measures include, for example, the purchase of electricity, gas, heat and compressed air, the in-house generation of secondary energy and building energy efficiency in the form of energy-saving lamps. Energy purchasing in sectors such as the automotive industry is generally already largely optimized. Since the majority of the energy required by a company is consumed

in production, demand-side measures in production in terms of green manufacturing, offer a major improvement lever.

Of course, energy-saving measures in production are not new. Most companies regularly check where energy consumption can be reduced in production
through technical measures such as the use of heat exchangers, amongst others.
Green manufacturing also aims to systematically smooth out any deviations in
the load curve, which means it tries to flatten the energy consumption curve.
Strong fluctuations in the load curve are typically expensive for the energy supplier because peak demand generally determines capacity requirements. This
is why very constant demand is typically much cheaper for the company. The
core of green manufacturing is therefore the fusion of classic steering concepts of
production planning and scheduling with load management in the energy sector.
In addition to load management, other parameters such as capacity, batch size,
sequence, adherence to schedules, etc. must also be taken into account. Suitable
work organization measures, such as raising the machines at the beginning of
a shift, are used to smooth the load profile and, in particular, avoid peak loads.

In individual cases, the use of *energy storage* devices can support this, even
though storage technology is still comparatively cost-intensive. In this context,
the integration of the company's vehicle fleet offers a promising approach by
absorbing or buffering excess capacities of the company's own generation of
electricity and peak demand via the storage facilities of the electric vehicles.
In addition, the performance of the batteries of electric vehicles decreases significantly in the course of their operation, so that batteries can also be used as
energy storage devices after they have been used in the vehicle.

In order to be able to connect the classic PPDS key figures with the load
curve management, a differentiated measuring system is required to record
the energy consumption. The demands on measurement technology increase
even more when service providers of energy supply and efficiency have to be
invoiced according to performance. The *smart meters* and electricity grids used
here are based on the same technology of cyberphysical systems as digital supply chains itself. Green manufacturing is also the subject of digital supply chain
management in this respect.

Intelligent energy supply and digital supply chains have many points of contact, especially in energy-intensive companies like process industries. Against
this background, the following project case shows how environmental protection and cost efficiency can be harmonized.

Project example: energy cost efficiency

Initial situation: In the past, a company in the manufacturing sector had
identified numerous measures to save energy costs. However, many of
these measures were not implemented because the economic efficiency
did not meet the company's standards. The majority of the measures

implemented were also on the supply side (e.g. structured purchasing of energy) and not in production. The latter was the main source of demand in the company.

Objective: In order to identify possible further savings in energy costs, the company set up a review. In addition to cost improvements, it was also the aim to use any marketing and image effects wherever possible.

Approach: The project team formed four workstreams, which were to identify and address improvement potentials in three steps. A first workstream focused on increasing the company's own generation of energy, including renewable energies such as photovoltaics (PV) and wind. A second workstream examined existing measures that had not yet been implemented due to their economic viability. Most of these measures were in the area of building energy efficiency. A third workstream dealt with the production area, i.e. a corresponding stabilization of the energy demand there. A fourth workstream examined fleet management. In the first step, the status was recorded, which means the energy consumption and corresponding drivers were documented. In the second step, starting points for improvement were collected and prioritized. And in the third step, the prioritized measures were handed over to those responsible and the planned savings effects coordinated with the controlling department.

Results and digital relevance: More than 15 percent of energy costs could be saved, although the company had already made extensive efforts in the past. The production area in particular offered significant cost savings potential. For example, the project team found that around 20 percent of the load was caused by 31 hours of demand alone. On the other hand, no electricity was consumed at all in 755 hours per year. The use of renewable energy enabled the company to present itself positively in terms of environmental protection. And by integrating suitable energy service providers, it was finally possible to reorganize numerous business cases or measures, even though these did not meet the company's economic efficiency standards. The service providers could be strongly tied to success, and their contribution to success was tracked by intelligent measurement technology.

Success factors: The success of this project was mainly due to three factors. First, the review of innovative savings ideas and the expansion of the scope of the study were critical to success. In the past, improvement levers such as load curve management in production were simply not considered. Secondly, knowledge of the service market was crucial. This market is currently very much in motion, and new suppliers are partly prepared to implement and finance measures despite moderate profitability. Such providers are exposed to other expectations on the part of the capital market or also have very lean medium-sized cost structures. Last but not least, the company's openness to see energy efficiency not only as a cost issue but also as a strategic marketing issue was very important.

Predictive maintenance

A not insignificant portion of production costs is caused by maintenance and repair processes. Predictive maintenance aims to make the corresponding activities for logistics and production capacities (but also for customer plants in the course of customer service) more efficient by controlling them according to demand through the use of networked sensors. The aim is to use the measurement of relevant data to identify *patterns in the machine park* that anticipate a probable machine breakdown and the corresponding maintenance requirements. Maintenance activities as well as shutdowns of production can be organized more efficiently, and available capacities in terms of the operational equipment effectiveness of production assets can be planned more reliably. Such predictive maintenance can be relevant both in the company's own production and supply chain operations as well as in customer service, which means in the customer's machine park. Many companies, on the other hand, plan their maintenance according to certain empirical values in time intervals or production quantities in order to anticipate failures based on their condition, so-called *time-based maintenance*, or only react in the event of failures.

Vogel-Heuser (2014) points out that within the framework of the fourth industrial revolution production units have the ability to monitor themselves and, if necessary, to counteract themselves appropriately. Schlick et al. (2014) see in this context four successive *stages of the intelligent behaviour* of production systems which correspond to the characteristics of digital supply chains (recursion, autonomy, redundancy and self-reference) that were discussed in Part 2 of this volume:

- Communication and distributed functionality (network of mechatronic systems)
- Adaptivity and autonomy (independent setup and autonomous processing)
- Context-sensitive, cognitive machine systems (dynamic environmental adaptation)
- Self-optimized systems (independent target definition for holistic optimization)

Integrated information logistics

Two typical extremes can be identified for information logistics (Figure 3.16). On the one hand, there is *isolated information logistics*. The lack of linking of administrative processes leads here to an increased realization of lagging order information. High throughput times of order processing justify a correspondingly stagnant flow of physical execution actions. The weakly pronounced change in information logistics is expressed in particular by the Industry 3.0 kind of production, for example in terms of traditional workshop production in the course of PPDS. On the other hand, there is the *integrated information logistics*, in which the networking of administrative processes allows a flow-oriented

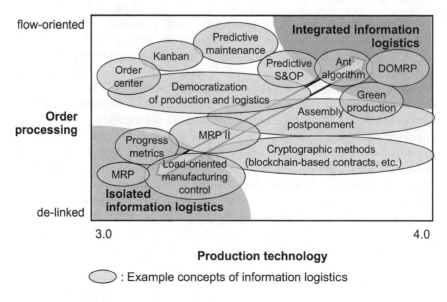

Figure 3.16 Change profile of information logistics

structure of the flows of goods, but also presupposes this in reverse. The supply chain structures in line with the organizational concept of flow production and Industry 4.0 technology. The change associated with them is correspondingly high. Due to its high system complexity, information logistics designed in this way are able to handle a large number of different processes while taking into account the principles of green manufacturing.

The area functions described so far basically characterize both the supply and the disposal side of supply chain processes in more or less equal measure. In addition to the collection and separation function of waste disposal logistics, which is not attached to the supply logistics, it is also characterized by other special features, so that the following separate consideration appears appropriate.

3.3.6 Logistics for the circular economy

Recycling

Disposal logistics characterize the "application of the logistics concept to residual materials" (Pfohl/Stölzle 1992, translated). Against the background of the theory of joint production (Riebei 1955; Bührens 1978), residual materials can be characterized as an output of operational processes in the broadest sense (production, logistics, administration, consumption, etc.) which has no direct relation to the objectives of the company and logistics in particular (Stölzle

1993). A distinction must be made between reusable and non-reusable residual materials. Reusable residues are suitable for recycling, which means for recovery or use. They are also referred to as *recyclables* or "wastes for recovery" (e.g. as per § 3 para. 1 KrW-/AbfG in Germany). In contrast to residual materials that cannot be reused, so-called *residues* or "waste for disposal", which are disposed of in an orderly manner, generally imply a technological feasibility and economic advantage of reuse. However, the transition between recyclable and non-recyclable residual materials is fluid, because with the increasing number of reuses due to the so-called *downcycling*, which means the diminishing quality of the residual material, the recyclability is reduced (Rautenstrauch 1993). And even the assessment of the technological representability and economic efficiency of recycling is probably not without a subjective moment, and so can be the differentiation between waste and distribution logistics, accordingly. Needless to say, the most efficient waste logistics are those that are never needed unless the *avoidance* of waste is not over-compensated by other harmful effects.

Synergy management

A special feature of waste logistics now arises from the fact that the flow direction of its processes is opposite to that of supply logistics, at least in the case of recycling and reuse. This offers corresponding connection potentials, so-called synergies, which extend beyond the field of waste logistics and refer to the connection of supply and waste logistics processes. The latter potentials can be described as external synergies, the former as internal synergies. The design of *internal synergy* potentials in waste logistics has hardly any special features compared to the supply logistics (in-depth Wehberg 1997). Its exploitation can therefore be traced back to the intra-process coordination task of supply chain management. In contrast, the use of external synergy potentials and thus inter-process coordination are more demanding (for the concept of "synergy" and its roots see Göpfert/Wehberg 1996).

External synergy potentials of waste logistics can be found in the form of *factor synergies* and *process synergies* as well as *result synergies*. Furthermore, it seems helpful to differentiate the synergies according to whether they are characterized by a high or short service life, large or small influenceability and to what extent the synergy effects occur directly or indirectly in terms of time.

Although the three forms of synergy must not be seen separately from each other, as they partly build on each other in the form of medium-purpose relationships, their separate consideration seems to be helpful at first. So how are the contents of the individual forms of synergy presented in concrete terms? With regard to factor synergies, which result from the linking of the input factors of the service production process, differentiation according to repeating and potential factors (Gutenberg 1983, translated) can be made, which can be specified both in their quantitative and qualitative dimensions. Repeat factor-induced synergies seem to be of less importance here, insofar as waste logistics is aimed precisely at minimizing the use of consumption factors through the implementation of the closed-loop concept or recycling. In the majority of cases, the avoidance of the use of repeating factors is bought at the expense of an increased use of potential factors, as can be seen from the example of returnable transport packaging. With regard to factor synergies, concentration on potential factors therefore seems appropriate. *Potential factor-induced synergies* are also generally characterized by a relatively long service life and great influence. The larger the range of services (Wehberg 1994) covered by the potential factors in the area of supply and waste logistics (qualitative dimension) and the smaller the sum of the capacity requirements of the two areas together (quantitative dimension), the higher they are. By way of example, any capacity overhangs can be reduced by adding waste logistics services, and the management know-how can also be made fruitful in the field of waste logistics. Göpfert and Wehberg (1996) provide a more in-depth description of the potentials and influencing factors of external factor synergies.

External process synergies are the result of linking the actual supply and waste logistics processes. The excesses of possible process energies are as complex as the manifestations of processes themselves. A systematization according to X- and Y-synergies thus facilitates the perception and design of such sources of advantage (based on Porter/Fuller 1989): *X-synergies* are the result of the interaction of different processes that complement each other, i.e. interlock with each other to a certain extent. Their starting point is the asymmetric course of supply chain processes. Paired transports between waste disposal and supply logistics can be cited as an example. With regard to the latter, however, the complete takeover of existing route plans will not always be possible if, for example, connections blocked for goods subject to declaration may no longer be used. If several customers are to be reached over the same area, it should also be noted from a transhipment perspective that shipments to be unloaded and loaded do not stand in each other's way. The latter is likely to be the case with pure hedge loading. Rear-side unloading and right-side loading is a practical alternative here, which, however, requires appropriate fleet equipment. In addition, if the goods to be removed are only dismantled and expanded in the course of time-consuming multi-man handling, the external synergy advantage of the transport pair can be overcompensated by the time disadvantage caused by this.

Y-synergies, on the other hand, are due to the linking of similar processes and are based on symmetrical process structures. Examples of this are the bundling of transports.

Pattern visuals

Irrespective of whether these are X- or Y-synergies, the recognition of such process synergies as well as factor synergies is in reality associated with great difficulties. These are highly complex facts. The erudition of such synergies thus becomes the task of pattern recognition. Due to the possible complexity of process relationships, the detailed analytical approach often offers only little assistance. The *recognition of synergy patterns* presents itself as a synthetic process that requires a great deal of creativity, but also the trust of management (Sprüngli 1981). It is based on the already mentioned methods of predictive data analysis. It has proved helpful to present muster in visual form. The human eye is the organ whose synthetic abilities are probably the most trained and developed. As a rule, vision takes place holistically. For the recognition of external synergy patterns, as of certain process patterns of the enterprise in general, the use of so-called pattern visuals seems to be particularly suitable. The visualization of process structures offers the management the possibility to uncover legal relationships. For the purpose of graphic representation, the relationship patterns are brought into two- and also, in particular with online graphics, three-dimensional representations. Possible description dimensions – not limited to identifying process synergies – are:

- Spatial dimensions (source, sink, transshipment points, direction, etc.)
- Time dimensions (hour, minutes, etc.)
- Supply chain objects (residual materials, intermediate products, end products)
- Supply chain subjects (cooperation partners, logistics service providers, etc.)
- Supply chain performance indicators (delivery time, transport cost, planning accuracy, etc.)
- Indicators for the description of the operational supply chain processes themselves (transshipment, transport, storage processes, etc.)

Corresponding *ways of visualization* include the following methods as examples:

- Tag clouds visualize text as weighted lists.
- Clustergrams show assignments to clusters.
- History flow charts document evolution.
- Spatial information flows show geographical links.
- Ramler plots show graphic pattern overviews.

In addition to factor and process synergies, there are also result synergies. They result from the overall view of the results of two or more supply chain processes and can be differentiated according to cost- and performance-oriented synergy effects. In particular, the cost advantages can be seen as a sequence of the factor and process synergies just explained. For example, they go hand in hand with an even utilization of logistical capacities. Performance synergies, i.e. earnings synergies located on the performance side, comprise both any higher strategic robustness and an improvement in the operational delivery service such as flexibility. Increases in robustness may be due to the fact that, despite a sudden increase in the volume of waste logistics, the company can dispense with capacity expansion due to external synergies and then be in a position to cover the capacity requirements that now exist from the supply logistics facilities. The external synergy potential here forms the basis for a flexible deployment potential (Wehberg 1994) for waste logistics. Some companies are also faced with the favourable situation of being able to offer waste logistics services to other companies. The high level of competence that has been built up in the field of waste logistics can then be marketed and, if necessary, allows the core business to establish another attractive business area. Such a diversification from a pure product manufacturer into the service sector also has the effects of increased robustness.

Irrespective of which form of recycling is chosen and whether it concerns internal and external waste logistics or the disposal of production residues, end products, transport and product packaging, the potential of factor, process and result synergies now also and especially depends on the *organization of the reusable system*. As an example, individual, bilateral and pool systems can be distinguished for the reuse of transport packaging (Lange 1994). Decisive factors here are primarily the degree of standardization of multi-way packaging and transport control in the area of waste logistics. Thus individual systems are characterized by company-specific packaging and transport flow solutions. In this way, they take the operational requirements into account to a high degree and create favourable conditions for the realization of external synergies. Bilateral reusable systems, on the other hand, are characterized by standardized reusable packaging on the one hand and company-specific logistics chains on the other. As *standards*, they regularly fall back on corresponding standards, such as DIN and VDI standards, which are often industry specific. As a rule in the course of a 1:1 exchange, a change of transport packaging between different logistics systems is possible due to standardization. In principle, this makes it possible to maintain a lower total stock of packaging as a whole, since short-term peaks in demand among the shareholders of this reusable system can be balanced out. The internal factor synergies here are comparatively high. Due to the individual transport control and execution, the disposal logistics processes can also be linked to supply logistics processes according to the situation, which can result in high external process synergies.

Finally, so-called pool systems are characterized by the fact that both the load carriers and the logistics chain, i.e. primarily the transport execution and control, are standardized and shared. The design of reusable packaging, as well as the residual material flows themselves, can be traced back to a common denominator, which is usually embodied in the form of a neutral *pool carrier*. The tasks of such a pool company are then to offer various logistical services and to acquire new members for its returnable solution, i.e. above all to maintain the openness of the pool system. Their aim is to ensure sufficient availability of packaging and rapid disposal, which does not have to be the case in the course of bilateral systems. Advantages of the pool system compared to bilateral and individual returnable systems are also possible bundling effects of return transports in the form of internal synergies. As in the case of the bilateral system, the total stock of reusable packaging can be reduced.

Integrated waste logistics

The overall view of waste logistics design options makes it clear that their change can be profiled above all in the form of the following two extremes (Figure 3.17): On the one hand, there is *isolated waste logistics*, which concentrates

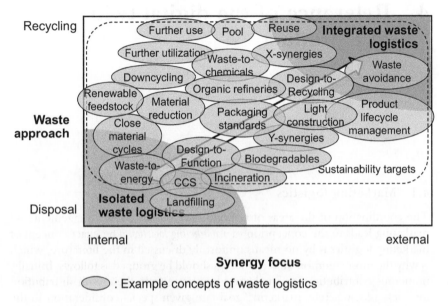

Figure 3.17 Change profile of waste logistics

on the disposal, i.e. landfilling and incineration, of residues. The starting points for exploiting synergies are limited to intra-process coordination. Any synergetic external relations remain unused. The structures of isolated waste logistics systems are correspondingly stability oriented. On the other hand, *integrated waste logistics* benefits greatly from the linking of its own processes with those of supply logistics. The high proportion of recycled residual materials corresponds to the development and exploitation of external synergies. In particular, reuse and recycling, which means the reuse of residual materials within their previous area of application, promotes such a synergy focus. Moreover, the avoidance of waste is being considered systematically. It becomes clear that integrated systems of waste disposal logistics imply a comparatively high change. In order to enable that change, integrated waste logistics make use of pattern recognition and self-control processes through the use of cyberphysical systems, comprehensively.

After the exemplary basic and area strategies of logistics management have been explained, the planning profile that reflects the relationships between logistics and marketing will be examined in the following.

Literature

Moore, G.E., *Cramming more components onto integrated circuits*. In: Electronics. Band 38, No. 8, 1965, Pg. 114–117.

4 Relevance of the digital twin of a product

4.1 Marketing logistics

The coordination of the areas of responsibility supply chain management and marketing leads to the conception of a *marketing logistics*. The exact concept of marketing logistics is by no means uniformly discussed in the literature, which is why the most common understandings should be grouped as follows: Initially, numerous contributions to marketing logistics equate these with distribution logistics tasks, whereby marketing goals are given special consideration in the course of coordinating the flow of finished products (Pfohl 1972; Traumann 1976). Such an understanding of terms is based on the recognition that the sales area in buyer market situations is usually the bottleneck area of the company (Delfmann 1990). If, however, procurement and sales are understood as "mirror-image transaction systems" (Meffert 1986, translated), then in principle both sides need a so-called balanced marketing (Nieschlag/Dichtl/Hörschgen 1991) of a corresponding coordination. Thus, procurement markets can also advance to become the central operational bottleneck, for example as a result of higher raw material prices (Bowersox/Closs/Helferich 1986). In addition to distribution, marketing logistics also refers to procurement (e.g. Krulis-Randa 1977; Poth 1973). It should be noted critically that the coordination of marketing logistics is not limited to the area of procurement and distribution, though. Rather, production and waste logistics also take on a variety of references to the market (Ihde 1978).

Now, marketing tasks can be structured by the 4 Ps; namely, product, price, place and promotion. Let's start with the placing and promotion part of it.

In the course of digitalization it is expected that there will be a renaissance of marketing logistics. Modern customer relationship platforms such as Salesforce bring marketing and sales organizations to the next level. *Placing* will be virtual and thus omnipresent via the Internet. *Promotion* develops from advertising to real-life experiences, which are shared in blogs by users. The discussion of the so-called customer journey becomes vital for marketing efforts to improve customer loyalty and value added. The more mature such concepts are the more comprehensively they tend to define the customer journey and are not limited to the sales process in the narrow sense. Delivering products at certain service levels and providing spare parts are also part of the journey in the way that they contribute significantly to the experience and thus satisfaction of a customer.

From a supply chain point of view, *product development* offers many chances to simplify logistics, for example, through modular sourcing and standardization of packages. At the same time, the trend of individualizing products in terms of mass customization is challenging the supply chain organization in many companies. In this context it is key to align both the digital twin of the supply chain and the digital twin of product development, production and the Internet of Things, which means the appliances on a users' level.

Let's talk about *pricing*: An important connection between marketing and logistics is the influence of logistics costs on pricing. Many companies do not adequately handle the complexity of logistics-relevant cost drivers, as the following case will illustrate. A so-called supply chain management–based pricing becomes vital.

Project example: supply chain management–based pricing

Initial situation: A company in the process industry found itself under increasing margin pressure due to the increasing commoditization of its products. The analysis of the cost structure showed that margins of numerous products and customers were insufficient and in some cases even negative. In the past, this was not transparent because costs in the logistics and service area were not allocated according to the cause. Instead of taking the specific cost drivers into account, the corresponding costs were distributed equally across all products and customers, i.e. averaged. This averaging resulted in the increased use of corresponding logistics and services in the sales department, without paying attention to cost-effectiveness. From the point of view of the individual sales employee, these services were, so to speak, free goods for which virtually no price was charged. As a result, the use of these services for the purpose of customer loyalty was exhausted to the point of a negative marginal benefit. There was a lack both of sufficient transparency about the actual profit contribution of individual customers and products as well as of a corresponding controllability in the sense of corporate objectives.

Objective: Against this background, the company launched an initiative to improve the margin structure. The aim was to ensure transparency about the "real margins" by allocating costs according to their origin, to put sales pricing on a new footing and to raise profitability in all product and customer segments to a minimum level. The new pricing system to be developed should above all sharpen the focus on the relevant cost drivers, because in B2B business the justification of price increases on the basis of cost-driver developments enjoys a high level of acceptance. In the future, the potential of value-based pricing should also be exploited to a greater extent by investigating the willingness of individual customers to pay more, beyond a full cost-based approach.

Approach: The initiative was divided into five steps. In the first step, the current situation was made transparent. An overview was created of key logistics and services, as well as the associated quantity and resource structures. The second step developed an appropriate allocation logic for the further development of cost type, unit and carrier accounting, so that the aforementioned services could be attributed to products and customers. Individual calculation examples with surprisingly poor margins acted as eye-openers and created the necessary momentum. The adjusted cost-accounting system was initially set up in a side calculation parallel to the current SAP cost accounting. On this basis, the sales pricing system was further developed in the third step. In this context, the price potentials per product and customer were determined in order to achieve an acceptable margin level for the company throughout. The customers' willingness to pay was taken into account on the basis of the sales department's assessment and validated in individual cases through discussions with customers. The fourth step involved piloting the new pricing strategy for selected products and customers, i.e. raising prices for products and customers or reducing additional services. The focus of this step was the task of proving the feasibility of the new pricing. The fifth step was to transfer the new pricing system to the line. Cost accounting was also permanently adapted in the SAP system. A new pricing regime (pricing tool) was introduced to support the calculation tasks of the sales department. Ongoing optimization based on a continuously improved understanding of willingness-to-pay and performance expectations was initiated and anchored in the organization.

Results and digital relevance: The company's margins were improved by an average of 1.8 percentage points and the overall result increased by a double-digit percentage. The transparency of costs and cost drivers in the supply chain area also offered significant improvements for the competitiveness of the company, because services could be offered flexibly and individually to customers and the network capability of the corporate logistics could be increased. Especially when supply and demand are coordinated in a decentralized manner, a system-based calculation of costs based on cost drivers is a prerequisite for a distributed negotiation process between self-organizing units.

Success factors: Three factors were decisive for the success of the initiative. The first was the technically correct mapping of costs and services in the SAP system. The second was the willingness of the sales department to participate. The third was the successful piloting of the pricing strategy with initial financial success at an early project stage.

4.2 Service competition and pioneer marketing

Marketing tasks can concentrate on the one hand on the material product and on the other hand on secondary services such as logistics. In this context, the development from a primary to a secondary competition triggered by the increasing homogeneity of product offerings leads to a shift in the marketing focus from the product to the logistics process. In a similar way, this kind of shift is being triggered by the upcoming stronger *service competition*. For example, Automotive OEMs are not building cars anymore but selling mobility. Specialty chemicals companies are not selling chemicals such as additives or catalysts any-more but performance. In extreme cases, marketing is limited almost exclusively to logistics or service content.

It is also conceivable, however, that due to the overall pronounced product focus of the branding activities, these and the tasks of marketing logistics will remain completely uncoordinated. With regard to the methodology of mar-keting, an experimental–creative working method can be distinguished from a systematic, almost technocratic one (Meffert 1988). Marketing tasks in rather static markets are often standardized by introducing administrative procedures. The decisions have to be backed up by appropriate analyses. Such a method of working usually aims to maintain the stability of the range of services and the earnings situation. It can be aptly described as "desk marketing". The experimental–creative working method is different. Especially in dynamic market fields such a methodology can be seen, which, pointedly said, can also be called *pioneer marketing*, suitable to provide the necessary degrees of freedom in the context of marketing analysis and planning. Among other things, cre-ativity techniques, explorative market research and correspondingly innovative segmentation approaches represent this second way of working. It includes methods of pattern recognition based on the explorative methods of predictive data analysis when it comes to understanding market-relevant behaviour pat-terns within the supply chain. And it makes potential use of the technologies of cyberphysical systems when it comes to implementing innovative segmentation approaches with the necessary flexibility and decentralization.

Finally, the change profile of marketing logistics can be presented in its two extreme forms, isolated and integrated marketing logistics (Figure 4.1). *Isolated marketing logistics* attempts to support product marketing by means of a systematic approach. The traditional marketing of benefits in kind corresponds here with a sophisticated set of marketing instruments and a correspondingly established methodology, which probably also affect logistics in the form of stability-oriented structures. The scope for behaviour in marketing logistics is relatively small here. On the other hand, *integrated marketing logistics* is character-ized by an experimental approach and instruments that promote creativity in order to offer appropriate assistance in focusing marketing on logistics services. In logistics in particular, marketing instruments as a whole are still underdevel-oped. For example, with regard to the transition from logistics segmentation to market segmentation, the theoretical foundation of a "logistics-oriented market

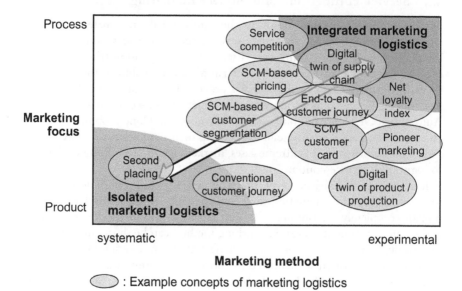

Figure 4.1 Change profile of marketing logistics

segmentation" (Pfohl 1977) is required. This demand on logistics becomes even more stringent when one considers the increasing tendency towards segmentation and niche formation in the course of digital operating and business models (Anderson 2007). The way of working in this area is correspondingly malleable and immature. The solutions to be implemented in logistics tend to be more differentiated and require a high degree of agility. The spectrum of methods and instruments used is therefore broader and explorative. Not least for this reason, integrated marketing logistics represents change-oriented behaviour patterns in the sense of resilience and digitalization. In practice, marketing logistics has so far often been implemented in isolated form (Duerler 1990). Because in many companies the process of a market-oriented formation of the supply chain system is only in the initial phase.

In the sense of integrated marketing logistics, the following application case shows how process and customer perspectives can be effectively linked.

Project example: logistics loyalty card

Initial situation: A plant engineering company was active in the project, service and product business. The company thought that a stronger link between the customer and the supply chain perspective offered potential for improvement, because many important customers received a rather average delivery service, whereas C customers were partly supplied with high priority. Overall, the delivery service focused more on how well the respective key account manager was able to channel his orders through the internal organization. There was no systematic prioritization according to the strategic importance of the individual customer.

Objective: Against this background, the company's goal was to offer a kind of "loyalty card" for A customers with a view to the delivery service. The company wanted to systematically differentiate the delivery service according to the strategic importance of its customers in order to position itself even more strongly in the market, especially in the project business. The delivery service and logistics were thus to become an important instrument of the company's strategic market development. The rather random dependence of the delivery service on the individual skills of individual key account managers should also be overcome.

Approach: The loyalty card for logistics was implemented in five steps. In the first step, the necessary transparency was created. Since customer contact in the project business was made via project development companies, a way had to be found to first know the customers of the various orders in order to prioritize the orders according to the importance of customers. For this purpose, an incentive system was designed for the project developers to pass on corresponding customer data. In the second step, additional logistics services were defined that were suitable for contributing to customer loyalty. On the basis of customer surveys, these services were determined from the customer's point of view in order to avoid the error of the company offering services from its own point of view that might not offer added value for customers. Examples for corresponding additional services were the activity of customs clearance and a shortened delivery time. Based on the defined catalogue of additional services, these were budgeted by the company in the third step and sub-budgeted to the various businesses (service, product, project). This was intended to counter the danger that the promised additional services might get out of hand and jeopardize the profitability of the company as a whole. In the fourth step, the customer segments to be prioritized were defined on the basis of objective criteria. This prevented individual key account managers from arbitrarily awarding additional services and undermining the customer loyalty strategy at the operational level due to opportunistic sales interests. Service-oriented B customers were also offered a higher level of service at an extra charge, so that the segments were permeable. The key account managers were trained in the new customer segmentation. In the fifth and final step, the connection to the established ERP system was ensured, so that the customer card for logistics could be integrated into the operative billing and ordering processes.

Results and digital relevance: The logistics loyalty card was able to make a significant contribution to customer satisfaction and positioning of the company, especially in the project business. Growth in the project business was almost doubled. Logistics was systematically instrumentalized for the implementation of the market development strategy. Transparency in the project business was also significantly increased, which was beneficial for more extensive marketing strategies. The definition of guardrails and technical system mapping ensured that the loyalty card was not introduced at the expense of the entrepreneurship of the individual key account manager. Rather, the customer card created clarity about the scope for awarding costly additional services and supported self-organization in the formulation of offers by sales.

Success factors: The decisive factor for the successful introduction of the logistics loyalty card was above all the integration of sales. After initial resistance, the sales staff quickly realized that such a binding and transparent performance promise could set new impulses in market development and raise cooperation with project developers to a new level.

In addition to an effective system building of marketing logistics and the supply chain structures in general, its resilience largely depends on the quality of the day-to-day coordination in terms of system coupling.

5 Coordination along the chain

5.1 Supply chain coupling

We have already discussed that self-organization is a conditio sine qua non in highly complex systems. But let's discuss the supply chain coupling, which is subject to operational supply chain controlling in more detail. Moreover, let's better understand why the (self-)coordination in an agile fashion is asking for a digital twin of the supply chain.

In principle, supply chain controlling can make use of exactly those coordination mechanisms in the course of system coupling that are also used for coordination tasks in the execution system (Weber 1993). This is essentially the coordination via personal instructions, through programs, plans and finally via self-coordination. Figure 5.1 shows the change profile of such supply chain coupling.

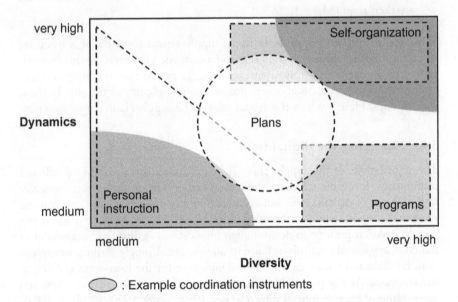

Figure 5.1 Change profile of supply chain coupling (based on Weber 1993, further developed by Wehberg 1994)

Self-organization uses its possibilities by effectively and efficiently linking the subsystems of a supply chain (management). Self-organization is characterized by its recursive, autonomous, redundant, and self-referential attachment (Wehberg 1997):

- Recursive, because certain characteristics of digital supply chains are similar on different factual hierarchy levels, i.e. recurrent. Such characteristics are not limited to the organization, but can include goals, functions, methods, instruments, etc. For example, modular structures can help to ensure the communication and compatibility of various units (e.g. plug-and-serve).
- Autonomous, because to a certain extent a digital supply chains manages or develops itself and seeks its own way for this, without there being a central unit for it (e.g. as a self-controlling drone). Controlling and the controlled unit are then one. At the same time, many units, so to speak, can perceive the control or development by a "swarm". Then, the control intelligence is also "swarm intelligence".
- Redundant, because in principle those units of digital supply chains have a controlling or developing influence, each of which has (the most or best) information. This means that, fundamentally, control-relevant information is available and shared for all relevant units.
- Self-referential, because the behaviour of a digital supply chain always reacts back to them and these feedbacks in a way that forms the basis for further behaviour. Accordingly, the system or its units themselves in part produce those characteristics that make up the system. The cause and effect merge into each other. Development in small steps and avoidance of oversteering are then required.

Self-coordination corresponds to digital supply chains insofar as it is based on its methodological or technological foundations, and vice versa. In this context, the varying character of self-organization suggests that the suitability of these coordination mechanisms also depends on the complexity of the supply chain relationships. Here is where the digital twin of the supply chain comes into play.

5.2   Mastering the digital twin

The digital twin of the supply chain helps to coordinate and develop relevant relationships. Since the relevant relationships can be very multi-layered, especially in the course of digitalization, self-coordination requires appropriate instrumental support. The positioning of the relevant interfaces in a corresponding *relationship portfolio* makes it possible to derive design implications against the background of the company-specific situation. Current and potential supply chain relationships must be evaluated with regard to their significance for the long-term viability of the company. At this point, the distinction between critical, reactive, active and inert relationships is helpful (Probst/Gomez 1989; Vester 1990; Wehberg 1994). The relevant elements are being captured by the so-called *digital twin of supply chains*.

How does the digital twin actually work? Critical system elements that exert a strong influence on third parties and at the same time are themselves subject to strong influences must be given high attention by supply chain management. The digital twin of the supply chain models relevant elements and their behaviour (Figure 5.2). It builds an optimization loop of two phases – *real-to-virtual* and *virtual-to-real* – in order to measure, understand, enhance and monitor the performance of supply chains. Specifically, the two phases of a digital twin summarize a road map of ten key milestones, where the progress from one milestone to another marks the achievement of specific supply chain objectives, and puts cybersecurity and digital traits at the core. Although the digital twin technically completes at milestone ten for a relevant supply chain element – like a logistics asset or operation – it must be broadened and started again to include a wider set of supply chain elements, assets or business segments, the entire organization and, ultimately, the end-to-end supply chain of a company, including external stakeholders. A comprehensive cyber-risk management initiative that is secure and resilient as well as a culture that would enable the evolution of the supply chain remain at the core of the digital twin.

Does the classical decision theory match with the requirements of a digital twin? In connection with the coordination decisions aimed at supply chain coupling, it is now also important to satisfy the holistic-evolutionary or resilient understanding of supply chain management and thus the process orientation in the broader sense. This is because interface management is directed against and even justified by isolated and mechanistic ways of thinking and acting.

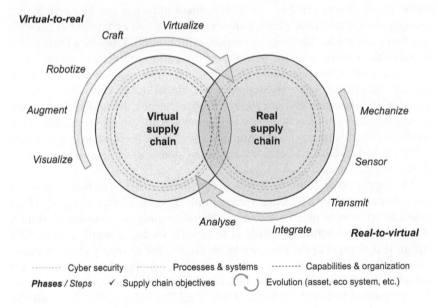

Figure 5.2 Digital twin of the supply chain

To this end, it is necessary to fall back on *decision-theoretical principles*. The classical decision theory models the business management decision field in the core on the basis of the so-called result matrix, which distinguishes an action (among other things functional and basic strategies), a state and a result space (target system) and can be more or less differentiated by the consideration of risk and uncertainty (Bamberg/Coenenberg 1991). It implicitly assumes that the elements to be assigned to the action and state space are exclusively influencing, i.e. active, elements and that the elements of the result space are exclusively influenced, i.e. reactive, elements. The decision maker himself stands above the system and pulls the strings.

What kind of theoretical basis fits the digital twin? Apart from the fact that the separation of decision maker and decision field does not take into account the operational unity of the supply chain, it must be critically stated with regard to the decision theory described here as classic that in reality such a clear distinction between active influencing variables and design parameters as well as reactive target variables will only be possible in a few cases and thus equates to a certain trivialization. Rather, reactive, active, critical as well as inert elements can be inherent in the so-called action as well as result and state space and play a decisive role in the overall context. Thus, result variables can be quite active, critical or sluggish in nature. Numerous framework conditions can also be influenced. It should also be remembered at this point that the *butterfly effect* stems from chaos research, which emphasizes that even small influences (butterfly strike) can have serious consequences (hurricane) due to their networking (e.g. Küppers 1993). The boundaries between action space, state space and result space become blurred. Instead, the distinction between endogenous system variables, on which direct influence can be exerted, and exogenous variables, on which indirect influence can be exerted at most, is appropriately made. The decision maker, who himself is usually a critical element of the system, now has to consider the entire interior and surrounding system as well as their networking. In summary, this suggests a new decision theory, which places the classical decision model on a cybernetic–systemic basis. The *behavioural decision theory* (Berger/Bernhard-Mehlich 1995), for example, can be understood as a first approach on the development track of such a new decision theory. And also the system methodology of Gomez (1985) is to be classified here. It satisfies the demands of process orientation in the broader sense.

The supply chain coupling as well as the supply chain formation have so far been examined primarily from a static point of view. However, supply chain relationships evolve over time and can therefore only be coordinated from a dynamic understanding, especially in the course of digital supply chains. This means that changes in the change profiles are also left to supply chain management. In the following fourth part, the dynamics of digital supply chains will therefore be discussed in more detail. First, typical development paths have to be categorized before the associated structural dynamics can be dealt with in more detail.

Literature

acatech/Arbeitskreis Smart Service Welt, Ed., *Smart Service Welt – Umsetzungsempfehlungen für das Zukunftsprojekt Internetbasierte Dienste für die Wirtschaft*, Abschlussbericht, Berlin 2015.

acatech – Deutsche Akademie der Technikwissenschaften, Ed., *Cyber Physical Systems*, Innovationsmotor für Mobilität, Gesundheit, Energie und Produktion, München, Berlin 2011.

Ackoff, R. L., Optimization + Objectivity = Opt Out, in: *European Journal of Operational Research*, 1 (1977), pp. 1–7.

Adam, D., *Kurzlehrbuch Planung*, 2nd ed., Wiesbaden 1983.

Anderson, C., *The Long Tail*, deutsche Übersetzung, München 2007.

Ansoff, I., *Management-Strategie*, München 1966.

Argyris, C., Schön, D. A., *Organizational Learning, a Theory of Action Perspective*, MA 1978.

Augustin, S., *Information als Wettbewerbsfaktor, Informationslogistik – Herausforderung an das Management*, Köln 1990.

Ashby, W. R., Information Flows within Co-Ordinated Systems, in: Rose, J. (Ed.), *Cybernetics*, London 1970, pp. 57–64.

Ashby, W. R., Measuring the Internal Information Exchange in a System, in: *Cybernetica*, 8 (1965) 1, pp. 5–22.

Ashby, W. R., Systems and Their Informational Measures, in: Klir, G. (Ed.), *Trends*, 1971, pp. 78–97.

Atteslander, P., Hauptlager Landstraße, in: *Wirtschaftswoche vom 28.8.1987*, 41 (1987) 36, pp. 78–82.

Backhaus, K., *Investitionsgütermarketing*, 2nd ed., München 1990.

Bahke, E., *Materialflußsysteme, Band III: Materialflußplanung*, Mainz 1976.

Bamberg, G., Coenenberg, A. G., *Betriebswirtschaftliche Entscheidungslehre*, 6th ed., München 1991.

Bauernhansl, T., Die Vierte Industrielle Revolution – Der Weg in ein wertschaffendes Produktionsparadigma, in Bauernhansl, T., ten Hompel, M., Vogel-Heuser, B. (Ed.), *Industrie 4.0 in Produktion, Automatisierung und Logistik*, Wiesbaden 2014, pp. 5–35.

Baumgarten, H., *Über technische und organisatorische Möglichkeiten zur Anpassung der Industriebetriebe an das Containersystem*, Berlin 1972.

Beckmann, H., Theorie einer evolutionären Logistik-Planung, Basiskonzepte der Unternehmensentwicklung in Zeiten zunehmender Turbulenz unter Berücksichtigung des Prototypingansatzes, in Kuhn, A. (Ed.), *Reihe Unternehmenslogistik*, Dortmund 1996.

Berger, U., Bernhard-Mehlich, I., Die Verhaltenswissenschaftliche Entscheidungstheorie, in: Kieser, A. (Ed.), *Organizationstheorien*, 2nd ed., Stuttgart 1995, pp. 123–153.

Bertodo, R, Implementing Strategie Vision, in: *LRP*, (1990) 5, p. 26.

Bircher, B., Planungssystem, in: *HwPlan*, Stuttgart 1989, pp. 1503–1515.

Blamauer, M., Just im Stau, Radikales Umdenken notwendig, in: *Jahrbuch der Logistik 1992*, Düsseldorf 1992, pp. 64–66.

Bleicher, K., *Das Konzept Integriertes Management*, 2nd ed., Frankfurt a.M., New York 1992.

Bleicher, K., *Das Konzept Integriertes Management*, 3rd ed., Frankfurt a.M., New York 1995.

Bleicher, K., Zum "Management of Change", in: *Technologie & Management*, 43 (1994) 2, pp. 65–69.

Bojkow, E., *Getränkeverpackung und Umwelt*, Berlin 1989.

Borkowsky, J., Computerunterstützung bei der Arbeit mit qualitativen Daten am Beispiel des Marketing, in: *zm*, 64 (1994) 3, pp. 313–332.

Bössmann, E., Volkswirtschaftliche Probleme der Transaktionskosten, in: *ZgS*, 138 (1982) 4, pp. 664–679.

Böttger, M., Ladeeinheiten bilden: Rational und verpackungsarm, in: *Jahrbuch der Logistik 1991*, Düsseldorf 1991, pp. 238–240.

Bousonville, T., Ameisenkolonien und evolutionäre Algorithmen zur Lösung logistischer Probleme, Präsentation an der Hochschule für Technik und Wirtschaft des Saarlandes, Systemwissenschaftliches Kolloquium, Saarbrücken 2009.

Bowersox, D. J., Closs, D. J., Helferich, O. K., *Logistical Management*, 3rd ed., New York, London 1986.

Bowersox, D. J., Smykay, E. W., LaLonde, B. J., *Physical Distribution Management, Supply Chain Management Problems in the Firm*, revised ed., New York 1968.

Bremermann, H. J., Optimization through Evolution and ReCombination, in: Yovits, M. C. et al. (Ed.), *Self-Organizing Systems*, Washington, DC 1962, pp. 93–106.

Bremermann, H. J., Quantum Noise and Information, 5th Berkley Symposium on Mathematical Statistics and Probility, Berkley, CA 1965.

Bührens, J., *Anpassungsmaßnahmen zur Harmonisierung von Produktions- und Nachfrageverhältnissen bei Kuppelproduktion unter besonderer Berücksichtigung der Absatzpolitik*, Hamburg 1978.

Büttner, K.-H., Anwendungsbeispiel Industrie 4.0 – Fertigung im Siemens Elektronikwerk Amberg, in: Bauernhansl, T., ten Hompel, M., Vogel-Heuser, B. (Ed.), *Industrie 4.0 in Produktion, Automatisierung und Logistik*, Wiesbaden 2014, pp. 121–144.

Carter, J. R., In Search of Synergy: A Structure-Perforrnance Test, in: *The Review of Economics and Statistics*, 59 (1977), pp. 279–289.

Clay, D., Mashall, J., Glynn, M., *Who Is Dawn?*, Lippincott 2017.

Coase, R. H., The Nature of the Firm, in: *Economica*, 4 (1937) o. Nr., pp. 386–405.

Cohen, W., Levinthal, D., Absorptive Capacity: A New Perspective on Learning and Innovation, in: *ASQ*, 35 (1990) 2, pp. 223–244.

Conant, R., *Informations Transfer in Complex Systems, with Application to Regulation*, Illinois 1968.

Corsten, H., *Betriebswirtschaftslehre für Dienstleistungsunternehmen*, München, Wien 1988.

Darr, W., *Integrierte Marketing-Logistik*, Wiesbaden 1992.

D'Aveni, R. A., *Hyperwettbewerb, Strategien für die neue Dynamik der Märkte*, Frankfurt a. M., New York 1995.

Delfmann, W., Integration von Marketing und Logistik, in: Bundesvereinigung der Logistik (Ed.), *Berichtsband zum 7. Dt. Logistik-Kongreß*, München 1990, pp. 154–186.

Delfmann, W., Marketing und Logistik integrieren, in: *Jahrbuch der Logistik 1990*, Düsseldorf 1990, pp. 10–15.

Diruf, G., Computergestützte Informations- und Kommunikationssysteme der Unternehmenslogistik als Komponenten innovativer Strategien, in: Isermann, H. (Ed.), *Logistik: Beschaffung, Produktion, Distribution*, Landsberg Lech 1994, pp. 71–86.

Duerler, B. M., *Logistik als Teil der Unternehmensstrategie*, Bern, Stuttgart 1990.

Dylick, T., *Management der Umweltbeziehungen, Wiesbaden 1989*, Nachdruck der ersten Auflage, Wiesbaden 1992.

Englander, E. J., Technology and Oliver Williamson's Transaction Cost Economics, in: *Journal of Economic Behavior and Organization*, 17 (1988) 10, pp. 339–353.

Fastermann, P., *3D-Druck/Rapid Prototyping: Eine Zukunftstechnologie – kompakt erklärt*, Berlin, Heidelberg 2012.

Fiol, M., Consensus, Diversity and Learning in Organizations, in: *Organization Science*, 4 (1993) 11, pp. 10–26.

Fischer, E., Just-in-Time, Sündenbock für das Vekehrschaos?, in: *Logistik Heute*, 15 (1993) 4, pp. 42–44.

Freemann, R. E., *Strategie Management: A Stakeholder Approach*, Marsfield, MA 1984.

Frerich-Sagurna, R., Zukunftsorientierte Verpackungsplanung: Strategien für den Vertrieb, in: *Jahrbuch der Logistik 1993*, Düsseldorf 1993, pp. 42–44.

Gaebe, W., *Zur Bedeutung von Agglomerationswirkungen für industrielle Standortentscheidungen*, Mannheim 1981.

Gebhardt, A., *Rapid Prototyping – Werkzeuge für die schnelle Produktentstehung*, 2nd ed., München 2002.

Gilbert, X., Strebel, P. J., Outpacing Strategies, in: *IMEDE-Perspectives for Managers*, 9 (1985) 2, pp. 73–89.

Goldratt, E. M., Devising Coherent Production/Finance/Marketing Strategy, in: *American Production and Inventory Control Society*, 1984, pp. 22–27.

Gomez, P., Systemorientiertes Problemlösen im Management, Von der Organizationsmethodik zur Systemmethodik, in: Probst, G. J. B., Siegwart, H. (Ed.), *Integriertes Management, Bausteine des systemorientierten Management*, Bern, Stuttgart 1985, pp. 235–260.

Gomez, P., Probst, G., *Vernetztes Denken im Management, Schriftenreihe: Die Orientierung, Nr. 89, hrsg. durch die Schweizerische Volksbank*, Bern 1987.

Göpfert, I., Interlining, Code-Sharing und Trucking, in: *WiSt*, 23 (1994) 9, S. 460–462.

Göpfert, I., Ed., *Logistik der Zukunft: Supply Chain Management for the Future*, Gabler Verlag, Wiesbaden 1999.

Göpfert, I., *Logistik – Führungskonzeption und Management von Supply Chains*, 3rd ed., München 2013.

Göpfert, I., Ökokologie und Logistikmanagement, in: Fickert, R., Hässig, K. (Ed.), *Megatrends, Schriftenreihe des Schweizerischen Verbandes für Materialwirtschaft und Einkauf*, Bd. 8, Bern 1992, pp. 149–170.

Göpfert, I., *Ökonomie und Ökologie in der Logistik – Wettbewerbschancen durch Innova-tion, Vortrag zu den 8. Internationalen Frankfurter Luftfrachttagen vom 22.9.1993*, Frankfurt a. M. 1993.

Göpfert, I., Wehberg, G., *Ökologieorientiertes Logistik-Marketing, Konzeptionelle und empirische Fundierung ökologieorientierter Angebotsstrategien von Logistik-Dienstleistungsunternehmen*, Stuttgart, Berlin, Köln 1995.

Göpfert, I., Wehberg, G., Synergiemanagement in der Entsorgung – Potentiale zwischen ent- und versorgungslogistischen Dienstleistungen, in: Lukas, G., Dutz, E., Wehberg, G. (Ed.), *Prozeßmanagement in der Entsorgung*, München 1996, pp. 61–85.

Göpfert, I., Wehberg, G., *Zur Diffusion von Logistikverständnissen, Ergebnisse einer schriftlichen Befragung, Arbeitspapier Nr. 8 des Lehrstuhls für Allgemeine Betriebswirtschaftslehre und Logistik der Philipps-Universität Marburg*, Marburg 1996.

Grochla, E., *Einführung in die Organizationstheorie*, Stuttgart 1978.

Gutenberg, E., *Grundlagen der Betriebswirtschaftslehre, Erster Band: Die Produktion*, 24th ed., Berlin u. a. 1983.

Habermas, J., *Theorie des kommunikativen Handelns, Bd. I, Handlungsrationalität und gesellschaftliche Rationalisierung*, Frankfurt a. M. 1981.

Hahn, O., Just-in-Time – ein Rückschritt in die Mangelwirtschaft, in: *Int. Verkehrswesen*, 43 (1991) 3, pp. 101–102.

Haken, H., *Erfolgsgeheimnisse der Natur – Synergetik: Die Lehre vom Zusammenwirken*, 3rd ed., Stuttgart 1983.

Haken, H., *Synergetics, an Introduction*, 3rd ed., Berlin u. a. 1983b.

Haken, H., Haken-Krell, M., *Entstehung von biologischer Information und Ordnung*, Darmstadt 1989.

Hätscher, A. M., *Unternehmensentwicklung durch strategische Partnerschaften*, München 1992.

Haussmann, F., *Einführung in die Systemforschung*, München 1978.

Heinemann, G., *No-Line-Handel – Höchste Evolutionsstufe im Multi Channeling*, Wiesbaden 2012.

Helfrich, C., Neue Kennzahlen für die Logistik, in: *io-Management-Zeitschrift*, 58 (1989) 7/8, pp. 69–73.

Herron, D. P., Buying Time and Saving Money with Air Freight, in: *TDM*, 8 (1968) 12, pp. 25–28.

Hesse, M., Neue Produktionskonzepte aus ökologisch-ökonomischer Sicht, in: *Logistik + Arbeit*, (1993) 1, pp. 45–47.

Hesse, M., *Verkehrswende: ökologisch-ökonomische Perspektiven für Stadt und Region*, Marburg 1993.

Heuger, M., Kückelhaus, M., Zeiler, K., Niezgoda, D., Chung, G., *Self-Driving Vehicles in Supply Chain Management*, Bonn 2014.

Hilbert, M., López, P., The World's Technological Capacity to Store, Communicate, and Compute Information, in: *Science*, 332 (2011) 6025, pp. 60–65.

Hirsch-Kreinsen, H., Weyer, J., Ed., *Wandel von Produktionsarbeit – Industrie 4.0*, Soziologisches Arbeitspapier, Nr. 38, Dortmund 2014.

Hodgson, G. M., *Economics and Institutions: A Manifesto for a Modern Institutional Economics*, Cambridge, Oxford 1988.

Höhler, G., Unternehmenskultur als Erfolgsfaktor, in: Königswieser, R., Lutz, C. (Ed.), *Das systemisch-evolutionäre Management*, 2nd ed., Wien 1992, pp. 341–350.

Höller, M., Informations- und Kommunikationstechnologien – Techniküberblick und das Potential zur Verkehrsvermeidung, in: Höller, M., Haubold, V., Stahl, D., Rodi, H. (Ed.), *Die Bedeutung von Informations- und Kommunikationstechnologien für den Verkehr, Beiträge aus dem Institut für Verkehrswissenschaft an der Universität Münster*, Heft 133, Göttingen 1994, pp. 7–58.

Ihde, G., *Distributionslogistik*, Stuttgart, New York 1978.

Ihde, G., Dutz, E., Stieglitz, A., Möglichkeiten und Probleme einer umweltorientierten Konsumgüterdistribution, in: *Marketing ZFP*, 16 (1994) 3, pp. 199–208.

Imai, M., *Kaizen, Der Schlüssel zum Erfolg der Japaner im Wettbewerb*, 9th ed., München 1993.

Jacoby, J., *Zielbeschreibung und Zielbestimmung für das Zeitmangagement in der Logistik*, München 1994.

Jansen, R., Die Verpackungstechnik als integraler Bestandteil der Logistik, in: *Fördertechnik*, 56 (1987) 11/12, S. 28–34.

Jordan, D., Integrale Logistik im Philips Konzern, in: *DGfL*, 1988, pp. 43–65.

Jöstingmeier, B., *Zur Unternehmensethik international tätiger Unternehmen*, Göttingen 1994.

Jünemann, R., *Materialfluß und Logistik*, Berlin u. a. 1989.

Kanter, R. M., *Mobilizing Corporate Energies*, St. Gallen 1993.

Kast, F. E., Rosenzweig, J. E., *Organization and Management, a Systems and Contingency Approach*, 4th ed., New York u. a. 1985.

Kern, W., *Industrielle Produktionswirtschaft*, 5th ed., Stuttgart 1992.

Kirsch, W., *Kommunikatives Handeln, Autopoiese, Rationalität, Sondierungen zu einer evolutionären Führungslehre*, München 1992.

Kirsch, W., *Organisatorische Führungssysteme, Bausteine zu einem verhaltenswissenschaftlichen Bezugsrahmen*, München 1976.

Kirsch, W., Esser, W.-M., Gabele, E., *Das Management der geplanten Evolution von Organisationen*, Stuttgart 1979.

Klaus, P., *Die dritte Bedeutung der Logistik, Nürnberger Arbeitspapier Nr. 3*, Nürnberg 1993.

Kleinaltenkamp, M., *Recycling-Strategien*, Bochum 1985.

Klimecki, R., Probst, G., Eberl, P., *Entwicklungsorientiertes Management*, Skript zur Publikation, 1994.

Klimke, W., Basis-Strategien zur Ausrichtung der Logistik-Konzeption eines Unternehmens, in: *DGfL*, 1983, pp. 215–218.

Kluckhohn, C., *Culture and Behavior*, New York 1962.

Koppelmann, U., Stichwort Verpackung, in: Kern, W. (Ed.), *Handwörterbuch der Produktionswirtschaft*, Stuttgart 1979, pp. 2129–2138.

Kracke, R., Hildebrandt, J., Runge, W. R., Voges, W., Güterverkehr- und -verteilzentren, in: Isermann, H. (Ed.), *Logistik: Beschaffung, Produktion, Distribution*, Landsberg Lech 1994, pp. 361–373.

Kroeber-Riel, W., *Beschaffung und Logistik*, Wiesbaden 1966.

Krulis-Randa, J. S., *Marketing-Logistik – Eine systemtheoretische Konzeption der betrieblichen Warenverteilung und Warenbeschaffung*, Bern, Stuttgart 1977.

Kückelhaus, M., Steck, S., Ortmann, F., Richter, K., Poenicke, O., *Low-Cost Sensor Technology*, Bonn 2013.

Kuhn, T. S., *Die Struktur wissenschaftlicher Revolutionen*, Frankfurt a. M., 1967.

Kummer, S., *Logistik für den Mittelstand*, München 1992.

Küppers, B.-O., Wenn das Ganze mehr ist als die Summe seiner Teile, in: *Geo Wissen: Chaos und Kreativität*, (1993) 11, pp. 28–31.

Lange, V., Mehrweg-Systeme im logistischen Umfeld, in: *Logistik im Unternehmen*, 8 (1994) 3, pp. 84–87.

Liebmann, H.-P., Struktur und Funktionsweise moderner Warenverteilzentren, in: Zentes, J. (Ed.), *Moderne Distributionskonzepte in der Konsumgüterwirtschaft*, Stuttgart 1991, pp. 17–32.

Lüder, K., Küpper, W., *Unternehmerische Standortplanung und regionale Wirtschaftsförderung*, Göttingen 1983.

Luttmer, G., Billig und schlecht verpackt kommt teuer zu stehen, in: *Handelsblatt vom* 12.5.1993, o. Jg. (1923) 93, pp. 27.

Malik, P., *Systemisches Management, Evolution, Selbstorganization*, Bern, Stuttgart, Wien 1993.

Mann, R., *Das ganzheitliche Unternehmen*, 6th ed., Stuttgart 1995.

Meffert, H., *Marketing*, 7th ed., Wiesbaden 1986.

Meffert, H., *Marketingforschung und Käuferverhalten*, 2nd ed., Wiesbaden 1992.

Meffert, H., *Strategische Unternehmensführung und Marketing*, Wiesbaden 1988.

Meffert, H., Kirchgeorg, M., *Marktorientiertes Umweltmanagement*, 2nd ed., Stuttgart 1993.

Merkel, H. H., *Simulationsmodelle für die Optimierung interdependenter logistischer Prozesse*, Bremen 1981.

Michaletz, T., *Wirtschaftliche Transportketten mit modularen Containern*, München 1994.

Nieschlag, R., Dichtl, E., Hörschgen, H., *Marketing*, 16th ed., Berlin 1991.

Nork, M. E., *Umweltschutz in unternehmerischen Entscheidungen*, Wiesbaden 1992.

Nyhuis, P., Heinen, T., Reinhart, G., Rimpau, C., Abele, E., Wörn, A., Wandlungsfähige Produktionssysteme: Theoretischer Hintergrund zur Wandlungsfähigkeit von Produktionssystemen, in: *wt Werkstatttechnik Online*, 98 (2008), pp. 85–91.

Pfohl, H.-Chr., *Logistikmanagement, Funktionen und Instrumente*, Berlin u. a. 1994.

Pfohl, H.-Chr., *Logistiksysteme, Betriebswirtschaftliche Grundlagen*, 4th ed., Berlin u. a. 1990.

Pfohl, H.-Chr., *Marketing-Logistik, Steuerung und Kontrolle des Warenflusses im modernen Markt*, Mainz 1972.

Pfohl, H.-Chr., Total Quality Management: Konzeption und Tendenzen, in: Pfohl, H.-Chr. (Ed.), *Total Quality Management in der Logistik*, Berlin 1992, pp. 1–49.

Pfohl, H.-Chr., Zur Formulierung einer Lieferservicepolitik, Theoretische Aussagen zum Angebot von Sekundärleistungen als absatzpolitisches Instrument, in: *ZfbF*, 29 (1977) 5, pp. 239–255.

Pfohl, H.-Chr., Stölzle, W., Entsorgungslogistik, in: Steger, U. (Ed.), *Handbuch München* 1992, pp. 571–591.

Porter, M. E., *Wettbewerbsvorteile*, Frankfurt a. M., New York 1986.

Porter, M. E., Fuller, M. B., Koalition und globale Strategien, in: Porter, M. E. (Ed.), *Globaler Wettbewerb*, Wiesbaden 1989, pp. 17–68.

Poth, L., Die perspektivischen und strategischen Herausforderungen an eine Systemvernet-zung, in: Pfohl, H.-Chr. (Ed.), *Logistiktrends '91*, Berlin 1991, pp. 59–109.

Poth, L., *Praxis der Marketing-Logistik*, Heidelberg 1973.

Probst, G. J. B., Organizationales Lernen und die Bewältigung von Wandel, in: Gomez, P., Hahn, D., Müller-Stewens, G., Wunderer, R. (Ed.), *Unternehmerischer Wandel*, Wiesbaden 1994, pp. 295–320.

Probst, G. J. B., *Selbst-Organization, Ordnungsprozesse in sozialen Systemen aus ganzheitlicher Sicht*, Berlin, Hamburg 1987.

Probst, G. J. B., Büchel, B., *Organizationales Lernen: Wettbewerbsvorteil der Zukunft*, Wiesbaden 1994.

Probst, G. J. B., Gomez, P., Die Methodik des vernetzten Denkens zur Lösung komplexer Probleme, in: Probst, G. J. B., Gomez, P. (Ed.), *Vernetztes Denken – Unternehmen ganzheitlich führen*, Wiesbaden 1989, pp. I–18.

Pümpin, C., Kobi, J. M., Wütherich, H. H., *Unternehmenskultur. Basis strategischer Profilierung erfolgreicher Unternehmen, Schriftenreihe: Die Orientierung, Nr. 85, hrsg. durch die Schweizerische Volksbank*, Bern 1985.

Rautenstrauch, C., Betriebliches Recycling, in: *Zffi-Ergänzungsheft*, (1993) 2, pp. 87–104.

Reese, J., Just-in-Time-Logistik, Ein umweltgerechtes Prinzip?, in: *ZfB-Ergänzungsheft*, (1993) 2, pp. 139–156.

Reißner, S., *Synergiemanagement und Akquisitionserfolg*, Wiesbaden 1992.

Rendez, H., *Konzeption integrierter Logistik-Dienstleistungssysteme*, München 1992.

Riebei, P., *Die Kuppelproduktion, Betriebs- und Marktprobleme*, Köln, Opladen 1955.

Ropella, W., *Synergie als strategisches Ziel der Unternehmung*, Berlin 1989.

Rössl, D., *Gestaltung komplexer Austauschbeziehungen, Analyse zwischenbetrieblicher Kooperation*, Wiesbaden 1994.

Sauerbrey, G., *Logistisch Denken, Perspektiven für die Organization von morgen*, Wiesbaden 1991.

Schäfer, E., *Die Unternehmung*, 10. Auf., Wiesbaden 1980.

Schaltegger, S., Sturm, A., *Ökologieorientierte Entscheidungen in Unternehmen*, Bern, Stuttgart, Wien 1992.

Schein, E., Coming to a New Awareness of Organizational Culture, in: *SMR*, (1984) Winter, pp. 3–16.

Schiffers, E., *Logistische Budgetierung, Ein Instrument prozeßorientierter Unternehmensführung*, Wiesbaden 1994.

Schlick, J., Stephan, P., Loskyll, M., Lappe, D., Industrie 4.0 in der praktischen Anwendung, in Bauernhansl, T., ten Hompel, M., Vogel-Heuser, B. (Ed.), *Industrie 4.0 in Produktion, Automatisierung und Logistik*, Wiesbaden 2014, pp. 57–84.

Schmidt, A., *Das Controlling als Instrument zur Koordination der Unternehmensführung*, Frankfurt u. a. 1986.

Schmidt-Bleek, F., Ohne De-Materialisierung kein ökologischer Strukturwandel, in: Altner, G., Mettler-Maibom, B., Simonis, U. E., von Weizsäcker, E. U. (Ed.), *Jahrbuch Ökologie*, München 1994, pp. 94–108.

Schneider, D., Die Unhaltbarkeit des Transaktionskostenansatzes für die "Markt oder Unternehmung-Diskussion", in: *ZfB*, 55 (1985), pp. 1237–1254.

Scholz, C., *Strategisches Management, Ein integrativer Ansatz*, Berlin, New York 1987.

Schreiter, C., *Evolution und Wettbewerb von Organizationsstrukturen*, Göttingen 1994.

Servatius, H.-G., Umsetzung umweltbewusster Führung als Prozess eines kulturellen Wandels, in: Zahn, E., Gassert, H. (Ed.), *Umweltschutzorientiertes Management*, Stuttgart 1992, pp. 95–118.

Soder, J., Anwendungsbeispiel Production: Von CIM über Lean Production zu Industrie 4.0, in: Bauernhansl, T., ten Hompel, M., Vogel-Heuser, B. (Ed.), *Industrie 4.0 in Produktion, Automatisierung und Logistik*, Wiesbaden 2014, pp. 85–102.

Spelthahn, S., Schlossberger, U., Steger, U., *Umweltbewußtes Transportmanagement*, Bern, Stuttgart, Wien 1993.

Sprüngli, R. K., *Evolution und Management, Ansätze einer evolutionistischen Betrachtung sozialer Systeme*, Bern, Stuttgart 1981.

Stahl, G., Konzeptionsmodelle für zu integrierende Verkehrssysteme – aber welche?, in: *Int. Verkehrswesen*, 46 (1994) 1/2, pp. 43–50.

Stahlmann, V., *Umweltorientierte Materialwirtschaft*, Wiesbaden 1988.

Steegmüller, D., Zürn, M., Wandlungsfähige Produktionssysteme für den Automobilbau der Zukunft, in: Bauernhansl, T., ten Hompel, M., Vogel-Heuser, B. (Ed.), *Industrie 4.0 in Produktion, Automatisierung und Logistik*, Wiesbaden 2014, pp. 103–119.

Stölzle, W., *Umweltschutz und Entsorgungslogistik, Theoretische Grundlagen mit ersten empirischen Ergebnissen zur innerbetrieblichen Entsorgungslogistik*, Berlin 1993.

Tempelmeier, H., *Quantitative Marketing-Logistik*, Berlin u. a. 1983.

ten Hompel, M., *Autonomik-Transfer: Industrie 4.0, Vortrag vom 31. Januar 2013*, Berlin 2013.

ten Hompel, M., Logistik 4.0, in: Bauernhansl, T., ten Hompel, M., Vogel-Heuser, B. (Ed.), *Industrie 4.0 in Produktion, Automatisierung und Logistik*, Wiesbaden 2014, pp. 615–624.

Thaler, S. P., *Betriebswirtschaftliche Konsequenzen der EG-Güterverkehrsliberalisierung für europäische Speditionsunternehmen*, Bern, Stuttgart 1990.

Thonemann, U., *Operations Management: Konzepte, Methoden und Anwendungen*, 2nd ed., München 2010.

Traumann, P., *Marketing-Logistik in der Praxis – Leitfaden für das Management in Industrie und Handel*, Mainz 1976.

Türks, M., Auftragsabwicklung, in: Klee, J., Wendt, P. D. (Ed.), *Physical Distribution im Modernen Management*, München 1972, pp. 65–85.

Turck, M., Hao, J., and First Mark Capitel – Big Data Landscape 2017.

Tuttle, T., Engineering the IoT, Embedded World Conference 2015.

Ulrich, H., Probst, G., *Anleitung zum ganzheitlichen Denken und Handeln*, 3rd ed., Stuttgart 1991.

Vester, F., *Ausfahrt Zukunft, Strategien für den Verkehr von morgen, Eine Systemuntersuchung*, 5th ed., München 1990.

Vester, F., *Crashtest Mobilität, Die Zukunft des Verkehrs*, München 1995.

Vester, F., *Denken, Lernen, Vergessen*, 21st ed., München 1994.

Vester, F., Ökologisches Systemmanagement, Die Unternehmung am Scheideweg zwischen Mechanistik und Biokybernetik, in: *Probst, Siegwart*, 1985, pp. 299–330.

Vester, F., *Neuland des Denkens*, Stuttgart 1980b.

Vogel-Heuser, B., Herausforderungen und Anforderungen aus Sicht der IT und der Automatisierungstechnik, in: Bauernhansl, T., ten Hompel, M., Vogel-Heuser, B. (Ed.), *Industrie 4.0 in Produktion, Automatisierung und Logistik*, Wiesbaden 2014, pp. 37–48.

von Hayek, F. A., *Die Theorie komplexer Phänomene (Deutsche Übersetzung)*, Tübingen 1972.

Warnecke, H. J., Kühnle, H., Bischoff, J., Produktionsplanung und -steuerung bei Gruppenfertigung, in: Isermann, H. (Ed.), *Logistik: Beschaffung, Produktion, Distribution*, Landsberg Lech 1994, pp. 309–318.

Weber, A., *Über den Standort der Industrien, I. Teil: Reine Theorie des Standorts*, Tübingen 1922.

Weber, J., *Einführung in das Controlling*, 4th ed., Stuttgart 1993.

Weber, J., Kummer, S., *Logistikmanagement*, Stuttgart 1994.

Wehberg, G., Logistik 4.0, in: *Komplexität managen in Theorie und Praxis*, Wiesbaden 2015.

Wehberg, G., Logistik-Controlling – Kern des evolutionären Logistikmanagement, in Jöstingmeier, B. et al. (Ed.), *Aktuelle Probleme der Genossenschaften aus rechtswissenschaftlicher und wirtschaftswissenschaftlicher Sicht*, Göttingen 1994, pp. 73–134.

Wehberg, G., *Ökologieorientiertes Logistikmanagement, Ein evolutionstheoretischer Ansatz*, Wiesbaden 1997.

Weick, K. E., *The Social Psychology of Organizing*, New York u. a. 1969.

Wiedemann, T., Bedeutung des Kombinierten Verkehrs (KV) und des Bahntrans-Projektes, in: *Int. Verkehrswesen*, 45 (1993) 10, pp. 575–579.

Wiendahl, H.-P., *Belastungsorientierte Fertigungssteuerung*, München, Wien 1987.

Wildemann, H., *Die Modulare Fabrik*, 4th ed., München 1994.

Wildemann, H., Produktionssteuerung nach japanischen KANBAN-Prinzipien, in: *WiSt*, 12 (1983) 11, pp. 582–584.

Williamson, O. E., *The Economic Institutions of Capitalism*, New York 1985.

Williamson, O. E., Economic Institutions: Spontaneous Order and Intentional Governance, in: *Journal of Law, Economics & Organization*, 7 (1991) 7, pp. 159–187.

Witte, E., Power and Innovation: A Two-Center Theory, in: *International Studies of Management Organization*, Spring (1977).

Wittmann, W., *Unternehmung und unvollkommene Information*, Köln u. a. 1959.

Wölker, M., Holzhauer, R., "Chaotische" Materialflußsysteme, in: *Jahrbuch der Logistik 1995*, Düsseldorf 1995, pp. 202–203.

Yunker, J. A., *Integrating Acquisitions: Making Corporate Marriages Work*, New York 1983.

Zäpfel, G., *Strategisches Produktions-Management*, Berlin, New York 1989.

Zeilinger, P., Just-in-Time – Ein ganzheitliches Konzept zur Erhöhung der Flexibilität und Minimierung der Bestände, in: Baumgarten, H., Bliesener, M., Falz, E., Holzinger, D. V. Rühle, H., Schäfer, H., Stabenau, H., Witten, P. (Ed.), *RKW-Handbuch Logistik, 12., ergänzende Lieferung*, Berlin 1987, Abs. 5310.

Zentes, J., Effizienzsteigerungspotentiale kooperativer Logistikketten in der Konsumgüterwirtschaft, in: Isermann, H. (Ed.), *Logistik: Beschaffung, Produktion, Distribution*, Landsberg Lech 1994, pp. 349–360.

Zhang, W.-B., *Synergetic Economics, Time and Change in Nonlinear Economies*, Stuttgart 1991.

Zibell, R. M., *Die just-in-time-Philosophie – Grundzüge*, Wirtschaftlichkeit, Berlin 1989.

Zibell, R. M., *Just-in-Time, Philosophie, Grundlagen, Wirtschaftlichkeit, Schriftenreihe der Bundesvereinigung Logistik*, Band 22, München 1990.

Zöllner, W. A., *Strategische Absatzmarktplanung*, Berlin u. a. 1990.

Part 4

How to develop digital supply chains

1   Typical paths of supply chain evolution

Supply chain development is the qualification of structural changes over time. It is an integrated part of the development of the company and is ultimately expressed in the fitness of supply chains, especially in the development and maintenance of success potentials (in the following: Bleicher 1992; Göpfert/ Wehberg 1996; Wehberg 1994).

1.1   Trend-sonar digital supply chains

Supply chain development is characterized by its dynamic nature. It offers managers an important orientation aid, especially in turbulent environments. In this respect, it can be understood as the reference point for supply chain management. To the extent that the supply chains aims at a certain development through its own addition, which means it tries to develop itself, supply chain development takes on an object character. It is then the result of *innovation* efforts and underlines the autonomous character of supply chain management. Companies that are pioneers in the implementation of digital supply chains take on a certain market maker function and set new standards in competition.

If, on the other hand, a supply chain is confronted with an obligation to adapt, the development becomes a regulator of supply chain management (similar to Kirsch/Esser/Gabele 1979). In this case, the company is a market taker and must adopt new standards in order to keep pace with the competition. The fact that the development of a supply chain is only "feasible to a limited extent" or cannot be completely mastered repeatedly results in deviations between the actual and desired development of a supply chain and thus in adjustment requirements. Overall, supply chain development is therefore a *co-evolutionary* process, i.e. supply chains and surrounding systems develop together.

Trends such as *digitalization*, which have a significant influence on the supply chain of the future, are a trigger for its development. For the practitioner it is not sufficient to understand new developments at a high aggregation level as a megatrend. In order to assess the influence of a trend and, if necessary,

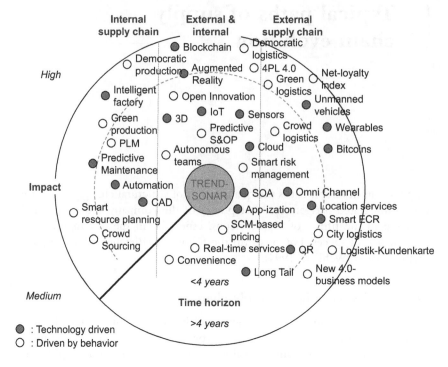

Figure 1.1 Trend sonar (similar to Bubner et al. 2014)

derive options for action, a more differentiated discussion is required at the level of concrete technological and behavioural trends. The latter can result from the behaviour of market participants or – more generally – from social behaviour. The *trend sonar* presented in Figure 1.1 provides an example of selected supply chain trends in the course of the fourth industrial revolution (see also the trend radar by Bubner et al. 2014). The sonar looks, so to speak, beneath the surface of the water in order to detect not only the tip of the iceberg, which is the obvious. Even a captain needs detailed information about the best way to navigate his ship in order not to be shipwrecked, to use this metaphor. Examples of individual waymarks or trends make the discussion tangible:

- *4PL 4.0*: The EU logistics project aims to improve the interoperability of logistics companies of various sizes and the competitiveness of Central European logistics hubs.
- *Real-time services*: Agheera offers innovative sensor technology and portal solutions for real-time tracking of shipments.

- *City logistics*: The Dutch inland-city service offers urban consolidation centres in 15 cities.
- *Omnichannel*: The service provider Hointer combines real with virtual shopping experiences through the on-site use of eTags with personalized content.
- *Crowd logistics*: DHL MyWays connects individuals for last mile delivery.

Trend analysis in the form of the trend sonar provides a basis for any discussion on the development of supply chains (Figure 1.2). Such discussion typically has to be sector and company specific because the influence of certain trends always has an individual character. And it provides the basis for concrete innovations, just because shaping the future requires an alternation of change and stabilization. Corporate supply chain managers must ask themselves how they can effectively organize suitable *scouting* of new trends if they do not want to be surprised by one or the other supply chain innovation. Especially in times of digitalization, supply chain development is a question of innovation with regard to individual processes, operations and business models.

As already mentioned, it can be assumed that change and stability cycles alternate in the course of supply chain development. This does not mean that the character of a digital supply chain is episodic. Rather, a development in the direction of a digital supply chain will take place in batches with *stabilizing intermediate phases*, each of which corresponds to a higher order. The change towards effective, market-driven structures and the efficiency-enhancing stabilization typically alternate.

Before such an interplay of a supply chain between stability and change orientation is to be examined in more detail, it seems appropriate to first answer the question of whether there are any *ideal-typical development paths* at all in which such a system behaviour of supply chains moves – paths, in other words, that supply chains repeatedly follow in an exemplary manner. The knowledge of such dynamic patterns offers a "conceptual overall view" (Kirsch/Esser/Gabele 1979) for the treading of existing paths, but also for the creation of new development paths. A prerequisite for the invention of new development possibilities, however, is the ability to engage in a corresponding *fundamental critique* (Kirsch/Esser/Gabele 1979), which characterizes the questioning of prevailing contexts. This requires problem views of supply chain management and confrontation with alternative contexts. What do these development paths look like now? In other words, which phases can be used to describe supply chain development? It will be explained in the following in its economic and technological dimension (for the dimensioning of logistics see Wehberg 1997).

1.2   Market development and supply chain evolution

The phases of the economically induced supply chain development can be illustrated by following Bleicher's model for corporate development (Göpfert 2013; Wehberg 1997). It is also conceivable, however, to make other life cycle

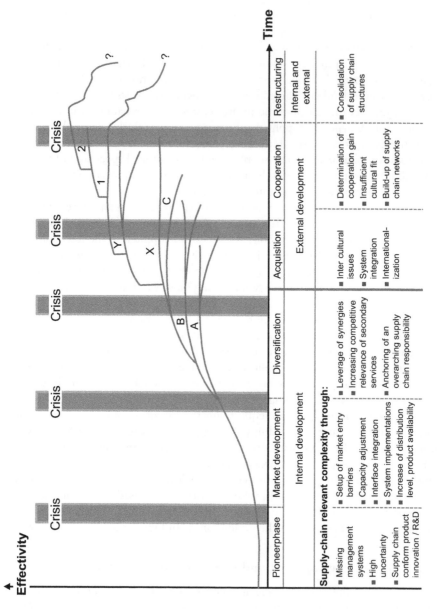

Figure 1.2 Phases of supply chain development (based on Bleicher 1992, changed and completed)

concepts "fruitful" for modelling supply chain development. Pümpin and Prange (1991) offer here a systematic overview of the models of corporate development that can be found in the literature. If we now take up the construction of Bleicher, we can sketch an ideal-typical supply chain development divided into *six phases*, which is shown in Figure 1.2 in its overall view (Bleicher 1991; Wehberg 1994).

In the *pioneering phase*, the development of the company is based on an innovation. The way the company thinks and behaves is therefore strongly influenced by the inventor, who is often identical with the owner (continued by Pümpin/Prange 1991). And also the employees of supply chain management are fixed on the model of the pioneer company. The service repertoire concentrates on a market niche or on a relatively narrow sales program for which new logistics channels have to be established. Success is measured primarily by technological and market parameters rather than financial ones. Technical start-up problems, for example, of packaging machines, can stand in the way of high supply chain efficiency. In addition, due to the absence of management systems, the operational process is controlled primarily through on-site information, personal instructions and improvisation. Information logistics is accordingly isolated. Furthermore, the often weak capital resources of pioneer companies result in the particular necessity that supply chains, especially through appropriate postponement strategies and the reduction of inventories, contributes to the reduction of capital tie-up. Furthermore, due to the high risk appetite and insecurity of the pioneer business, the supply chain structures must be planned open to use (Wehberg 1994), which means they should be able to offer a rather broad range of services and sufficient capacity reserves.

As the volume of services increased, the improvising behaviour of the multinational company was increasingly unable to meet the supply chain requirements. The integration of the flows of goods and their stronger orientation towards market events are becoming the focus of interest here. The transition from the pioneer phase to the market development phase in logistics is particularly likely to be marked by the following *signs of crisis*: Inadequate competence of supply chain management, non-existent technical systems of information logistics, technologies that have not been tried and tested to a great extent, overstraining of capacities through reworking, flow structures that have not been adapted to the needs of the process because they have evolved over time, as well as logistical inadequacy of product characteristics. The aim of the company in such a situation must be to create the economic conditions for handling supply chain problems through the broader diffusion of its product.

In the course of the *market development phase*, the company opens up broader customer groups, which go far beyond the originally worked market niche. The buying of further owners, which is often accompanied by growth, can justify a corporate culture that is now less focused on a single person. In order to secure the company's growth, barriers to market entry must be created. Logistics-induced barriers to entry can result, for example, from the occupation of certain distribution channels through exclusion contracts with sales agents. The realization of a price advantage within the framework of penetration strategies also offers corresponding starting points. The capacity adjustment of logistics resources primarily involves the specialization of the range of services with simultaneous flexibilization of the application potentials (as to the resource strategy of Logistik Wehberg 1994). Solution-oriented learning strategies are used for this purpose. Only product changes, the main cause of which is to be seen in the attempt to further differentiate oneself from imitating competitors, counteract the specialization of the service spectrum. The capacity adjustment in the supply chain is also aimed at preventing losses in market share due to inadequate readiness to deliver. It is thus the central bottleneck factor for the company.

In order to counter the risk of the top management being overburdened by operational activities, it is particularly incumbent on the cross-divisional function of supply chain management to coordinate the interfaces with the functional organization typical of a growth company. Due to the increasing size of the company, the coordination of performance activities is increasingly determined by programs and plans rather than by personal instructions. The *crisis potential of growing companies* is much smaller than that of pioneering companies. Nevertheless, mistakes in adapting to possible growth, for example through the realization of so-called lost sales, can offer the competition opportunities for market entry and thus jeopardize the development of the company as a whole. In addition, the development of logistical overcapacities (for the use of experience effects) as well as the neglect of new success potentials hold a high crisis potential of the market development phase, which introduces the diversification phase.

In the *diversification phase*, the company or logistics applies its previous experience and know-how to new technological and/or market areas in order to exploit synergies in the further development of the company and to create a risk balance between the areas of application that arise. In supply chain management, examples are the transfer of knowledge from supply logistics to waste logistics and the implementation of supply chain principles in research and development. If fields of application are developed that do not show any relationship to the previous ones, the new self-image must be incorporated into the philosophy of supply chain management or the company. The differentiation of the company in terms of performance policy can be seen not only in the diversification of primary benefits in kind but also in the corresponding refinement of secondary logistics services. If one considers that the company's product offerings in this life cycle phase are largely homogeneous in relation to the competition, it is precisely the differentiation of logistics services that offers opportunities for profiling in competition. Delivery service and environmental compatibility in particular should be mentioned in the first place. Although digital supply chain can, in principle, play a role in any other phase, it is therefore particularly relevant in diversification. In such a situation, the development of a supply chain tends towards self-controlled, flexible structures in which the synergy of supply chain activities, such as the bundling of goods flows or the realization of paired transports, must be taken into account by decentralizing and self-coordination.

Above all, the *crisis potential of diversifying activities* lies in the lack of realization of synergies between the existing and newly added logistics services, but also other corporate functions. The higher order of digital supply chains, for example, must lead to concrete customer and efficiency advantages for the company in order to be sustainable. Simply being more complex, more flexible and technologically up to date has no value for the company. The ideal way to manoeuvre out of such crises is to develop external opportunities, which means to exploit the potential of other companies through appropriate acquisitions or cooperations.

The *acquisition*, i.e. the takeover of companies, represents a first opportunity for the external development of a company or supply chain in particular. If the company in question sees the takeover not only as a financial investment object but also as an attempt to supplement its own portfolio of services, regions and resources with the acquired business, the extent to which synergies can be exploited depends to a large extent on the extent to which the parties concerned are compatible with each other in the sense of a committed reorientation. Particularly in the case of mergers, the corporate cultures that have grown differently must be brought closer together and the new ways of thinking and behaving must be stabilized. With regard to the supply chain subculture, the core of such an acculturation can lie in the harmonization of different competence levels. Possibly, for example, in the context of the takeover of Rolls-Royce by the BMW Group, the British advanced supply chain expert had to be introduced to the Bavarian supply chain professional. Depending on the degree of integration sought between the acquired and the parent company, the technical supply chain systems will also have to be aligned. The possible *crisis potential of acquisition efforts* thus lies above all in a lack of integration. In order to overcome the crisis – true to the motto "if you can't beat him join him" – a cooperation relationship can be entered into.

Similar to acquisitions, *cooperations* also aim to complement the service, regional and resource portfolios appropriately. However, less adjustment pressure can be exerted on a cooperating company than on an acquired one, so that within the framework of the cooperation phase there is considerably less "compulsion" to realize a cultural fit. In the cooperation phase, supply chain management tends to change-oriented behaviour patterns, especially if the gain in cooperation results from the synergies of flexible network structures. However, management profiles that are also geared to change are also necessary if the cooperation is to be regarded as having failed. In this case, supply chain management is confronted with a complete reorientation or restructuring of the normative, strategic and operational areas in order to enable their further development.

Finally, during the *restructuring phase*, supply chain management is attempting to open up new options for its development and for the development of the company in general – virtually by jumping into one of the aforementioned phases. If the company does not succeed in tapping new potential through appropriate restructuring, its existence will be endangered. In the course of an external "development", the company in question may then be taken over by others.

1.3 Technology development and supply chain evolution

Technology-induced supply chain development characterizes the qualification of the technologies used in supply chains over time. It is the result of technological progress and innovation strategies in supply chains in particular. In order to understand the dynamics of supply chain–relevant technologies, their development can be described using the S-curve concept known from innovation research (Krubasik 1988; in conjunction with Wehberg 1994). The starting point of this concept is the consideration that for every technology used in supply chains and the services provided with it there are certain performance limits that cannot be overcome. Once this limit has been reached, there is no further development, i.e. improvement, in all supply chain management efforts, unless the technology concerned is replaced by a new, more efficient one. For supply chain management it is therefore important to recognize the *weak signals of possible replacement technologies* from the corporate environment at an early stage and to transfer them into the company's own supply chain in good time. Substitution technology can, however, also be the product of the company's own innovation efforts.

The ideal-typical course of technology development describes a path from pacemaker to key to basic technologies. Basic technologies mark the end of the *S-curve*. They are therefore particularly endangered by new key technologies. The latter are characterized by high competition relevance because they are not yet standard, but on the other hand, unlike pacemaker technologies, they already offer a high performance potential. Digital supply chains and the technologies associated with it (cyberphysical systems, clouds, predictive data analysis, etc.) are key for supply chain development in this sense. Their *degree of maturity from a technological point of view* can also be classified on the basis of the following levels, which also correspond to the competence types presented in the chapter on learning strategy (similar to acatech 2015; Wehberg 1997):

- *Pre-mature*: No use of cyberphysical systems or similar in the supply chain.
- *Digitally interested*: Selected features like configuration and maintenance of the supply chain are digitally enabled.
- *Digital beginner*: Condition-based tracking provides supply chain transparency.
- *Digitally forward*: Supply chain analysis and foresight offer selected benefits.
- *Digital professional*: Integration into the core business of an end-to-end supply chain.
- *Post-digital*: Supply chain facilitates intelligent services and business models.

As already mentioned, digital supply chains should by no means be limited to technological dimension. The use of new technologies is a necessary prerequisite because it enables decentralized control and self-coordination. The effective use of digital supply chains also requires a holistic, coherent overall concept that takes all other dimensions of supply chain development into account. In connection with the technology life cycle, Bauernhansl (2014), for example, also proposes the *product, factory and order life cycle* as relevant classification criteria for the chronological sequence.

Overall, the description of the supply chain development makes it clear that it may well take on a life of its own in relation to the company's development, or even become the *motor for the company's development*. For example, supply chain management can enter into cooperative obligations to establish a network, while the company as a whole is characterized by growth phenomena. The presented ideal type of supply chain development as an integrated part of company evolution must therefore always be critically questioned. It must not restrict the creativity of supply chain management in the search for new development paths.

1.4   New business models and digital supply chains

The discussion of aforementioned maturity levels shows that new business models prove the highest maturity and offer the largest potential. Supply chain management itself can be subject to such new business model development if logistics is the core business of the company or logistics service provider. On the other hand, digital supply chains are a key enabler for new business models in the manufacturing industry. In both cases a comprehensive journey for a business-led technology transformation is vital for the success of the digitalization strategy of the company, combining business and technology perspectives.

Regardless of who has the best prerequisites to establish themselves as a post-digital leader and which functions are affected, digital business models are generally characterized by (some of) the following *key characteristics* (Anderson 2007, 2012; Reichwald/Piller 2009; Wehberg 2015), which can also apply to digital supply chains:

- *LaaS*: Logistics as a service has its intelligence in the cloud, so that the control algorithms are not revealed by its sole use.
- *Combination of software and hardware*: Proprietary hardware solutions can represent market-entry barriers that support the achievement of critical sizes, for example, corresponding service platforms.
- *Knowledge as new core*: Through "sharing" and accumulation of empirical knowledge, comparative competitive advantages (e.g. USP – Unique Selling Proposition) are created, not necessarily through patents. Knowledge is only created through the application of the right algorithms, i.e. not through the accumulation of data itself.
- *Long tail*: Logistics for niche products in the sense of Anderson (2007) can in sum be profitable business. The definition of the niche can arise from the needs of the primary (product) and/or secondary service (logistics) (for details the triple-long-tail strategy see Wehberg 2015).
- *B2B follows B2C*: Examples for suitable business models come in particular from the B2C sector, because here data security is less problematic and the variety of ideas broader, so that appropriate scouting of ideas makes sense.

In the area of digital business model innovations, the B2B area follows the B2C area. At the same time, many B2C business models are still looking for their economic basis. An economic benefit in the B2B area is often more likely to be realized, which also explains the disproportionate growth of this area.

• *Democratization of logistics*: In extreme cases, logistics solutions can be offered for everyone, which means the "Maker" initiative by Anderson (2012) can be transferred from production (e.g. 3D) to the supply chain function (e.g. crowd supply chain management), including the sales function (e.g. Omnichannel) and so-called open innovations in the sense of Reichwald and Piller (2009).

• *Freemium*: The market penetration of many new digital business models is driven by the fact that certain basic services are offered free of charge, while additional services with additional benefits are invoiced.

Specifically, new business models in the logistics service provider market are likely to be driven both internally, which means by participants in the logistics market, and externally, i.e. by market convergence. Practice will show in the coming years which models will prove to be particularly competitive.

1.5   LogTechs – start-ups in the logistics service provider market

Over the course of the last five years there has been a significant push of supply chain management and logistics related to the market, so-called LogTechs. For decades the *logistics industry* has been dominated by giants such as UPS, FedEx and Deutsche Post DHL. These players typically have a proven, holistic offering that covers a variety of integrated services along the global supply chain. In addition, they regularly act as an integrator that accumulates resources, capabilities, and technologies to provide comprehensive solutions to customers. As a result, they now house a huge number of employees globally, high market shares and significant market capitalization. Economies of scale – secured via scaled assets – has been a key competitive advantage that is typically raising large entry barriers to new players in the market. This is changing now (hereto and in the following Buchholz/Wehberg/Zimmermann 2017).

1.5.1   Asset-light business models

Technological advances, increasing levels of connectivity, industry convergence and digitalization are disrupting the logistics service market. Emerging Log-Techs are leveraging these trends and often have an Internet of things (IoT), analytics or digital-related background. Their business model typically builds upon an agile, asset-light, technology-driven backbone, allowing them to reach scale and often even grow exponentially with a very lean infrastructure and at limited risk. Uber and AirBnB are two prominent examples that illustrate that exponential growth is not tied to the amount of capital. This principle seemingly starts to extend to industries such as the logistics service market as well.

At the same time, *customer expectations* in the logistics service market are continuously on the rise – convenience becomes key. Ever faster delivery times, ongoing price optimization and higher flexibility in terms of modes, pickup locations or specific delivery slots are expected. This is driving demand for innovative and specialized solutions, especially in the urban delivery and medium-haul market. Young LogTechs often can take better advantage of their lean structure and are coming up highly targeted. Such start-ups often are innovative and customized supply chain firms compared to their more traditional peers, which sometimes lack the flexibility and speed in responding quickly to changing dynamics and new technology.

Over the last ten years, there has been a significant increase in the number of LogTechs. Correspondingly, the amount of investment deals and related company valuations has been raising. For example, more than US $5 billion in *venture capital* was invested in LogTechs in 2016.

Recent surveys of LogTechs reveal that three quarters of those surveyed had been founded only within the last five years. The majority are located in *North America*, along the typical start-up clusters in Silicon Valley, New York, Atlanta and Chicago. About one third are based in Europe, the Middle East or Africa. Within this region, *Germany* can be seen as key market. A number of LogTechs have been founded in the country over the past ten years in cities like Berlin, Munich, Cologne and Hamburg. The companies' average headcount ranges between 50 and 100 employees.

The go-to-market strategy of LogTechs often represents an "unbundling" of supply chain services. Although a number of LogTechs provide services across multiple customer segments, the majority take a much more *focused approach* to offerings and concentrate on providing a very specialized type of service. This is a major difference to the more integrated business models of traditional logistics service providers. Nonetheless, large parts of the physical transport of goods remain with established players, as they own the assets required to execute deliveries. LogTechs thus own and develop an increasing share of the customer interaction, rather than disrupting the entire value chain at once.

Let's look at some examples: A large number of LogTechs focus on freight brokerage, last mile delivery, convenient solutions and supply chain analytics. A few examples will illustrate their innovative, very distinct offerings. Companies like *Flexport, Haven* and *Roadie* operate platforms for price comparison and booking services for freight shipments. LogTechs such as *Postmates, Flirtey* and *Rickshaw* focus on short-distance transport in metropolitan areas. Their offering is to secure the urban logistics within a few hours via either courier, drone or self-driving robotic vehicles. *InstaFreight, Shyp* and *Swapbox* provide combined easy-to-use services including pick-up, packing, labelling and warehousing. This is often part of an e-commerce solution. Route optimization, tracking of shipments and other analytics belong to the offering of firms like *Routific, Supply Vision* and *OptimoRoute*.

Most of these LogTechs do have a digital footprint with elements of IoT, connectivity, analytics, mobile apps or easy-to-use web portals. They typically have three major *advantages* compared to their more traditional peers:

- LogTechs operate with *asset-light* or in some cases asset-zero infrastructure and corresponding business models. Making use of new technologies, they challenge historic assumptions of the logistics market.
- While creating online marketplaces, interfaces and dashboards, they effectively connect the demand with the supply side. Hereby they gain *ownership of the customer interfaces* via customer data, and further supply chain transparency.
- Eventually, their *post-digital* character more naturally embraces lean structures and a resilient working style. This leads to a very high degree of agility and flexibility when working with customers and serving customer needs.

1.5.2 *Typical LogTech clusters*

Analyzing a number of LogTechs enables identification of typical clusters of business models and customer segments. A significant proportion of LogTechs focus on providing on-demand *brokerage platforms*, single marketplaces or bundles of multiple marketplaces. These typically enable customers in bidding and bargaining for the best option in terms of transportation modes, etc. An example that very well illustrates this cluster is the firm Transfix. It provides a brokerage platform that facilitates smaller logistics companies and individual truck drivers to offer free capacities on a digital marketplace. The most significant benefit brokers or aggregators typically provide is to create greater, real-time transparency with respect to rates and logistics options along the long tail of demand and supply.

Another significant cluster of LogTechs provides *supply chain analytics*, ranging from descriptive analytics (e.g. better visualization of data), KPIs and dashboards towards advanced analytics solutions. ShipHawk, for example, promises to enhance buyer experience, logistics automation and shipping intelligence. This is managed by summarizing more than 200 delivery options and rates in a cloud solution. The company analyzes spend and shipping performance by carrier to give advice on how to optimize packaging strategies and profitability. LogTechs in the segment of analysts typically focus on increased transparency, simplified workflows and better decision making for customers to handle their orders.

A third cluster of LogTech business models is the *niche player*. These firms usually provide a one-stop-shop solution for selective customer segments or within a limited regional coverage (often focused on major metropols). Shyp, as example, integrates its solution into customers' fulfilment operations. It provides carrier comparison services, labelling printing, pickup and packaging support that can be integrated into existing e-commerce solutions. The company's pickup and packaging offering concentrates on major cities in the US. Pricing models change based on the number of shipped items per month.

Such niche operators provide an increased level of flexibility in payment modes (e.g. switching on-demand or subscription models) and response cycles towards changing customer needs.

Last but not least, a fourth business model cluster of LogTechs acts as *technology provider*. Firms in this space typically develop and market technology that bridges a gap between traditional customers and logistics service providers. Cardrops is one example company of this kind that sells and installs small hardware devices in an end-user's car. The technology allows logistics partners to remotely open a car's trunk and deposit deliveries. Moreover, the start-up collects mobility data through their device and conducts analytics in order to improve delivery slots and locations over time. Companies in this cluster are innovators at the very heart of the industry. They target at holistically disrupting the modes of transportation or types of packaging and improve the customer journey or cost efficiency.

The climbing number of agile LogTechs might easily be perceived as a threat by established players as well as overwhelm customers with the sheer number of new names and offerings. Nonetheless, upcoming LogTechs equally offers plenty opportunity to both groups alike. Established logistics service providers as well as industry firms can benefit from this development by *leveraging new business models* via proper collaboration, incubation, investments and acquisitions.

Beyond the modelling of the life cycle phases of the various logistics dimensions, it can be assumed that there are generalized, i.e. phase-independent characteristics, for supply chain development. In the following, these are to be worked out against the background of its evolutionary theoretical foundations.

2　Key principles of supply chain evolution

For the foundation of the dynamics of supply chains, one can refer to corresponding approaches of organizational theory. These approaches suggest design principles that offer assistance to handling complex supply chain phenomena and digital supply chains in particular. All approaches have in common the assumption of limited information and processing capacity as well as "blindness" in that they cannot be planned synoptically.

2.1　Perspectives of organizational theory

2.1.1　Industry perspective

One approach to describe, explain and shape the structural dynamics of industries, i.e. entire classes of organizations, is the population ecology approach (Hannan/Freeman 1977). The most important *representatives* of this approach include Hannan and Freeman as well as Aldrich, Kaufman and McKelvey. These authors are particularly concerned with transferring the mechanisms and taxonomy of the evolution of biological systems to social structures (in the following, for example, Semmel 1984 and McKelvey 1982).

The central concept is the *population*. It is a polythetic group of organizations that have largely similar basic skills, so-called comps, to ensure their existence. The sum of all comps of an organization indicates the "genotype". The similarity of *genotypes* stems from the fact that all the members of a population fall back on a common repertoire of population-specific knowledge and skills, which is also known as the *compool*. From the common source of basic skills, similar appearances, i.e. structural forms of the organizations of a population, called *phenotypes*, regularly follow. The population-specific organization can therefore be understood from two different perspectives, on the one hand by describing the phenotypic forms of expression and the genotypic conditions that explain them on the other.

In order to understand the long-term change of organizations in a population, it must now be taken into account that both phenotypes and genotypes are influenced by their environment. The *environment* is to be understood as a set of external forces that impose constraints on an individual organization or a population and are outside its ability to influence them (McKelvey 1982). In interaction with the environment of individual organizations, a change in the phenotypes and genotypes of a population occurs. The *mechanisms* include, in particular, variation, selection and preservation (Aldrich 1979; Hannan/Freeman 1977; Kaufman 1975; McKelvey 1982, and others).

The application of population-ecological fundamentals to supply chain management leads to the following picture: The consideration of entire classes of logistics systems is in the foreground here, for example, to the CEP services market. From a population-ecological point of view, all logistics-related competences together characterize the pool of the population. The development of supply chains is attributed above all to the evolution of its basic skills (genotypic concept of supply chain) and structural forms (phenotypic concept of supply chain). This also and especially applies to digital supply chains. For example, the diversity of supply chain variants takes into account the need for resilience, which is derived from the *inertia* of supply chain structures. In many cases such structures cannot adjust as fast as environmental changes occur (for further analogies see Wehberg 1997).

Population ecology records the development of entire industries. The logistics sector will make use of the opportunities offered by Logistics 4.0 and the new business models and services associated with it, as the following case illustrates.

Project example: smart logistics services (acatech 2015, translated)

The economic environment of internationally operating seaports is characterized by global competition, high cost pressure and great dynamism with regard to the actors to be involved. The pressure on the port infrastructure is growing (increasing freight volumes with little scope for physical expansion).

Individual players use smart processes and partial infrastructures, but there is a lack of optimization of the overall system. The cooperation of the actors, such as port management, shipping companies, operators of container terminals, logistics network operators, forwarders and railway companies takes place only on a bilateral basis. The most important drivers for an increase in efficiency and effectiveness on the basis of intelligent, data-based networking are:

- Inefficiency in transport operations due to long downtimes of vehicles in port
- Strong increase in traffic with limited infrastructure growth (port can only grow geographically to a limited extent)
- Demand for intelligent goods and order tracking in global supply chains
- The need to link goods with traffic flows in supra-local transport infrastructures

- Increasing importance of smooth and time-saving container handling
- So far only limited picture of the traffic and infrastructure situation for decisions (marketplace/eco-system) . . . .

A synergetically designed Smart Services system designed for the interaction of port operations in a dynamic business network contributes to the overall optimization of port infrastructure utilization. The key performance indicators (KPIs) of the individual operations can be mapped, the port eco-system as a whole can be improved and economic benefits can be generated.

Smart Services enable port operators, service providers and transport and logistics companies to place their own transport orders in real time, the aim is to monitor media and routes in order to transport goods more efficiently and safely and, as a result, to increase the satisfaction of all parties involved, in particular end customers.

The implementation of Smart Services takes place through the processing of own, external and reporting data. Data protection requirements are controlled by access regulations and personal characteristics. There are different data providers depending on the seaport. Local business partners for Smart Services are taken into account by an activation and deactivation concept and can be integrated as required. Participating business partners and authorities receive a real-time and forward-looking view of the respective status of the infrastructure used (roads, bridges, waterways) and the resulting resource requirements. Marketplace mechanisms are used to lay the foundation for the self-sustaining expansion of this approach into a port eco-system that includes other related businesses. IT-technically, functions will be combined that are currently offered in isolated web portals and smart device apps. They are easy to use for all players as software "as a service" offerings. Each participant can share information and services with the other network participants at flexibly definable conditions and benefit from them. Through a smoother processing of traffic and goods flows in the port and beyond, inter- and multi-modal logistics chains can be closed in a service-oriented way, thus enabling further innovative business models.

The economic eco-system in seaports is characterized by different actors whose interaction is necessary in order to achieve efficiency gains in container handling and traffic flow. In the value creation network, the seaport operator assumes the task of port management. He is responsible for official matters, port communication, water and land infrastructure, road and bridge network as well as the safety of ship traffic and real estate management.

Other important roles are: Container terminal operators . . ., hauliers . . ., parking providers . . ., business network operators. . . .

The overall optimization of logistics processes (from port logistics to the destination of the transported goods) is the common benefit for all players (also in Smart Cities/Smart Countries). It is an overall logistics concept that can be transferred and extended to any logistics hub, such as airports or freight stations, in addition to seaports. The decisive factor is that the individual value propositions are sufficiently relevant for each actor; only if all actors along the transport chain use the Smart Services and contribute their share of the required data can the overall benefit be achieved. A gradual expansion based on the principle of a service marketplace will continuously create new added value for the various user groups.

2.1.2 Corporate perspective

In contrast to population ecology, the so-called *organizational process approach* brings together a group of scientists who, in the context of their numerous publications, have endeavoured to shed light on the processes that take place within organizations by transferring evolutionary theoretical findings (in the following, Semmel 1984; Wehberg 1997). It therefore directs its efforts above all to the level of the individual enterprise. This group includes Bigelow, Röpke and Zammuto, but also Dyllick and other organizational theorists.

At the centre of the organizational process approach is the effort to gain the deepest possible understanding of the three mechanisms of evolution within goal-oriented social systems. A peculiarity of this approach is that it does not want to understand the evolutionary phenomenon to such an extent that it is restricted to certain facts, like the genotypes and phenotypes of a population. Thus, it basically includes all levels within a factual-hierarchical organizational system, for example, the organization as a whole, subsystems, etc. (similar to Semmel 1984). Instead of the term hierarchy, the term *recursion* is also used if the different hierarchical levels of a system assume they are similar with regard to certain structural properties (Bleicher 1995).

The integration of the organizational process approach and supply chain management leads to a focus on populations of variants, which can also address certain behaviours (such as disposition practices, warehousing principles), ideas (process innovations) and other artifacts of individual supply chains.

The inclusion of the respective higher level in the objective hierarchy, for example, the question of how rush orders are integrated into the transport and production control of the other supply or production program, reveals the emergent characteristics (Dyllick 1982; Röpke 1977) of the considered supply chain (sub)system, which only arise through interaction with other (sub)systems. In contrast to function logistics, the networking of supply chain relationships is therefore not considered ex post, but through the interplay of selection, variation and preservation. Coordination in this sense means *co-evolution* of the "main strands" of logistic-relevant change processes, more precisely, the design of mechanisms for such a joint development. Due to its secondary performance character of supply chain management in industry and trade, particular attention must be paid to the relationship between primary and secondary services (e.g. logistics-oriented product design vs. product-oriented logistics design).

The advantages of an objective hierarchy of supply chains, which also explains its widespread use, can be illustrated by the example of two suppliers of turn signal systems for the automotive industry, *Blinki* and *Leuchti* (Simon 1978). Both of them produce turn signal systems, each consisting of 1000 individual parts. Leuchti assembles his turn signal systems piece by piece. If he wants to take a break or is disturbed, he has to start all over again. In contrast, Blinki assembles ten parts into a subsystem. In a second step, he constructs another subgroup out of ten of these subsystems. Blinki's turn signal system consists of ten such subgroups. In the worst case, Blinki has nine steps to recover in the event of an interruption. Assuming that a fault occurs in 100 steps, Leuchti needs about 4000 times more time to build a system. When Blinki works one day, it takes Leuchti 11 years to produce the same quantity. According to Dyllick (1982, translated):

> This time difference shows the difference in the performance of the hierarchical method. It is based on the effect that the existence of stable intermediate forms has on the evolution of complex forms. By shortening the "stride length" of progress, the probability of finding successful further developments is increased and the extent of failure is limited.

In this sense, hierarchical structures that "grow" slowly over time and are typically only partially modified instead of being completely rebuilt offer the greatest opportunities for the development of digital supply chains.

The objective hierarchization of logistics also finds its expression in concepts such as modular sourcing (by Eicke/Femerling 1991), modular factory (Wildemann 1994), fractal factory (Warnecke 1992), modular principle, modular packaging, modularization of supply chains (Pfohl 1994) and others. It will often also play an important role in digital supply chains. And it explains why borrowed and *incremental variations* are particularly suitable for creating complex relationship in supply chains. It is probably precisely these two forms of variation that take advantage of hierarchization. Incremental variations find their expression in praxi, among others, in the kaizen concept (Imai 1993). The idea of a step-by-step improvement in the sense of kaizen contrasts with revolutionary innovation in the form of an original variation. The realization of borrowed variations can be favoured in particular by the instrument of benchmarking (such as Camp 1989; Sander/Brackmann 1995; Walleck/O'Halloran/Leader 1991). In the course of digital supply chains, engineering is supported by suitable assistance systems and the availability of relevant data and their correlations (Vogel-Heuser 2014).

At this point the necessity of a holistic coordination of the selection of development mechanisms becomes clear. For the variation as well as for the selection and preservation there are numerous *mechanisms* available which have to be selected depending on the situation and have to be driven coherently to each other (Figure 2.1).

Type	Evolution mechanisms		
	Selection	**Retention**	**Variation**

Supply chain capabilities	• Horizontal career
	• Talent management
	• Scoring models
	• Senior hires
	  Recruiting
	• IT testing
		• MBO: Efficiency
		  targets
		• Learning of
		  solutions
		• Algorithms
		• SC academy
			• MBO: Market
			  targets
			• Learning of new
			  capabilities
			• Crowd-/
			  outsourcing

Supply chain structures	• Field tests/piloting
	• Innovation funnel
	• Employee
	  suggestion scheme
	• Internal competition
		• Performance mgt.
		• Guidelines/
		  procedures
		• Certification/
		  standards
		• Best practices
			• Benchmarking
			• Kaizen
			• (Open) innovation
			• Multi-channel
			• Change
			  management

Figure 2.1 Selected evolution mechanisms of supply chains

Triggered by the increasing need for resilience in digital supply chains, the focus is shifting from execution to (meta-)management, from control algorithms to the adaptation of these through *meta-algorithms* and from operative content to normative, such as anchoring the desired competitive advantage in the supply chain philosophy. Due to their complexity-generating "power", the latter are of great importance for integration.

The following case on *innovation management* shows how the evolution mechanisms of the organizational process approach can be implemented quite practically. The core element is the innovation funnel, which produces, evaluates, selects and, if necessary, introduces or preserves new variants. Innovation management is a core component of every digital supply chain.

Project example: Innovation management for supply chains

Initial situation: A company in the automotive supply industry has always had supply chain management in mind as a competitive factor. The discussion about the possibilities of Industry 4.0 motivated the company to also play a leading role in digital supply chains. The company had already implemented a number of smaller use cases. Due to technological developments in the field of cyberphysical applications and the ongoing gains in experience with corresponding operating models, however, the company could not be sure that it would continue to be at the cutting edge of technology in the future.

Objective: The aim of the initiative was to set up a process to keep the company up to date in connection with the Industry 4.0 discussion and digital supply chain in particular, to discover new possibilities, to consider promising starting points and to position the company as a leader in the field of supply chain management. The company was aware that such a process has to integrate external sources in a comprehensive way. But also that the internal coordination for the selection and evaluation of new ideas under the heading Industry 4.0 should be structured even better.

Approach: The initiative was implemented in three phases. In a first phase, an innovation strategy "digital supply chain" was developed in the cornerstones, i.e. the development needs of supply chain management based on market and customer requirements were coordinated with the technological possibilities of digitalization. In this way, selected innovation focal points could be identified that were considered particularly relevant from the point of view of the company and from which corresponding criteria for the evaluation of new ideas or projects were derived. In the second phase, a process for the identification, evaluation, selection, development and implementation of new ideas was set up, quasi an "innovation funnel". This innovation funnel was characterized by clearly defined milestones, which support the economic efficiency and transparency of the procedure. In the third phase, the ongoing use of the innovation funnel was implemented with the involvement of customers, suppliers and other service providers and responsibility was transferred to the line. The ideas developed for innovations included new products and services as well as innovative processes and business models.

Results and digital relevance: As a result of the initiative, more than 100 ideas were collected each year, more than 20 of which were pursued in the form of feasibility studies on the topic of digital supply chains. The time-to-market, i.e. the period from idea collection to implementation, was more than halved. The so-called hit rate of innovations, i.e. the ratio of evaluated to successfully introduced ideas, was improved tenfold.

Success factors: The following two factors were decisive for the success of the initiative. On the one hand, the definition of the innovation funnel ensured that the ideas that were included for relevant impulses for further development in the sense of a digital supply chain were not limited to the logistics department. Almost all functional areas of the company, suppliers, customers and cooperation partners were integrated into the process of the innovation funnel at a suitable point. And beyond this, a broader community of experts was also involved through innovation competitions. On the other hand, the understanding of innovation was not limited to the technological dimension. Rather, innovations in processes, the operating model, external presentation, etc. were explicitly sought and promoted. Such a broad understanding of innovation allows the participants to think and go completely new ways with a lot of creativity, without being limited by existing structures and habits.

2.1.3 Self-organization and autopoiesis

The self-organization approach represents the work of a group of scientists who focus their efforts on the phenomenon of self-organization of or in targeted social systems. In contrast to the organizational process approach, the self-organization perspective increasingly turns to the biological foundations of organizational theory. Among others, the *autopoiesis theory* of the neurobiologists Maturana and Varela has a great influence here (Maturana/Varela 1980). However, self-organization research is also influenced by other natural sciences and socio-cultural evolution theory, in particular the concept of the *spontaneous formation of order* by von Hayek (1969) (Probst 1987). From a business management perspective, the self-organization approach has been developed and developed to this day primarily by two scientific circles, the *St. Gallen School* under Ulrich and the *Munich School* under Kirsch.

The idea of self-organization accentuates the fact that management's scope for exerting influence is rather limited. The development and order of an organization are largely determined by itself or by its immanent "own life" in the form of self-design and self-direction. In contrast to population ecology, which derives the deterministic moments of the evolution of organizations from their environmental conditions (environmental determinism), this is rather a system immanent lack of freedom (system determinism). This shows a certain similarity to the organizational process approach, which also focuses on internal organizational processes.

However, the phenomenon of self-organization reflects a rather *institutional* phenomenon (Kirsch 1992). This distinguishes it from the functional consideration of the approaches of organizational theory processed so far. Moreover, it is typically not a mechanistic view in the sense that it places the mechanisms of evolution, i.e. selection, variation and preservation, at the centre of its interest. Rather, it concentrates on the self-dynamics in organizations that emerge without such interventions.

Now we have to realize that self-organizing social systems always also include moments of third-party organization, the exact opposite of self-organization, i.e. there is a complementarity between the two phenomena (zu Knyphausen 1988). In this respect, organizations will always have an autopoietic and allopoietic character. An "autopoie-sis-allopoiesis-interplay" (Andrew 1981) in this sense is a constitutive characteristic of "living" or existential organizations. Kirsch (1992, translated) suspects: "Perhaps 'evolutionary management' consists (among other things) in creating 'initial conditions' in an third-party-organizing way . . . which are conducive to self-organizing processes, but also influence these processes". And Probst (1987) finally notes characteristics of self-organizing systems, which were already briefly discussed in the second and third parts of this volume.

Self-organization in supply chains now means *implementing suitable framework conditions* in the sense of the characteristics just described in order to enable and promote the "self-development" of certain desired results (in more detail Wehberg 1997). This requires a minimum of appropriate external organization of supply chain execution by supply chain management or a meta-level, respectively. In the course of digital supply chains, for example, this can affect the process of introducing new algorithms for self-management.

It turns out, however, that an increasing self-organization of supply chain management is less a question of the extent of externally imposed rules than of the way in which external interventions take place and follow the requirements of the above characteristics of self-organization (Kieser 1994). In this context, abstract regulations that take effect at the level of the norm are more likely to enable self-organization than concrete specifications that regulate the operative. In this sense, the supply chain manager – as an institution – becomes, so to speak, the *catalyst* (Malik/Probst 1981) of the development of the management system for the flow of goods. Similarly, zu Knyphausen (1988) speaks generally of "modulation". Using the example of the introduction of new control algorithms, this can mean that these are developed and applied by the company itself, but their quality is checked and approved by a third party.

For a differentiated understanding of such "catalysis", or modulation, it is advantageous to first consider system-forming and system–coupling tasks separately. The *polarization* of the system coupling between third-party and self-organization as well as the system formation between specialization and generalization then leads to a conception, as shown in Figure 2.2. Generalization and specialization, unlike self-organization or third-party organization, express a primarily functional viewpoint.

In principle, generalized supply chains can be just as organized by a third party as a specialization may be self-organized. However, it should be noted that generalization and self-organization tend to correspond to change-oriented structures and process patterns of supply chain management, whereas specialization and third-party organization correspond to stability orientation. Because the high complexity of self-organizing coupling processes probably finds the necessary *degrees of freedom* in generalized management structures, as they were approximated in the course of the third part on the basis of the change-oriented structural discussions for supply chain management (similar to Kirsch 1992). Future-oriented and extroverted supply chain cultures can even be understood as *implicit coupling patterns* (von der Oelsnitz 1995) due to their integrating character.

What does guided self-organization mean in practice? The following case offers an example of the *setting of guardrails*, in the course of which the cooperation of different units of production, delivery and sales is organized

Coordination	Change	
	Stability oriented	Complexity oriented
System building	Specialization	Generalization
System coupling	Third-party organization	Self-organization

Figure 2.2 Basic alignments as a function of change

comparatively autonomously. Supply chain management already sets the guardrails here today and pays attention to adhering to the given rules of the game along the value chain, but does not control every single order on a detailed level. The case also shows that self-organization and the setting of guardrails is not limited to the use of cyberphysical systems.

Project example: Guardrails for the supply chain organization

Initial situation: A company in the process industry is exposed to a strong commoditization of its products in competition and correspondingly shrinking margins. The organization is strongly functionally divided into the areas of purchasing, production, sales, etc. An initial analysis of the supply chain potential shows that the lack of coordination along the value creation chain leaves significant savings opportunities untapped.

Objective: In addition to mobilizing innovation activities for the company, supply chain potentials are to be addressed above all by anchoring a corresponding supply chain management function in the organization. In addition to realizing efficiency gains, the functional definition of the responsibilities between the functions has the highest priority from the management's point of view, because one does not want to "disturb" the well-rehearsed organization by introducing a new functionality. In any case, a competence wrangling is to be avoided, in the course of which nobody sees itself more responsible for arising errors in the organization. Rather, the new organization is seen as a platform to enable more efficient cooperation along the value chain in the future.

Approach: The new supply chain management function was introduced in the course of a three-stage procedure and the corresponding potentials were addressed. In the first stage, the current situation was baselined and the desired result derived from selected KPIs. This means that a business case was developed for supply chain management (as a function), which was supported by all participants. In the second stage, a draft of the future organizational structure and principles for cooperation were developed. The principles of the organization were based on a supply chain segmentation, i.e. the future rules of the game were developed separately for each supply chain model. The organizational structure was detailed on the basis of corresponding organizational charts, resource estimates and job descriptions. In the third stage, the new organization was introduced step by step, the employees were trained and the implementation of savings potential was monitored. Among other things, the new responsibilities of supply chain management were appointed, with the project manager assuming the management task of this new function in the line. Last but not least, the organizational principles were integrated as far as possible into the existing IT system, for example, into the PPDS of production and the price calculation of sales.

Results and digital relevance: As a result, the new supply chain management enabled cost savings of 12 percent and inventory reductions of up to 45 percent depending on the product areas and supply chain segments. The transition to an organization that is more closely aligned with the value chain went smoothly thanks to the introduction of rules for cooperation. The self-organizing approach helped maintain entrepreneurship and market focus in the line while improving alignment between line functions. Self-organization on the basis of organizational principles can be understood as a preliminary stage of self-organization on the basis of algorithms, i.e. an initial technical concept and the basis for a digital supply chain had been laid.

Success factors: Three factors were decisive for the successful introduction of supply chain management. First, the decentralized organizational approach helped to secure the buy-in and acceptance of the established executives. Secondly, the goal-oriented approach from the very beginning was decisive in ensuring that the project did not run the risk of being (mis) understood as a pure organizational project. And thirdly, cross-functional cooperation made it possible to realize significant improvement potential because it was not satisfied with island solutions. The relevance and extent of these potentials also supported the acceptance of the project.

2.1.4   Cybernetics

The cybernetic approach comprises the description, explanation and design of the development of organizations from the perspective of control loop theory. In addition to dealing with processes that maintain equilibrium (first-order cybernetics), it also and above all deals with *imbalances* in the sense of second-order cybernetics. With regard to the type of regulation, this means that the cybernetic approach deals not only with negative, but primarily with positive feedback in regulation systems (Sprüngli 1981). The former stabilize a desired state in the long term by preventing deviations from a certain controlled variable. They are doing so by damping them to a certain extent through negative feedback, and in a way by punishing them. Numerous structures, no matter whether in economy, society, technology etc., cannot be kept constant for a long time due to their openness and the complexity of their environment. Especially in the management of organizations, not only "punishment and damping", but also "confirmation and reward" of deviations play an important role. The latter, the positive feedback, characterizes the destabilization of systems in the form of increasing feedback loops (similar to Sabathil 1993). They lead to increasing system complexity.

Positive and negative feedback in the development context are now typically in a complementary relationship to each other; stabilizing and destabilizing moments of organizational structures always alternate. Such an interplay of feedback mechanisms can also be documented by the concept of the *equilibrium of flow* originally coined by von Bertalanffy (1953), a phenomenon to which the cybernetic approach pays special attention. Systems that can adapt their control mechanisms in this way are "adaptive control systems". A distinction must be made between "ultra-stable" and "multistable" control loops (especially Ashby 1974; Beer 1966, 1970; Krieg 1971; Pask 1972 and especially for the application of theoretical considerations of control loops in supply chain management Wehberg 1997).

One of the probably most significant design principles of the cybernetic approach is the *law of the required variety* by Ashby (1956): "only variety can destroy variety". According to this, the minimum variety of a degree of target achievement of a considered supply chain presents itself as the quotient of the variety d of an influencing environment and the variety r, which the considered supply chain can oppose to the environmental system, provided that for the considered supply chain to achieve its targets an adjustment is necessary with any changes of the environment: $o \geq d/r$. The "variety" can be understood as a measure for the concrete characteristic of the system complexity. To this extent, it may also be translated with the term "change" used in this publication and borrowed from the St. Gallen management concept. Unlike the concept of change, however, "variety" expresses a direct connection with the theoretical foundations of control loops.

The variety law can be applied both in terms of recording and handling the complexity of the supply chain. The starting point for the corresponding handling of supply chain organizations, also known as "variety engineering", is now the establishment of adequate feedback mechanisms or control systems (general Probst 1981; Schwanninger 1994). They can basically be transferred to the supply chain and are particularly interesting in connection with digital supply chains because they provide a good basis for the development of algorithms or meta-algorithms, respectively. In particular, the digital twin of a supply chain is essentially a control loop.

However, it is not only the number of supply chain–relevant variables themselves (quantitative dimension) that determines the manageability or controllability of the overall system. Rather, it also depends on the concrete content of the change possibilities (qualitative dimension). The respective forms of appearance of the supply chain and the surrounding system must fit together in terms of content. It should also be noted that absolute control of a supply chain is impossible in the majority of cases because the variety of the surrounding system is too great (in general Luhmann 1990). It can also be economically viable to limit the variety of a supply chain (differently e.g. Kieser 1995). Here, the (opportunity) costs of setting up a variety are contrasted with the gains in resilience (Wehberg 1994). The latter efficiency considerations then stand in the way of the highest possible effectiveness of supply chains. In order to solve this tradeoff, therefore, no minimum, but rather an appropriate variety gap and a (probably) satisfactory level of effectiveness should be striven for. At the same time, the digital supply chain opens up the possibility of realizing such a satisfactory fit at a higher (effectiveness) level.

2.2 Integration of perspectives and key design principles

Most of the design perspectives just discussed are not related to each other in any way. Rather, they usually complement each other. For example, it may be useful to design the (meta-)evolution of development mechanisms (organizational process approach) in a largely self-organizing way (self-organization approach). This can then generate the supply chain variety that is needed in turbulent environments to absorb the external variety (cybernetic approach).

The dichotomization of supply chain structures in change and stability orientation carried out in the course of this volume is in principle compatible with cybernetics, but also with the further approaches of holistic evolutionary organizational theory. There are, for example, parallels between the measures of variety and change. In this respect, the previous theoretical foundations can be incorporated into the digital supply chain through the frame of reference on which this work is based. Ultimately, it is always a question of *profiling the supply chain between stability and change orientation* or of creating the "right" degree of complexity according to the situation.

2.2.1 Umbrella for key design principles

In this sense, Figure 2.3 summarizes the common directions of the different approaches of holistic-evolutionary organizational theory, as well as other concepts. Of course, this is not a complete conceptual consolidation of the different evolutionary approaches of management, but rather the classification into a frame of reference, which does not hide their differences and diverging fields of application. The suggested frame of reference rather tries to emphasize the common denominator of relevant perspectives. The attempt to integrate the various approaches of holistic-evolutionary organizational theory would probably also be pre-mature, as they are still predominantly in the early stages of their development. It is precisely the multi-conceptual perspective of the frame of reference that makes it possible to convey a deeper understanding of the concept of a resilient supply chain management. The reference framework of the digital supply chain presented here thus represents a kind of *umbrella concept*. It is open for the integration of further concepts.

Against the background of such multi-conceptual structure of the frame of reference, three essential basic interrelations can be summarized, which concern the evolution of the supply chain:

- What does the coordination principle of self-organization mean for the digital supply chain, specifically?
- What is the connection between change and fitness of the supply chain, and what is the effect of digitization?
- What are fundamental behavioural strategies for the evolution of digital supply chains in the course of a resilient understanding?

	Complexity decrease	Complexity increase
Ashby, 1956	Low variety	Large variety
Bleicher, 1991	Stability orientation	Change orientation
Campbell, 1975	Preservation, propagation	Variation
Hannan, Freeman, 1977	Selection, retention	Variation
Von Hayek, 1972	Competitive selection, multiplication	Variants
Kirsch, 1992	Allopoiesis	Autopoiesis
Probst, 1987	Third-party organization	Self-organization
Popper, 1973	Correction of errors	Trial
Röpke, 1977	Selection, retention	Variation
Wehberg, 1994	Third-party org., specialization	Self-organization, generalization

Figure 2.3 Common directions of selected theoretical concepts

2.2.2 Design principles of self-organization

Let's start with the first question, what does the coordination principle of self-organization specifically mean for the digital supply chain? As already mentioned, self-organization has four characteristics: recursion, autonomy, redundancy and self-reference. For the digital supply chain, this translates into design principles for digital supply chains, which suggest (Figure 2.4):

- The *steering* has to be consistent on different levels (in line with actual supply chain models). The *modularization* across hierarchy and *standardization* across sites are key for digital supply chains. Together, they support the recursion of a supply chain, which means certain characteristics are similar on different factual hierarchy levels.
- Responsibilities need to be *end-to-end* (rather than an organization, e.g. for SCOR functions with split-responsibilities). *Online-transparency*, an

Recursion	• Consistency of steering
	• Modularization across hierarchy
	• Standardization across sites
Autonomy	• End-to-end responsibility
	• >95 percent online
	• Enforced alignment
	• No management intervention
Redundancy	• Real-time transparency
	• Sharing
	• One data lake
Self-reference	• Dynamic forecasting
	• Continuous improvement
	• Machine learning

Figure 2.4 Selected design principles for digital supply chains

    enforced alignment (so that there is one aligned approach to coordination between functions and escalation mechanisms, accordingly) as well as *no management intervention* are required. All this together enables autonomy. The supply chain manages or develops itself and seeks its own way for this, without there being a central unit for it. Controlling and controlled unit are then one.

• Relevant information has to be openly *shared*. The sharing needs to be on a *real-time* basis and with means of *one data lake* as one source of truth. This makes sure that those units that have influence, each of which has (most or best) information, which means redundancy.

• Last but not least, digital supply chains have to *continuously improve* with means of *dynamic forecasting* and *machine learning* technology, amongst others. This is to make sure the behaviour always reacts back to it and these feedbacks in a way that forms the basis for further behaviour in terms of self-reference.

Considering these design principles, digital supply chains can absorb a huge amount of change because they can create significant resilience themselves without becoming chaotic or unreasonably complex. Needless to say, the aforementioned principles represent some key requirements from a self-organization viewpoint. They are not necessarily complete. Today, these principles are not being considered in a huge number of supply chain organizations, if not the majority of them.

2.2.3   *Supply chain fitness*

What is the ideal basic relationship, then, between the change in the supply chain on the one hand and its effectiveness and efficiency on the other? It should be noted that with increasing changes in a supply chain, its efficiency regularly decreases (see Figure 2.5). Above all, highly stabilized structures lead to *specialization gains* and economies of scale with regard to the cost structure. In contrast, change usually causes complexity costs and is therefore (ceteris paribus) associated with efficiency losses.

On the other hand, the effectiveness increases, against the background of the law of variety, with increasing changes in the supply chain. However, this behavioural relationship cannot be applied in every case with extremely high complexity. In this respect, the variety law can have a limited validity with regard to supply chains. With very high uncertainty and frequency, as well as

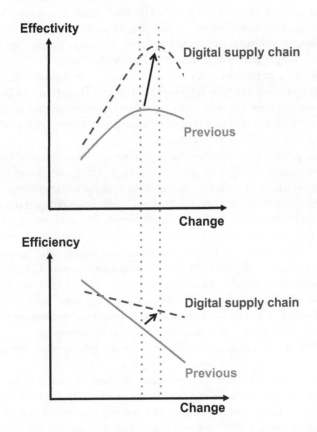

Figure 2.5 Relationship between the change, effectiveness and efficiency of a digital supply chain (illustrative)

correspondingly low compatibility, the principle of the *ecological niche width* can presumably guarantee a higher effectiveness (deepening Wehberg 1997).

Figuratively speaking, the position of the effectiveness and efficiency functions cannot be influenced in any way. By considering new potentials, such as new technologies like cyberphysical systems, it is possible to proactively shape the results of a supply chain. Thus, the digital supply chain improves the efficiency behaviour in the case of medium to high changes. With low changes, the *complexity costs* of the digital supply chain are at the expense of efficiency, because the *resilience* of the digital supply chain remains untapped. And the effectiveness function of the digital supply chain also offers advantages if the desired supply chain goals, such as delivery flexibility and reliability, can be better achieved with high changes.

The *fitness of the supply chain* now results from the overall view of the various efficiency and effectiveness functions of its individual subsystems. As a rule, as the supply chain under consideration changes, fitness initially increases and then decreases again at a critical point. The low fitness of supply chains with a maximum or minimum degree of complexity stems from the consideration that extremes, here change, are in the majority of cases "deadly" for a system, i.e. it can no longer perform its function (generally Probst 1987). Apart from the extremes of a minimum and maximum change considered here, the exact position of the fitness function is by no means fixed. Rather, it can be assumed that there are different patterns with regard to the effectiveness of the supply chain, each describing different typical behaviours of a subsystem of the supply chain. The same applies to their efficiency.

This static perspective must now be supplemented by a dynamic view of the typically oscillating changes in supply chains (Göpfert/Wehberg 1996). For example, adaptations to a change in the supply chain environment, as well as self-initiated innovations, require a sufficient change orientation if the effectiveness of a supply chain is to be further guaranteed. Change-oriented structures are useful, for example, in the transition from the market development phase to the diversification phase, but also in numerous other upheaval and transition phases for the supply chain. If supply chain management fails to anticipate changes and initiate suitable measures, such a misfit can lead to "crises" that threaten the existence of the company and leave no time for integrated and planned solutions. The rigid connection to suppliers and the wrong location of a large warehouse can be exemplary triggers of crisis situations.

Pfohl (1994, translated) speaks similarly of *crisis-oriented supply chain management*:

> In crisis-oriented logistics management, the analysis and solution of logistics problems is not yet carried out continuously on the basis of the logistics concept. . . . Logistics problems are not actively uncovered in time by logistics management, but are merely reacted to obvious symptoms that show the existence of bottlenecks (weak points, disruptions). Such symptoms are, for example, eye-catching frequent restacking of pallets, long queues of lorries at the ramps of a warehouse during the delivery of goods, or many cross journeys between delivery warehouses.

The prerequisite for avoiding or overcoming such crises is consequently a minimum degree of change-oriented orientation of logistics management.

However, as already mentioned, a change orientation has to be bought regularly through losses in efficiency (adjustment costs). Once the "right" structures to ensure effectiveness have been established, it is therefore a matter of increasing the economic efficiency of the supply chain again through rather stability-oriented measures. As a rule, what has been newly learned must first be deepened by supply chain management before it can be used efficiently. This also applies in principle to self-organizing cyberphysical systems of digital supply chains. More stability-oriented orders can prove advantageous, for example, in the transition from the pioneer to the market development phase. The spectrum in which such an interplay between change and stability orientation takes place – which is reminiscent of the phenomenon of the flow equilibrium – defines the adjustment area of supply chain management.

2.2.4 Strategies of supply chain evolution

What are fundamental behavioural strategies for the digital supply chain in the course of a resilient understanding? In order to minimize the dilemma between efficiency on the one hand and effectiveness on the other, there are three basic approaches to supply chain evolution (Figure 2.6).

First, it can be attempted to exert a corresponding influence on the development of the environment in the sense of *co-evolution* in order, for example, to stabilize supply chain–relevant parameters. Among other things, the outsourcing of logistics services can contribute to the stabilization of the environment if the complexity of the relevant influencing variables for the supply chain under

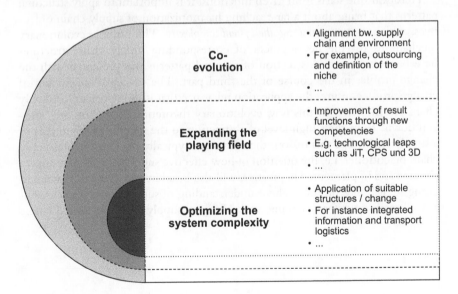

Figure 2.6 Evolution strategies of digital supply chains

consideration is reduced in this way. The principle of ecological niche-wide support offers assistance in defining the suitable niche. True pioneers will also be tempted to set dynamic accents in competition and new market standards through appropriate innovative behaviour in order to realize corresponding first-to-market profits in the medium term. The strategy of co-evolution should therefore be interpreted dynamically. It does not exclude the evolution strategies described in the following, but is to be understood rather spreading.

In addition to attempting to exert a favourable influence on the supply chain environment, it can also be promising to influence the effectiveness and efficiency functions of supply chains yourself. For example, it can be targeted so that the degree of efficiency conflicts as little as possible with a major change in the supply chain. It is about *expanding the playing field* for supply chain management, specifically about improving its functional relationships between change and its results by introducing new supply chain competences such as digitalization. The possible evolution mechanisms for the development of corresponding capabilities have been explained previously. In this way, new standards are set for the effectiveness and efficiency of the supply chain of the company under consideration, but possibly also absolutely in the form of a new state of the art. Relevant starting points offer in particular technological leaps such as the use of flexible manufacturing technologies, DOMRP, Just-in-Time and Postponement. It has also already been explained why a digital supply chain is suitable for expanding the playing field of supply chain management in this sense, i.e. offering new options for action in the form of the development of networks. It will not always be possible to differentiate between the adaptation of the change in supply chains and an adaptation of its efficiency or effectiveness function, because the latter includes new possibilities for the former.

Thirdly, if one starts from given functions, it is important to apply structural patterns that bring about a far-reaching harmonization of supply chain objectives, which means *optimizing the system complexity*. The possible evolutionary mechanisms for the development of corresponding supply chain structures have been explained. A selection of essential patterns was presented with the change profiles in the course of the third part. The in-depth breakdown of change profiles ensures the application relevance that is so important for supply chain practitioners. In this way, evolutionary theoretical statements are "broken down" from their high level of abstraction to the specific problem area of a supply chain. For this reason, the next steps typically relevant for the supply chain practitioner, i.e. the question of how effective supply chain structures are planned and implemented in practice, will also be addressed in the following. In doing so, it builds on the resilient understanding of supply chain management as well as on the reference framework of digital supply chains presented here.

3 Next steps for the digital supply chain

3.1 Overall approach to digitalization of the supply chain

How to get started? All that has been discussed thus far is only meaningful if it is used for making digital supply chains happen. So, the question is how to actually do it. In reality, many discussions on digital supply chains focus on leveraging new technologies. However, while better understanding the current situation and starting point of the respective company, in many cases one finds out that digitalization is not necessary the next step. This is just because the respective supply chain is not really mature enough and well prepared to face digitalization. In other words, the company is pursuing a supply chain understanding other than a resilient one. Basics need to get fixed first in terms of a process-oriented or demand-driven understanding. On the other hand, a subsequent approach that first takes care for basics takes too much time and does not support a proper time-to-market of digitalization concepts. This is especially critical because digital supply chains are key facilitator for new business models and digital offerings. The right timing often decides who will takes the system lead in certain markets, for example, as platform operator. A typical approach, therefore, is to fix the basics while digitalizing the supply chain in parallel.

Of course, introducing a digital supply chain based on a resilient understanding requires an *agile* approach. The proposed steps shown in Figure 3.1 are therefore not to be interpreted in a subsequent manner; rather, they are based on sprints and consider the design-thinking methodology. The first three steps of the approach, the baselining, maturity assessment and target operating model definition, thus follow this kind of methodology for exactly that reason.

Moreover, introducing a digital supply chain is never a one-off exercise but rather a continuous effort. At the same time, it is value adding to schedule a comprehensive transformation journey and "slice the elephant" via a realistic implementation roadmap and waves. In order to succeed one has to think big, start small and scale fast.

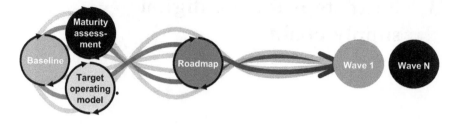

Figure 3.1 Typical approach for supply chain digitalization

3.2   Baselining and assessing maturity

Anyone who wants to develop supply chains in the direction of digitalization must first understand the development to date, the status and the key factors influencing future development. As a rule, a series of *fundamental analyses* in the sense of a baselining of supply chain (management) structures are available to support the answering of the aforementioned questions, for example:

*   Evaluation of relevant trends using trend sonar
*   Review of corporate strategy and desired competitive advantage
*   Environmental analyses, including supplier and competition surveys
*   Customer and employee satisfaction analyses
*   Survey of service levels for internal and external customers
*   Process maps to illustrate the value creation structure
*   Assessing the maturity of supply chain (management) processes
*   Evaluating supply chain performance with means of process mining
*   Understanding the cultural readiness to change and digitalization
*   Resource surveys (costs, employees) on the basis of a process framework and organizational structure

Often, a lot of information and tools are already available in the company, so that a comprehensive survey of all the aforementioned aspects can be dispensed with. When recording the *maturity* level of a supply chain, the focus is on the ability to cope with complexity or to generate complexity itself in an orderly manner. Figure 3.2 shows an overview of a corresponding methodology.

3.3   Defining the target operating model

When deriving the target state in the direction of digital supply chains, the same dimensions of supply chain management can be used as for maturity measurement. The desired operating model (target operating model) of the supply chain is to be defined holistically in the form of an end-to-end view, including supply chain information, planning, personnel management, organization, monitoring and control(ling).

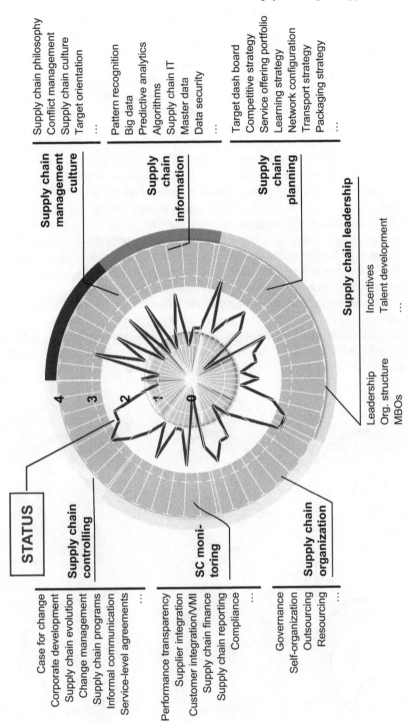

Figure 3.2 Maturity assessment for digital supply chains

In terms of supply chain evolution, the establishment of responsibilities for the supply chain of a company is often a first step in development. The way supply chain management is anchored within the organization typically says a lot about the appreciation of it as well as the supply chain governance. Once a *supply chain governance* is installed, this goes hand in hand with the desire to create more transparency about supply chain processes. *Transparency*, for example, about the actual costs of supply chains, often offers a kind of "aha" effect about their actual significance. In many companies, supply chain costs are limited to the transport department, for example, and are not seen as process related. Once the importance of supply chain management has been understood, this is the basis for tackling improvements and systematically planning them. The logic of different *supply chain models* is being understood. The focal points of such improvements are to be worked out individually by sector and company. A solid supply chain planning process is then the basis to understanding its implementation. For this reason, many companies focus on the control system. A comprehensive establishment of the digital supply chain requires not least a suitable development of both the personnel management and values, respectively. The latter are indispensable for the sustainable anchoring of a corresponding control philosophy in the minds of the employees.

Figure 3.3 shows such typical supply chain structures and evolution stages using exemplary patterns. Of course, it may also be expedient for the company under consideration to adapt the sequence of the addressed supply chain subsystems or to bring the entire supply chain management to a medium degree of maturity before it takes the idea of digitalization into account.

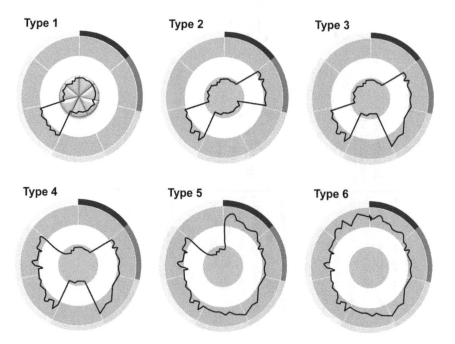

Figure 3.3 Example patterns of typical supply chains

Phase	Step	R&D	Procurement	Operations	Distribution	Disposals
Real-to-virtual	Mechanize	o				o
	Sensor			o		
	Transmit		o		o	
	Integrate					
	Analyse	x		x		
Virtual-to-real	Visualize					x
	Augment				x	
	Robotize		x			
	Craft					
	Virtualize					

O ⟶ x : Current status and 3y-target

Figure 3.4 Assessment of the digital twin of a supply chain (example)

In order to drive supply chain evolution and improvements associated, it is vital to have a proper approach to the operational supply chain coordination in place. As mentioned earlier, the digital twin of the supply chain is facilitating this kind of optimization loop with means of ten key milestones. To target and measure the progress from one milestone to another, an assessment as well as target definition of the digital twin helps to keep transparency and *track for the build-up of the digital twin* on a milestone-specific basis. Figure 3.4 shows a respective monitoring chart with respect to the end-to-end supply chain as an example. This is typically a key input for tracking a business case and thus providing evidence for the commercial viability of the transformation towards a digital supply chain. In this context it is important to understand that in not just a few cases the baseline data for building a business case is poor. In this case it is important to double-check the baseline performance at a later stage with means of digital twin measurements, and to update where needed. Otherwise, it can happen that improvements seem to be even negative just because actual figures are compared against wrong baseline data.

3.4 Planning the implementation roadmap

As you make your bed, so you sleep. Implementation planning is therefore a step in supply chain development that should not be underestimated. Many practitioners run comparatively unconsciously into an adventure if they do not systematically consider the desired target status nor the prerequisites, implementation steps, resources and employees necessary for its realization. Due to a planning of the "big throw", many companies also tend to define the implementation steps too big, too confusing and too ambitious. In both cases, there is a risk of a nasty awakening. Often the concept is then seen as the cause of failure, although it was not the "what" but the "how at the what". An agile implementation in clear steps is more promising here, but does not mean that an overall big picture would not be necessary, where the company would like to go in the result (Figure 3.5).

Last but not least, a fundamental decision about the implementation strategy has to be made in the course of the implementation planning: If the new *supply chain responsibilities* are to be established first in order to be able to take them into account for implementation ("lift–drop–change") or if the improvements from a project are to be addressed in order to then hand them over to the new responsibilities ("lift–change–drop"). In many cases lift–drop–change has proven itself in practice, because the implementation is directly driven by those responsible at a later stage and therefore a different level of motivation and sense of responsibility is supported. One could also say that those who have to spoon out the soup will also ensure that it tastes good. But there may also be reasons for an adapted approach, for example, in the sense of a lift–change–drop. If the supply chain capabilities are missing, for example, it can be reasonable to train future responsibles during the transformation and install the new roles based on a proven project path. A change–lift–drop, on the other hand, is seldom promising.

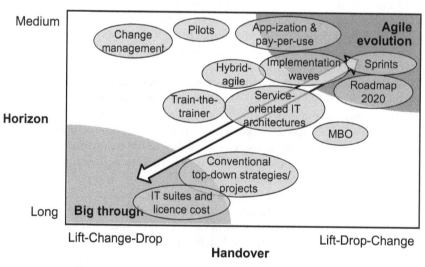

Figure 3.5 Implementation strategies

The following case is intended to serve as an example for the temporal structuring of the implementation of the target image on the basis of an implementation timetable.

Project example: supply chain roadmap

Initial situation: A company in the manufacturing industry segment faced intense competition both in terms of its product range and external growth. Due to the pressure on margins, the company was looking for potential savings in all directions. At the same time, the possibilities of digitization were to be examined, because growth and innovation potential was suspected here. Due to the pronounced product and technology focus in the past, corresponding potentials were expected above all in the area of the supply chain, in particular in the redesign of the value-adding structure. Due to the neglect of supply chain issues in the past, the range of possibilities in this area was particularly wide. At the same time, the decision makers and opinion leaders in the company disagreed as to where best to start and in what order the topics should be dealt with.

Objective: Against this background, the company management initiated a preliminary project to order, prioritize and project the possibilities for improvement in the supply chain area. The goal was a well-thought-out roadmap (Figure 3.6), supported by everyone, that would chart the path of supply chain development over the coming years. At the same time, a step-by-step approach would ensure that each step was self-contained and offered sufficient benefits – also seen in isolation.

Approach: The procedure for drafting the roadmap consisted of three steps. First, the current state was to be reviewed, which already existed in many respects but was incomplete. The approach was pragmatic because the company did not see any actual benefit in much analysis activity. Rather, they wanted to complete the required data. Secondly, potential improvements were assessed in the form of rough first business cases. Here, too, the 80:20 principle was applied pragmatically. In order to ensure that no significant opportunities for improvement were forgotten, the company put this exercise on a broad basis, attached great importance to the involvement of those affected at all levels and also initiated comparisons with other companies. The possibilities for improvement were arranged according to the management areas of the supply chain, for example, the information system, planning, organization, etc. The improvement possibilities were also evaluated. Thirdly, each business case was concretized with regard to responsibilities, resource requirements,

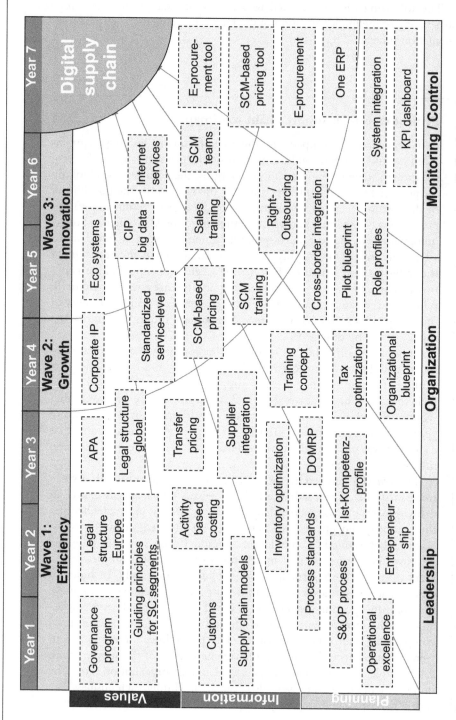

Figure 3.6 Example supply chain roadmap

exact milestones, etc. and an overall roadmap was drawn up by consolidating the various milestones. In addition to the targeted interim results, the milestone planning also included communication and the necessary resources. The roadmap was divided into three waves: Wave 1 stood for efficiency improvements and a state-of-the-art organization, wave 2 for growth and concentration on core competencies through outsourcing and wave 3 for innovation and new services.

Results and digital relevance: The roadmap summarized more than 35 projects with over 400 milestones over a period of seven years. Thus, the company's journey towards the introduction of a progressive supply chain function was fully structured. Due to the existence of the roadmap, the company's journey was well thought out, so to speak, in every stopover and to the end, even before the start of the journey. The sum of the business cases resulted in a net present value in the higher three-digit million range. Efficiency (inventory, etc.), growth (pricing, etc.) and innovation topics (new services, etc.) were equally taken into account.

Success factors: The success of the roadmap was demonstrated above all by the successful implementation of its milestones. Three success factors were decisive for the quality of the roadmap development: participation, competence and evolution. Participation meant bringing all important decision makers and those operationally affected on board. Without their expertise, feasibility, comprehensiveness and acceptance would have been in jeopardy. Competence means defining the roadmap within the framework of the company's capabilities and available capacity. Ambitious but unrealistic project plans are of no use to anyone. Rather, it is the reliability of the roadmap that is important, especially when considering the situation over several years, in order not to get out of hand right from the start. Evolution therefore means structuring the roadmap into smaller, controllable steps with corresponding intermediate successes that do not lose momentum over the years of implementation.

Literature

acatech/Arbeitskreis Smart Service Welt, Ed., *Smart Service Welt – Umsetzungs-empfehlungen für das Zukunftsprojekt Internetbasierte Dienste für die Wirtschaft*, Abschlussbericht, Berlin 2015.

Aldrich, H., Organizational Boundaries and Interorganizational Conflict, in: *Human Relations*, 24 (1971) 4, pp. 279–293.

Aldrich, H., *Organizations and Environments*, Englewood Cliffs 1979.

Anderson, C., *The Long Tail, deutsche Übersetzung*, München 2007.

Anderson, C., *Makers, Das Internet der Dinge: die nächste industrielle Revolution*, München 2012.

Andrew, A., Autopoiesis–Autopoiesis Interplay, in: Zeleny, M. (Ed.), *Autopoiesis: A Theory of Living Organization*, New York 1981, pp. 157–166.

Ashby, W. R., *An Introduction to Cybernetics*, London 1956.

Ashby, W. R., *Einführung in die Kybernetik*, Frankfurt 1974.

Bauernhansl, T., Die Vierte Industrielle Revolution – Der Weg in ein wertschaffendes Produktionsparadigma, in: Bauernhansl, T., ten Hompel, M., Vogel-Heuser, B. (Ed.), *Industrie 4.0 in Produktion, Automatisierung und Logistik*, Wiesbaden 2014, pp. 5–35.

Beer, S., *Decision and Control*, New York 1966.

Beer, S., *The Heart of Enterprise*, Chichester u. a. 1979.

Beer, S., *Kybernetik und Management*, Frankfurt 1970.

Bigelow, J. D., Approaching the Organizational Navel: An Evolutionary Perspective of Organizational Development, in: Cummings, T. G. (Ed.), *Systems Theory for Organization Development*, Chichester 1980, pp. 339–353.

Bigelow, J. D., Evolution and Middle Range Theories: Towards a Matrix of Organizational Modes, in: Pinder, C. C., Moore, L. F. (Eds.), *Middle Range Theory and the Study of Organizations*, Dordrecht, 1980, pp. 157–168.

Bigelow, J. D., *Evolution in Organizations*, Case Western Reserve University 1978.

Bleicher, K., *Das Konzept Integriertes Management*, Frankfurt a. M., New York 1991.

Bleicher, K., *Das Konzept Integriertes Management*, 2nd ed., Frankfurt a. M., New York 1992.

Bleicher, K., *Das Konzept Integriertes Management*, 3rd ed., Frankfurt a. M., New York 1995.

Boulding, K. E., *Ecodynamics: A New Theory of Societal Evolution*, Beverly Hills 1981.

Bretzke, W. R., *Der Problembezug von Entscheidungsmodellen*, Tübingen 1980.

Brittain, J., Freeman, J., Organizational Proliferation and Density Depent Selection: Organizational Evolution in the Semiconductor Industry, in: Kimberly, J. R., Miles, R. H. (Ed.), *The Organizational Life Cycle*, San Francisco 1980, pp. 291–338.

Bubner, N., Bubner, N., Helbig, R., Jeske, M., *Supply Chain Management Trend Radar*, Bonn 2014.

Buchholz, H., Wehberg, G., Zimmermann, P., *Supply Chain Start-Ups Are Coming of Age*, Düsseldorf 2017.

Camp, R. C., *Benchmarking, the Search for Industries Best Practices That Lead to Superior Performance*, Milwaukee 1989.

Campbell, D. T., On the Conflicts between Biological and Social Evolution and between Psychology and Moral Tradition, in: *American Psychologist*, o. Jg. (1975) 12, S. 1103–1126.

Caroll, G. R., Organizational Ecology, in: *ARS*, 10 (1984) o. Nr., pp. 71–93.

Chesnut, H., *Prinzipien der Systemplanung*, München 1970.

Darwin, C., *The Origin of Species*, Cambridge, MA 1967.

Dyllick, T., *Gesellschaftliche Instabilität und Unternehmungsführung, Ansätze zu einer gesellschaftsbezogenen Managementlehre*, Bern, Stuttgart 1982.

Ferguson, A., *An Essay on the History of Civil Society*, Edinghburgh 1966.

Fischer, M., *Die ökologische Dimension der Logistik, Evolutorisch-entropische Systemanalyse ökonomischer Prozesse*, Wiesbaden 1995.

Freichel, S. L. K., *Organization von Logistikservice-Netzwerken, Theoretische Konzeption und empirische Fallstudien*, Berlin 1992.

Giesen, B., *Makrosoziologie: Eine evolutionstheoretische Einführung*, Hamburg 1980.

Göpfert, I., *Logistik – Führungskonzeption und Management von Supply Chains*, 3rd ed., München 2013.

Göpfert, I., Wehberg, G., Logistikentwicklung – Ein pulsierendes System wechselnder Profilierung, in: *Logistik im Unternehmen*, 10 (1996) 3, pp. 92–93.

Grunwald, W., Wie man Vertrauen erwirbt: von der Mißtrauens- zur Vertrauensorganization, in: *io Management Zeitschrift*, (1995) 112, pp. 73–77.

Hannan, M. T., Freeman, J., *Organizational Ecology*, Cambridge, MA 1989.

Hannan, M. T., Freeman, J., The Population Ecology of Organizations, in: *AJS*, 82 (1977), pp. 929–964.

Hannan, M. T., Freeman, J., Structural Inertia and Organizational Change, in: *ARS*, 49 (1984), pp. 149–164.

Hejl, P., Kybernetik 2. Ordnung, Selbstorganization und Biologismusverdacht, Aus Anlaß der Kontroverse um das 'Evolutionäre Management', in: *Die Unternehmung*, 37 (1983) 1, pp. 41–62.

Imai, M., Kaizen, *Der Schlüssel zum Erfolg der Japaner im Wettbewerb*, 9th ed., München 1993.

Jantsch, E., *Die Selbstorganization des Universums, München, Wien 1979, als erweiterte Neuauflage*, Wien 1992.

Kaufman, H., The Natural History of Human Organizations, in: *Administration and Society*, 7 (1975) 2, pp. 131–149.

Kerber, W., German Market Process Theory, in: Boettke, P. J. (Ed.), *The Elgar Companion to Austrian Economics*, Vermont 1994, pp. 500–507.

Kieser, A., Evolutionstheoretische Ansätze, in: Kieser, A. (Ed.), *Organizationstheorien*, 2nd ed., Stuttgart 1995, pp. 237–268.

Kieser, A., Fremdorganization, Selbstorganization und evolutionäres Management, in: *ZfbF*, 46 (1994) 3, pp. 199–228.

Kirsch, W., *Kommunikatives Handeln, Autopoiese, Rationalität, Sondierungen zu einer evolutionären Führungslehre*, München 1992.

Kirsch, W., Esser, W.-M., Gabele, E., *Das Management der geplanten Evolution von Organizationen*, Stuttgart 1979.

Krieg, W., *Kybernetische Grundlagen der Unternehmensgestaltung*, Bern 1971.

Krubasik, E., Technologiemanagement für überlegene Innovationsstrategien, in: Henzler, H. A. (Ed.), *Handbuch strategische Führung*, Wiesbaden 1988, pp. 443–461.

Krystek, U., *Unternehmenskrisen, Beschreibung, Vermeidung und Bewältigung überlebens-kritischer Prozesse in Unternehmungen*, Wiesbaden 1987.

Levins, R., *Evolution in Changing Environments*, Princeton, NJ 1968.

Levins, R., Theory of Fittness in a Heterogeneous Environment, I: The Fitness Set of Adaptive Function, in: *American Naturalist*, 96 (1962) November/December, pp. 361–378.

Luhmann, N., *Ökologische Kommunikation*, 3rd ed., Opladen 1990.

Luhmann, N., *Soziale Systeme, Grundriss einer allgemeinen Theorie*, 4th ed., Frankfurt a. M. 1991.

Malik, F., Gomez, P., Evolutionskonzept für unternehmerische Entscheide, in: *io*, 45 (1976) 9, pp. 308–312.

Malik, F., Probst, G., Evolutionäres Management, in: *Die Unternehmung*, 35 (1981) 2, pp. 121–140.

Malik, P., *Systemisches Management, Evolution, Selbstorganization*, Bern, Stuttgart, Wien 1993.

Mann, R., *Das ganzheitliche Unternehmen*, 6th ed., Stuttgart 1995.

Maturana, H. R., Biologie der Sprache, in: Maturana, H. R. (Ed.), *Erkennen: Die Organization und Verkörperung von Wirklichkeit, Ausgewählte Arbeiten zur biologischen Epistemologie*, Braunschweig u. a. 1982., pp. 236–271.

Maturana, H. R., Varela, F. J., *Autopoiesis and Cognition: The Realization of the Living*, Boston 1980.

Maturana, H. R., Varela, F. J., Autopoietische Systeme: eine Bestimmung der lebendigen Organization, in: Maturana, H. R. (Ed.), *Erkennen: Die Organization und Verkörperung von Wirklichkeit, Ausgewählte Arbeiten zur biologischen Epistemologie*, Braunschweig u. a. 1982, pp. 170–235.

McCulloch, W. S., *Embodiments of Mind*, Boston 1965.

McKelvey, B., Organizational Speciation, in: Pinder, C. C., L. F. Moore (Ed.), *Middle Range Theory and the Study of Organizations*, Boston u. a. 1980, pp. 169–186.

McKelvey, B., *Organizational Systematics: Taxonomy, Evolution, Classification*, Berkeley 1982.

McKelvey, B., Aldrich, H., Populations, Natural Selection and Applied Organizational Science, in: *ASQ*, 28 (1983) 1, pp. 101–128.

Mesarovic, M. D., Macko, D., Takahara, Y., *Theory of Hierarchical Multilevel Systems*, New York 1970.

Osterloh, M., Das 'Gesetz der erforderlichen Varietät' und die hierarchische Struktur von Entscheidungssystemen, in: Schiemenz, B., Wagner, A. (Ed.), *Angewandte Wirtschafts- und Sozialkybernetik, Neue Ansätze in Praxis und Wissenschaft*, Berlin 1984, pp. 149–181.

Pask, G., *An Approach to Cybernetics*, London 1972.

Pfeffer, J., Barriers to the Advancement of Organization Science: Paradigm Development as a Dependent Variable, in: *AmR*, 18 (1993) o. Nr., pp. 599–620.

Pfohl, H.-Chr., *Logistikmanagement, Funktionen und Instrumente*, Berlin u. a. 1994.

Popper, K. R., *Objektive Erkenntnis, Ein evolutionärer Entwurf*, Hamburg 1973.

Probst, G. J. B., *Kybernetische Gesetzeshypothesen als Basis für Gestaltungs- und Lenkungsregeln im Management*, Bern, Stuttgart 1981.

Probst, G. J. B., *Selbst-Organization, Ordnungsprozesse in sozialen Systemen aus ganzheitlicher Sicht*, Berlin, Hamburg 1987.

Pümpin, C., *Das Dynamik-Prinzip: Zukunftsorientierungen für Unternehmer und Manager*, Düsseldorf 1989.

Pümpin, C., Dynamisches Management und Controlling, in: Horvath, P. (Ed.), *Synergien durch Schnittstellen-Controlling*, Stuttgart 1991, pp. 25–49.

Pümpin, C., Unternehmenseigner und Unternehmensentwicklung, in: Gomez, P., Hahn, D., Müller-Stewens, G., Wunderer, R. (Ed.), *Unternehmerischer Wandel*, Wiesbaden 1994, pp. 273–292.

Pümpin, C., Prange, J., *Management der Unternehmensentwicklung, Phasengerechte Führung und der Umgang mit Krisen*, Frankfurt a. M., New York 1991.

Reichwald, R., Piller, F., *Interaktive Wertschöpfung*, 2nd ed., Wiesbaden 2009.

Röpke, J., *Die Strategie der Innovation*, Tübingen 1977.

Sabathil, K., *Evolutionäre Strategien der Unternehmensführung*, Wiesbaden 1993.

Sander, U., Brockmann, K.-H., Benchmarking oder zwischenbetrieblicher Vergleich, in: *Logistik im Unternehmen*, 9 (1995) 112, pp. 72–74.

Schiemenz, B., *Betriebskybernetik: Aspekte des betrieblichen Managements*, Stuttgart 1982.

Schiemenz, B., Stichwort betriebswirtschaftliche Systemtheorie, in: Wittmann, W., Kern, W., Köhler, R., Küpper, H.-V., Wysocki, K. (Ed.), *Handwörterbuch der Betriebswirtschaft, Teilband 3*, 5th ed., Stuttgart 1993, pp. 4127–4140.

Schmidt, J., In Netzwerken denken und handeln, in: *Gablers Magazin*, (1993) 617, pp. 28–31.

Schreiter, C., *Evolution und Wettbewerb von Organizationsstrukturen*, Göttingen 1994.

Schwanninger, M., *Managementsysteme*, Frankfurt a. M., New York 1994.

Semmel, M., *Die Unternehmung aus evolutionstheoretischer Sicht, Eine kritische Bestandsaufnahme der Organizations- und Managementtheorie*, Bern, Stuttgart 1984.

Servatius, H.-G., *Vom strategischen Management zur evolutionären Führung*, Stuttgart 1991.

Simon, H., Die Architektur der Komplexität, in: Tärk, K. (Ed.), *Handlungssysteme*, Opladen 1978., pp. 94–120.

Sprüngli, R. K., *Evolution und Management, Ansätze einer evolutionistischen Betrachtung sozialer Systeme*, Bern, Stuttgart 1981.

Susman, G. 1., *Autonomy of Work*, New York 1976.

ten Hompel, M., Logistik 4.0, in: Bauernhansl, T., ten Hompel, M., Vogel-Heuser, B. (Ed.), *Industrie 4.0 in Produktion, Automatisierung und Logistik*, Wiesbaden 2014/2015, pp. 615–624.

Ulrich, H., Probst, P., *Anleitung zum ganzheitlichen Denken und Handeln*, 3rd ed., Stuttgart 1991.

Varela, F., Autonomie und Autopoiese, in: Schmidt, S. J. (Ed.), *Der Diskurs des Radikalen Konstruktivismus*, Frankfurt 1987, pp. 119–132.

Vester, F., *Neuland des Denkens*, 2nd ed., Stuttgart 1981.

Vester, F., Ökologisches Systemmanagement, Die Unternehmung am Scheideweg zwischen Mechanistik und Biokybernetik, in: Probst, G. J. B., Siegwart, H. (Ed.), *Integriertes Management, Bausteine des systemorientierten Management*, Bern, Stuttgart 1985, pp. 299–330.

von Bertalanffy, L., *Biophysik des Fließgleichgewichts*, Braunschweig 1953.

von der Oelsnitz, D., Individuelle Selbststeuerung – der Königsweg "moderner" Unternehmensführung?, in: *DBW*, 55 (1995) 6, pp. 707–720.

von Eicke, H., Femerling, C., *Modular Sourcing, Ein Konzept zur Neugestaltung der Beschaffungslogistik*, München 1991.

von Hayek, F. A., Arten der Ordnung, in: von Hayek, F. A. (Ed.), *Freiburger Studien, Gesammelte Aufsätze*, Tübingen 1969, pp. 32–46.

von Hayek, F. A., *Die Theorie komplexer Phänomene (Deutsche Übersetzung der englischen Originalfassung 'Theory of Complex Phenomena' aus dem Jahre 1964)*, Tübingen 1972.

Walleck, A. S., O'Halloran, J. D., Leader, C. A., Benchmarking World-Class Performance, in: *McKinsey Quarterly*, 28 (1991) 1, pp. 3–24.

Warnecke, H.-J., *Die Fraktale Fabrik, Revolution der Unternehmenskultur*, Berlin u. a. 1992.

Weber, J., Kummer, S., *Logistikmanagement*, Stuttgart, 1994.

Wehberg, G., *Die Triple Long Tail Strategie*, Köln/Düsseldorf 2015.

Wehberg, G., Logistik-Controlling – Kern des evolutionären Logistikmanagement, in: Jötingmeier et al., 1994, pp. 73–134.

Wehberg, G., *Ökologieorientiertes Logistikmanagement, Ein evolutionstheoretischer Ansatz*, Wiesbaden 1997.

Wildemann, H., *Die Modulare Fabrik*, 4th ed., München 1994.

Wildemann, H., Organisatorisches Lernen, Das Geheimnis des Erfolges, in: *Logistik Heute*, 9 (1995), pp. 52–57.

Young, R. C., Is Population Ecology a Useful Paradigm for the Study of Organizations?, in: *AJS*, 94 (1988) 1, pp. 1–24.

Zammuto, R. F., *Assessing Organizational Effectiveness*, Albany 1982.

zu Knyphausen, D., *Unternehmungen als evolutionsfähige Systeme, Überlegungen zu einem evolutionären Konzept für die Organizationstheorie*, München 1988.

Part 5

Over and beyond digital supply chains

This book offered an initial basis for digital supply chains, including both practical experience as well as a theoretical-conceptional foundation. The problem of managing complexity has so far only been dealt with rudimentarily in the supply chain literature.

Writing a final publication on integration, comprehensiveness and complexity management in logistics is probably a contradiction in terms. From a systemic point of view, there can be no "big bang". It should therefore be pointed out that the frame of reference of this volume is open in principle. The latter is to be understood as a "first step" towards a theoretical foundation of digital supply chains and its resilient understanding. And even against the background that organizational-theoretical evolutionary research has "only" tried to establish itself for about forty years, it is not surprising that the need for research in this area, measured by its significance for supply chains as well as for management in general, is comparatively great. Numerous questions were raised in this volume. However, a final answer could – of course – not be offered. In particular, the following continuing research tasks can be highlighted:

- The admissibility of transferring statements from basic sciences (such as biology, neurology, etc.) to supply chains needs to be examined in greater depth.
- The evolutionary mechanisms of supply chains and their development need to be explored more extensively.
- Typical behaviour patterns need to be developed in a more differentiated way.
- The social and technological dimensions of supply chain development in particular need to be further conceptualized.
- The complexity management of supply chains should be further shaped in such a way that tool-supported work is expanded.

In addition, the empirical testing of model hypotheses should be promoted. Together, additional theoretical-conceptual work as well as a stronger empirical foundation promise the expansion of our understanding of digital supply chains and their resilience.

At the end of the day, all the answers to be worked out will have to prove themselves in the light of practice. Without offering such added value in practice, it is merely a scientific activity as an end in itself. In this respect, supply chain management is called upon to prioritize the above questions from a practical perspective. In addition, practical considerations for the respective company come in the form of numerous W questions regarding digital supply chains, for example:

- What are the customer benefits and values of digital supply chains in the various segments?
- What are practical learnings that have to be incorporated in order to sharpen the framework?
- What kind of economic viability does the use of cyberphysical systems typically offer?
- What initial investments are required to set up a digital supply chain?
- What do the (meta-)algorithms for digital supply chains look like?
- Which way can digital supply chain solutions be implemented holistically?
- When is an organization ready for the introduction of a digital supply chain?
- What implementation risks must be managed with regard to digital supply chains?
- What are typical success factors for the implementation of digital supply chains?
- Which is the best way for digital supply chains to be organizationally anchored in the company?
- What kind of digital supply chain competences are required?
- What does a digital supply chain mean for the outsourcing strategy?
- What more can we learn from other application examples?
- Which is the best way to answer questions of data security satisfactorily?

The practical desire for suitable support to answer the relevant questions is obvious. Digital supply chains will certainly play a role in the course of the fourth industrial revolution. As I suggest, we all can very much look forward to our next steps and shared learnings in our joint digitalization journey.

The ten biggest errors as to digital supply chains

Sometimes the best way to describe something is to say what it isn't. In this sense, I would like to conclude by summarizing in a pointed way the ten biggest mistakes regarding digital supply chains.

Error No. 1: Digital supply chains will be important, but will not revolutionize our lives.

Wrong, digitalization offers the potential to build supply chains completely differently and to develop new business models. The Internet of Things is revolutionizing logistics, among other things.

Error No. 2: Digital supply chains help to reduce complexity.

Wrong, complexity can only be handled with complexity. The answer to increasing environmental and market requirements (customer expectations, regulations, scarcity of resources, etc.) is therefore resilience and flexibility.

Error No. 3: Digital supply chains mean maximum self-organization.

Wrong, the delegation of responsibility and decentralization of decisions do not mean the complete abandonment of design and development possibilities. It depends on the right scope and degree of self-organization as well as the right guardrails.

Error No. 4: Digital supply chains are an efficiency engine, but not a growth engine.

Wrong, the use of the Internet of Services in the field of supply chains offers potential for many new services and business ideas. This offers growth opportunities for companies and regions.

Error No. 5: Digital supply chains are what I do by doing a bit of cyberphysics.

Wrong, digital supply chains are more than a new technology. Cyberphysical systems make many things possible. However, digital supply chains can be implemented as a holistic management concept for individual companies. It affects all areas of management.

Error No. 6: Digital supply chains mean finding the right algorithm for forecasting.

Wrong, the relevant procedures typically offer a whole series of algorithms for a specific question. The all-healing algorithm does not exist. And not everything can be forecasted.

Error No. 7: Digital supply chains mean collecting as much data as possible.

Wrong. It is not about a comprehensive consideration of as much data as possible, but about the integration of the relevant sources. Relevant are those data that serve to achieve the supply chain goals such as forecast accuracy or resilience.

Error No. 8: Digital supply chains require big data and CPS competence but no supply chain management knowledge.

Wrong. The analysis and management of complex supply chains require not only the necessary IT and analytical competence, but also an understanding of logistics, flows and value chains, because this is precisely where judgement and business knowledge are required.

Error No. 9: Digital supply chains are already covered by the current Industry 4.0 Initiative.

Wrong. The degree of maturity of supply chains in industry is very different. Quite a few companies first have to implement minimum standards in the field of supply chain management before they can devote themselves sensibly to the subject of Industry 4.0. An Industry 4.0 without sufficient supply chains does not work.

Error No. 10: Digital supply chains are not a matter for the CXO, but a task for the logistics department.

Wrong. Digitization belongs on every board agenda. The design of the company's value creation structure and business model is strategic and critical of competition.

Index

Note: Page numbers in *italics* indicate a figure on the corresponding page.